The Communications Revolution in Politics

The Communications Revolution in Politics

Proceedings of
The Academy of
Political Science

Volume 34
Number 4

ISSN 0065-0684

Edited by Gerald Benjamin

New York, 1982

Library of Congress Catalog Card Number 82-72550
Cover design by Clare Francis
Printed by Capital City Press, Montpelier, Vermont

Contents

Preface

Miracles of technology have revolutionized communications. We take for granted the use of facilities that were undreamed of only a few years ago. The new methods of communication have altered, often radically, domestic and foreign policy decision-making. Political processes, and the substantive outcomes to which they lead, have been modified in ways that call for careful scrutiny. The end of this revolution is not in sight.

Professor Robert H. Connery, president of the Academy, combining his broad knowledge of governmental affairs with an awareness of the significance of technological advances, developed the first stages of planning of this series of studies. Professor Gerald Benjamin, of the State University of New York College at New Paltz, then undertook to define topics and engage experts to write about them.

The views expressed in this volume are those of the authors and not necessarily those of any organization with which they are associated. The Academy is a forum for the discussion of public policy issues, but as an organization it makes no recommendations on political questions. This volume is the 136th in a series that started in 1910.

A grant from the John and Mary R. Markle Foundation along with funds from the Academy's own resources financed this project. The Academy wishes to express its deep appreciation for the outside support while making explicit the fact that the sponsors of free inquiry have no responsibility for the contents.

William Farr, John Tone, and Leonard Smith copy edited the manuscripts and supervised the publication of the volume.

C. Lowell Harriss
Executive Director

Contributors

ERIK BARNOUW, formerly Chief, Motion Picture, Broadcasting and Recorded Sound Division, Library of Congress, is Professor Emeritus of Dramatic Arts, Columbia University. He is the author of *A History of Broadcasting in the United States.*

GERALD BENJAMIN is Professor of Political Science, State University of New York College at New Paltz. He is the coauthor, with Robert H. Connery, of *Rockefeller of New York: Executive Power in the State House.*

JOAN BIEDER, formerly Producer, Canadian Broadcasting Corporation, and Associate Producer, ABC-TV News, is Assistant Professor, Columbia University Graduate School of Journalism.

RICHARD CLUTTERBUCK, Senior Lecturer in Politics, University of Exeter, served as Major General in the British Army. He is the author of *The Media and Political Violence.*

ROBERT F. COULAM is Assistant Professor of Social Science and Public Policy, Carnegie-Mellon University. He is the author of *Illusions of Choice: The F-111 and the Problems of Weapons Acquisition Reform.*

WILLIAM H. DUTTON is Associate Professor of Communications and Public Administration, Annenberg School of Communications, University of Southern California. He is a coauthor (with James Danziger, Rob Kling, and Kenneth Kraemer) of *Computers and Politics.*

DAVID H. EVERSON, Director, Illinois Legislative Studies Center, Sangamon State University, is the author of *Public Opinion and Interest Groups in American Politics.*

STEPHEN FRANTZICH, Associate Professor of Political Science, U.S. Naval Academy, is the author of *Computers in Congress: The Politics of Information.*

DORIS A. GRABER is Professor of Political Science, University of Illinois at Chicago. Formerly Editor, College Department, Harper & Row, she is the editor of *The President and the Public.*

C. LOWELL HARRISS is Professor Emeritus of Economics, Columbia University; Executive Director, the Academy of Political Science; Economic Consultant, Tax Foundation, Inc.; and Associate, Lincoln Institute of Land Policy.

STEPHEN HESS, Senior Fellow, The Brookings Institution, is the author of *The Washington Reporters.*

PATRICIA A. KARL, is Instructor of Political Science, Vassar College, where she teaches a course on the media and international relations.

THOMAS E. PATTERSON, Professor and Chairman of the Department of Political Science, Syracuse University, is the author of *The Mass Media Election.*

ITHIEL DE SOLA POOL is Professor of Political Science, Massachusetts Institute of Technology. He is the author of *The Social Impact of the Telephone.*

CHRISTOPHER H. PYLE is Associate Professor, Department of Politics, Mount Holyoke College. He is the coauthor, with Richard M. Pious, of the forthcoming *President, Congress, and the Constitution.*

HARRY HOWE RANSOM is Professor of Political Science, Vanderbilt University. He is the author of *The Intelligence Establishment.*

CHARLES ROLL, formerly Study Director, The Gallup Organization, is President, Polls, Inc. He is the coauthor, with Albert H. Cantril, of *Polls: Their Use and Misuse in Politics.*

LEONARD R. SUSSMAN is Executive Director, Freedom House. He is the founder of the journal *Freedom at Issue* and the author of *Mass News Media and the Third World Challenge.*

Innovations in Telecommunications and Politics

GERALD BENJAMIN

In the Middle East, American-built "Hawkeye" battle-management airplanes employing computer-supported radar systems gave Israeli F-15 fighters, with complementary equipment, a decisive edge in engaging the Syrian air force in battle over Lebanon. In Washington, media experts pondered whether President Reagan's nine-day trip to Europe, beamed back to the United States via satellite, would boost his political fortunes. Also in Washington, the first patent for a computer program used in the financial field was granted to Frederick C. Towers after a ten-year-long legal battle. Meanwhile, in New York City, a telecommunications company that had been denied a cable franchise for the borough of Queens by the city council announced plans to bypass local regulations by providing programming via satellite. Also in New York, the Western Union Company, freed by deregulation to provide international services, signed an agreement with West Germany to offer "telex" high-speed computerized message transmission between there and the United States.

On Saturday, June 12, 1982, these five stories all appeared in an ordinary issue of the *New York Times*, itself compiled and edited using computers and dependent on the continuous transmission of information via satellite. All of the stories dealt with some kind of government involvement with communications. In their diversity, they illustrate the multiplicity of ways in which the communications revolution is transforming politics and government in the United States and in the world.

There are several interacting components of this revolution, which some analysts have compared in magnitude to the Industrial Revolution of the eighteenth and nineteenth centuries. The first component is the incredible advance in information processing over the past three decades. A computer that filled a room and cost about $1 million to manufacture before the widespread adoption of transistors in the early 1950s is now the size of a postage stamp and costs about $20. Over this period, too, the speed of large scientific computers has doubled about every two years, allowing their usage for an ever-widening array of tasks. In 1982 the fastest computers were able to process over 100 million operations a second. Simple description cannot evoke the extent of technological change this represents. In order to dramatize the change, Stanford University economist Edward Steinmuller drew a hypothetical comparison: "If airlines had progressed as rapidly as this technology, the Concorde would be carrying half a million passengers at 20 million miles an hour for less than a penny a piece."[1]

The gains in microelectronics based on miniaturization and concomitant cost reduction are expected to continue in the decades ahead, allowing not only the building of more efficient mainframe computers but also the general distribution of inexpensive personal machines throughout society. Advances in technology and programming will make computers "friendly," responsive to voice commands, and usable by people without any technical training. In 1980 about half of the United States gross national product involved information-processing activities. The number of computer systems at work in the United States reached half a million, doubling since 1974. Michael Blumenthal, chairman of the Burroughs Corporation, has projected that 7 million systems will be in use by 1984. And by the year 2000, fully two-thirds of the United States economy will be bound up in some way with the new "information society."

Advances in information processing have been paralleled by the impact of microelectronics on a wide array of information-gathering and dissemination activities—for example, the development of highly portable lightweight television cameras, the rapid spread in the use of audio- and video-cassette players, and, above all, the widespread availability of inexpensive radio and television receivers. But most significant are breakthroughs in satellite-based information gathering and transmission. Employing advanced electronic and photographic techniques and sensing equipment, satellites are now used for gathering military intelligence and scientific information with a vast range of uses, both commercial and political. After a period of experimentation in the late 1950s and early 1960s, the United States orbited the first geosynchronous satellite in 1963 for communications transmission purposes. On an equatorial orbit at a height of 22,300 miles, the geosynchronous satellite remains "stationary" over one point on the earth's surface. Three such satellites, located symmetrically around the equator, allow the reception of signals and their transmission for instantaneous communication between any two points on the earth's surface.

Fiber optics, developed from laser technology at about the same time as the first earth satellite was launched, also has great implications for the transmission and processing of information. Pulses of light traveling through fiberglass cable over long distances can be used to transmit large volumes of information accurately and cheaply, in the future perhaps more efficiently than satellite-based transmission. The adaptation of telephone systems from analog to digital

[1] Quoted in Edward Cornish, "The Coming of an Information Society," *The Futurist* 15 (April 1981): 17.

technology (the binary system on which all computer processing is based) has made the use of fiber optic cable possible and has also made the existing telecommunication infrastructure compatible with computers both for its internal operation and for transmission purposes. In the future, too, fiber optics may be the technological base for a new generation of ultrahigh-speed computers.

The synergistic effect of these technological breakthroughs is the very definition of the "communications revolution." The barriers between the methods for gathering, processing, and transmitting information have dissolved, bringing into question conceptual approaches that assume their separateness. One indicator of the turmoil in this field is the search for a new vocabulary—the emergence of words like *teleinformatics*, for example—to describe a result that is greater than its parts. The implications for politics, as for every other area of domestic and international life, are profound. As President John Kennedy once commented, "every time scientists make a new invention, we politicians have to invent new institutions to cope with it."[2]

The Political Process

At least since the rapid and widespread penetration of American society by television, analysts have been aware of the implications of technological change for the domestic political process. Television has eclipsed newspapers as the principal source of political information, and office seekers make great efforts to shape and time their public pronouncements so as to gain free access to television news programs. Paid television advertising has become essential for any campaign for a major political office. The concomitants of these two developments are enormous. Reporters and others who make decisions about television news coverage have assumed a gatekeeper role in the political process formerly held by party officials. Media consultants who can design effective campaign advertising and advise candidates on strategies for obtaining television coverage have displaced old-fashioned politicians as central campaign figures. The endorsement of some media consultants may be more important in legitimizing a candidacy than the backing of party leaders. For example, David Garth's decision to become involved in John Anderson's presidential campaign in 1980 lent great impetus to Anderson's candidacy. The costs of politics have risen enormously. Without public financing for most races, candidacy is limited to people who can either meet these costs themselves or can obtain support from groups that supply campaign funds.

Advances in the technology of television, speeding news coverage and making it more immediate, enhancing the visual appeal of political news through the use of computer-based graphics, continue to have incremental impacts on the political process. Limited in the time and resources allotted to its news organiza-

[2] Quoted in David F. Linowes, "Political Economy and Public Policy," *Vital Speeches*, vol. 47 (August 15, 1981), p. 665.

tions, however, network television remains dependent on the press to define "the news." Changing technology has, in part, altered this definition. Newspaper and television sponsorship of public opinion polls, for example, conducted over the telephone and analyzed with the aid of computers, has altered the political context. Nevertheless, although computerized operations and satellite communication have made it possible for daily newspapers to reach national and international audiences, as Stephen Hess points out in his essay in this volume, newspapers still depend for their substance on reporters who think and act much as they have in the past.

Perhaps the two greatest domestic political effects of the communications revolution have been the disintermediation and the nationalization (or at least delocalization) of American politics and government. For years, political parties have been weakened by the growth in the importance of primaries and by the decline in citizen identification with parties. By means of television, polling, and computer-based mail, candidates can enter into a direct relationship with citizens, bypassing the mediating institution of the party. Often organized according to local government boundaries made irrelevant by strict court-enforced standards for legislative apportionment, parties are less and less needed for campaign organization, voter mobilization, and even fund raising.

Two-way cable television promises to continue this process of disintermediation, with effects not only on parties but also on representative institutions. Spurred by the success of California's Proposition 13 in 1978, citizen initiatives and referenda have in recent years become increasingly important in United States politics below the national level. The use of one-way television in combination with large-scale community organization and polling has been tried with some success in Canada and in the states of Washington and Colorado. Now, interactive television, already in place in some jurisdictions in the United States and in Canada, France, and Japan, can be used either for "flash polling" or, after extensive effort to organize and involve the citizenry, to "obtain informed and deliberate opinion from a representative sample . . . on complicated issues."[3]

Theodore Becker, a political scientist at the University of Hawaii who has experimented widely with the use of television in politics in both his home state and in New Zealand, has concluded that "future experimentation will bring us closer to implementing pure electronic democracy in a real life situation and allow us to transform public opinion as developed and measured by teledemocratic means into the law of some lands."[4] But surely safeguards will be needed in such a situation to avoid the unbalanced presentation of information or the administration of biased questions. Technological advance to date has been paralleled by lower, not higher, political participation: the availability of the

[3] Ted Becker, "Teledemocracy: Bringing Power Back to the People," *The Futurist* 15 (December 1981): 7.

[4] Ibid., 8.

means to "talk back" does not guarantee that they will be used. In addition, participation through television is isolating. It tends to remove from citizenship the idea of collective social action. To participate in politics through interactive media, individuals must have the wherewithal to acquire the technology and pay monthly charges, dividing citizens into technological "haves" and "have nots." Finally, one need only recall the arguments in *Federalist No. 10* on the dangers of unrestrained majorities to realize that the potential for "pure electronic democracy" is, at best, a mixed blessing.

Politics is also delocalized by the communications revolution because appeals made in one place or to one group may be immediately communicated regionally or nationally. Thus the distributive politics of particular appeals to particular groups can no longer be made by candidates without their first calculating the possible effects on other groups in their electoral coalitions. In addition, nationalization of politics also occurs because groups with a single issue or interest are no longer geographically limited but can use computer-based technology to comb the entire nation for support. Single-issue politics is a product of technological change and gains much of its importance from two other effects of that change — the decline of political parties as mediating institutions and the dependence of politicians on high-cost media campaigning.

But when the combined effects of nationalization and disintermediation of politics are considered together, the future for political parties in America may not be as grim as it first appears. For example, the Republican National Committee (RNC) has sought to employ the new communications technology to revitalize itself and has had major successes in fund raising through computerized direct mail. In 1980 the party had 870,000 contributors (giving an average of $26 each), compared to 34,000 less than a decade earlier. The RNC has made itself a consulting center on modern campaign methods for party candidates at every level (though, aware of its institutional stakes, it will not share its mailing lists with them!). In addition, it used its resources to mount a national party-oriented advertising campaign in conjunction with the 1980 elections to help build state Republican organizations and to influence candidate selection in targeted districts at the state and local levels (an area in which the federal structure of parties previously blocked effective involvement). The party's work is given additional leverage by the tendency of many political action committees (PACs), supposedly antiparty organizations, to follow the party's lead in supporting candidates in incumbent-free elections.

If these developments are indicative of future trends — and the Democratic National Committee has expressed a desire to follow a similar organizational path — what may be happening is not the disappearance of the major parties at all. Rather, the parties may be changing in form from decentralized federal organizations to centralized unitary ones. And they may be changing in function so as to assume a service rather than a mediating role in the American political system.

Governance

Computers have become ubiquitous in American government at all levels. Some functions—the massive and increasing data-handling tasks of the Social Security Administration and the intricate calculations required by the National Aeronautics and Space Administration for manned space flight, to cite two examples—could not be performed without computers. Advanced data-processing machines are valuable for diverse tasks, ranging from the planning of energy-efficient school bus routes to the development of policy alternatives for meeting projected future needs. Computer models are used by the Department of Defense to consider the implications of alternative strategic choices and by the Department of State to help anticipate the effect on United States interests of expected resource scarcity in various parts of the world.

Both centralizing and decentralizing consequences for the location of political power in the United States have been projected as the result of increased use of advanced communications technology. Executives at all levels of government are natural focal points for the reporting of public affairs when compared to less-visible, decentralized legislatures; and, as a result, the media may in its day-to-day routine enhance the role in governance of one branch over the other. Most of the government's new communications machinery is often less understood by elected officials and senior civil servants than by experts. Thus, technological change may shift power from elected to appointed officials and disperse it throughout the middle of the permanent bureaucracy. Within the federal system the location in Washington of a preponderance of computer expertise and of resources to obtain the new technology and make it available, conditionally, to other levels of government may enhance already evident centralizing tendencies. But the proliferation of inexpensive, small computer systems, the ability of more political and administrative actors to store and retrieve enormous amounts of information, and the great difficulty of keeping secrets in an information age may have a decentralizing effect.

For an example of the effect of computer models on the locus of power, one need only consider the process of federal budget-making for fiscal 1983. With different assumptions about prices, unemployment, and economic growth for the coming year—themselves computer generated—White House and Congressional Budget Office analysts projected quite different revenue levels, expenses, and deficit figures. Disputes erupted over which computer printouts were most accurate and which should be the basis of executive-legislative budget negotiations. (Indeed, it might be fair to say that the disagreement over projections, and the resultant political conflict, had an impact on the economy that made everyone's projections less accurate.) In the end, the compromise, later abandoned, between the White House and the House of Representatives on which figures to start from was reached on the basis of political rather than econometric considerations. Although technical experts helped define the parameters of the debate, their work served—it did not control—the elective policymaking chiefs and their agents.

This example is indicative of the reality at the state and local levels as well. As with Congress, many state legislatures have hired expert staff and outside consultants to provide technological support for budget-making and other tasks, thus offsetting the former monopoly control by state executives over these resources and altering the political balance at that level of government. As for cities and counties, after exploring four models of the potential power shifts that might occur in them as a result of the widespread adoption of computer technology, William H. Dutton and his associates concluded that the principal effect was the reinforcement of already dominant elites.[5] Technological change favors incumbent officeholders.

Federal incentives, if sufficiently large, may result in centralization of information networks in some policy areas, as in the case of law enforcement. State mandates may occasionally result in forced uniformity for local jurisdictions because of the technical requirements of statewide systems. It does seem, however, that if institutional arrangements ensure a dispersion of power, as they do in most American jurisdictions, the new technology will ultimately be distributed through the systems so as to reinforce rather than overcome this dispersion. Dominating concentration of power solely as a result of changes in communications technology, either in the hands of elected officials or technocrats, will not occur.

Rapid technological change also raises a host of issues for communications as an object of public policy. Invasions of privacy are more and more likely as a result of both governmental and nongovernmental action. Constitutional provisions and laws written and interpreted in an earlier era may not provide adequate safeguards. Other legal issues are enormously diverse, ranging from the patent status of the softwear needed to operate the new machines to dealing with crime committed with the assistance of computers or with computers and their data bases as targets.

The threat of computer crime has made the arcane field of cryptography commercially viable, but open reporting of developments in this field (the research often sponsored by the National Science Foundation) has troubled the national security establishment. Some have suggested that the results of all research on this subject, and in some other computer-related areas as well, be classified. As a compromise position, offered before he resigned as deputy director of the Central Intelligence Agency, Admiral Bobby Inman suggested the establishment of a security technical information center in the National Security Agency so that developments in computer security could be shared with the government while protecting the proprietary rights of industry.

In the area of national defense, James Fallows has raised the question of whether the very availability of complex communications systems causes them

[5] James Danziger et al., *Computers and Politics: High Technology in American Local Governments* (New York: Columbia University Press, 1982).

to be adopted for their own sake, though the results may be counterproductive.[6] Strategic theorists worry, too, about the "electromagnetic pulse" that will result from the atmospheric use of nuclear weapons. This phenomenon, which disrupts ionized layers in the atmosphere, may completely upset all vulnerable means of electronic communication, cutting local commanders of strategic weapons off from the chain of command and making all deterrence scenarios that depend on centralized control questionable.

The de facto combination of the activities of a heretofore unregulated information-processing industry with the activities of the regulated information-transmission industry raised questions about the appropriate role for government in the resultant telecommunications environment. The thrust toward deregulation has been fueled by a belief in the value of competition, combined with a recognition that resource scarcity, the basic premise that underlay government regulation of broadcasting, has been invalidated by technological change (for example, cable television). Historically, however, major changes in communications technology have always been followed by an increased regulatory role for government.

Then there is the question of the unanticipated consequences of technological change that might generate new areas of governmental action or alter the scope or nature of action in established areas. For example, the rapid and widespread adoption of television had social effects apart from its principal overt goal, mass entertainment. One such effect was to turn the attention of people inward, to alter their former orientation to the streets and other places outside the home as focal points for social life. Consequently, street traffic and informal surveillance of communities by residents diminished—and opportunities for crime on the streets increased. Developments in telecommunications may well enhance this inward orientation and tendency toward social disintegration by allowing even more to be done at home. Much of the day's work and many of the sundry errands that now take people out may no longer do so in an era of two-way cable television and minicomputers. Instead of picking up the newspaper at the corner store, some subscribers will simply tune in the telex service on two-way cable. Instead of going to the supermarket, many shoppers will order over the cable and make payment by an electronic transfer of funds.

Speculation is possible, too, about the implications for some other social service areas. Massive capital investments will be needed in education to provide telecommunications literacy for a population, both in school and outside, that will work in an "information society." Teachers with different skills will be required, and the public sector will have to compete with industry for suitably trained people. Education costs will rise, even as the school-age population decreases. The resultant political tensions should be apparent. In the workforce, there will be major dislocations as the science of robotics advances and as older

[6] James Fallows, *National Defense* (New York: Random House, 1981).

people untrainable to function in a transformed economy become unemployed. Some fear the rise of structural unemployment and major new demands for governmentally provided alternatives to work. Economists familiar with the history of the impact of technological advance are more sanguine. They point out that the price system can work to increase consumption and employment where costs decline and quality increases, as has been so dramatically the case with computers.

International Implications

It has long been recognized that domestic political protesters, lacking other significant resources, are heavily dependent on access through the media to decision-makers for the achievement of their goals. In the international sphere, revolutionaries and terrorists also depend on newspapers, television, and radio to report their activities and transmit their demands and views. The Iranian terrorists holding the American hostages at the United States Embassy in Tehran communicated with the American people and government directly, by satellite and through the American media, during a time when the conventional channels of intergovernmental contact were closed. The use of the media to bypass normal diplomatic channels was a defining feature of that year-long crisis. Governments engaged in crisis management are aware of the central need to control the information flow as part of their overall strategy—for example, the Soviet Union in Afghanistan, the Poles during the crackdown on Solidarity, and, more recently, the British and Israelis while at war.

The more conventional conduct of international politics is affected by media advances as well. Faster, fuller, and more accurate communication may diminish the likelihood of conflict but may also lead to information overload or, on occasion, to pressure for action in haste. Heads of state who can be in instant communication with ambassadors abroad or military commanders in the field are less likely to delegate broad discretion for the execution of policy, increasing the burden on themselves and diminishing the attractiveness of those posts. While private negotiations between diplomats go forward, public appeals directed to the citizens of other nations may be attempted to alter the context of the discussions. Advanced technology makes keeping secrets more difficult, thus contributing to a potentially destructive dynamic of developing increasingly complex communications technology to overcome already existing technology, a sort of "informatics race."

Altered means of communications have not only changed the process of international politics but have also become its object. Critics in less-developed countries have long contended that exported American films and television shows carried with them an indirect but substantial political message. More recently, however, Western organizations' dominance of news gathering and reporting, enhanced by technological change, has been the focus of the attack on "the extension of colonialism by other means." At several recent UNESCO conferences,

Third World nations have sought to promote "responsible reporting" through a process of international regulation and licensing of reporters, and to generate alternative sources of news about developing countries through such cooperative efforts as the nonaligned news pool. The Western reaction to this thrust of the New World Information and Communication Order (NWICO) has been a vigorous defense of the free flow of information, most recently expressed in the May 1981 Declaration of Talloires.

A second aspect of the NWICO deals with Third World access to two finite communications resources, space on the electromagnetic spectrum, and the use of satellites for transmission of data and communications. Though technological developments have allowed more efficient use of the spectrum, allocations of which are controlled by the International Telecommunications Union (ITU), the spectrum remains finite. At recent World Administration Radio Conferences, developing countries, over the objections of the United States, sought distribution of frequencies for direct broadcast satellites for nations not yet able to use them, an abandonment of past practices of "controlled squatters rights." Anthony Smith has written that this reflects "a deliberate policy of trying to restrict the technological advantages which accrue to countries which develop early the economic and industrial capacity to exploit a world resource. . . ."[7]

The free flow of information is an issue not only in news gathering but also in commerce. It is here that the vulnerabilities of nationalism confront those of multinationalism. Governments are concerned because they are subject to information gathering, storage, and transmission techniques that may give others knowledge about their resources and nationals that even they themselves do not possess. Large-scale business organizations feel vulnerable because of the ever-present potential of interruption at national borders of the flows of data on which their operations rely. By mid-1981, twenty-two nations had adopted laws concerning the registration and licensing of data banks, time limits on the retention of records, and rights to be notified about personal records, to have access to them, to correct them, and to authorize their transmission abroad.

Recently, American companies have become suspicious that, in some nations, legitimate concerns about privacy may become "smoke screens for protectionism." A case in point is the Council of Europe convention on the subject, already adopted by several member nations and currently before the parliaments of others. The convention, which focuses on the privacy of information rather than of persons (as is the practice under United States law), also extends rights to corporations as "legal persons," and thus may force American companies to reveal proprietary information to competitors identified in their data banks. Though it provides that countries not interfere with data flows solely to protect privacy when data are going into the territory of another country that is party

[7] Anthony Smith, *The Geopolitics of Information* (New York: Oxford University Press, 1980), p. 122.

to the agreement and therefore has adequate safeguards, the convention allows such interruptions if the destination country is not a signatory. Since the United States is, of course, not in the Council of Europe, it cannot be a signatory, and its companies are thus potentially subject to this exception.

Working with the Organization for Economic Cooperation and Development, the United States has sought to develop privacy standards with which American companies can voluntarily comply without being placed at a commercial disadvantage. But these restrictions are not the only "invisible barriers to invisible trade" that have emerged recently. American companies providing information services have encountered difficulty in Japan and Europe in obtaining and retaining leased transmission lines for flat rates. Government-owned telecommunications monopolies wish to link rates to usage, thus making it more difficult for an American business to compete in foreign markets. In another development, Alain Medoc in France has done considerable work on the possibility of taxing information as a commodity in international trade. In Japan, West Germany, and Canada, restrictions have been implemented that will force multinationals to do more data processing within their borders and less in vast United States-based facilities. Part of the reason for this is to foster national development in communications by generating jobs and expertise. But part, too, is the fear in both developed and less-developed countries of American information power, with 56 percent of the non-Communist world's computers and 80 percent of its data banks located in the United States.

It has been estimated that the world market in the next ten years for communications equipment and services will reach $640 billion. Japan has developed a $300-million, ten-year national plan to enter the information age. It is proceeding with direct and indirect government support of corporate research and development efforts in a pattern similar to that used earlier in other industries. The European Economic Community has declared as a goal the obtaining of one-third of the world market in communications-related trade by 1990. In France, a national telecommunications policy has been devised and a special institute, initially funded at $17 million and directed by Jean Jacques Servan-Schreiber, has been established to address the communications needs of disadvantaged groups and Third World countries.

Clearly, United States dominance in world telecommunications is already being challenged and will be further challenged in the decade ahead. In response, some American companies, led by the Control Data Corporation, have sought to combine their research and development efforts for greater efficiency, though IBM, with its vast resources, continues to operate alone. A strong United States government effort will be needed to ensure that markets abroad are not closed to American companies, either by direct or by other means (such as inexpensive government financing to help competitors enter markets). International telecommunication standards that work against American companies (as in the case of color television) must be opposed vigorously. To date, United States policy has seemed uncertain and is not clearly centered in a single agency. Developing such a focal point and a comprehensive policy is a major and imperative challenge before American policymakers for the immediate future in the area of international communications-related trade.

The essays in this volume explore in greater detail some of the consequences of the communications revolution touched on in this introduction. The authors have focused on subjects to which each has been attentive in the past as a scholar, teacher, or practitioner. The intent was to have experts explore for the general reader the implications of change in telecommunications in three broad areas: the American political process, governance in the United States, and the process and substance of international relations. As is inevitably the case when the compass is so broad, limitations of space and time have militated against an exhaustive treatment of the subject. Nevertheless, these essays demonstrate how technological changes are revolutionizing communications in politics.

Historical Survey of Communications Breakthroughs

ERIK BARNOUW

Euphoric predictions greeted the advent of Morse's telegraph and the communication wonders that followed it—telephone, wireless, radio, television, and others. Each was seen to have special significance for a democratic society: each seemed to promise wider dissemination of information and ideas. It can be argued that this has happened, as predicted. But other results, in a contrary direction, were not so readily foreseen. Each new medium offered new possibilities for the centralization of influence and control, and introduced new monopoly possibilities. This essay examines the conflicting tendencies—inherent, to a large extent, in the technologies themselves—and may help in assessing the impact of new technological breakthroughs.

The invention of the telegraph made it possible for the first time to link distant areas by wire. The telegraph industry was founded by both large and small entrepreneurs, but the larger tended to absorb or otherwise eliminate the smaller. Soon after the Civil War the Western Union Telegraph Co. achieved a dominant position—it became virtually a monopoly. By 1873 its wires reached into thirty-seven states and nine territories and constituted the only nationwide web.

It is difficult to reconstruct the impact of the Western Union monopoly, but historians of the telegraph indicated that it yielded extraordinary wealth and power. In 1875, Representative Charles A. Sumner of California charged that news of sudden changes in market prices was repeatedly withheld from San Francisco until insiders had made large profits. Control of the flow of information apparently provided even more advantages than the profits made from the message business, which, monopoly-priced, was a bonanza in itself. Proposals to end the monopoly power by creating a government telegraph service linking United States post offices by an alternative web of wires—an idea that took hold in Europe—were repeatedly introduced in Congress in the decades after the Civil War, but Western Union always mustered crushing opposition. It worked in close alliance with the old Associated Press, which relied on Western Union wires. Newspapers aspiring to effective national or international coverage were totally dependent on these two monopolistic allies. It is said that newspapers backing postal telegraph proposals found their rates raised or service canceled. Publishers, editors, and reporters got accustomed to the idea that discussing postal ("socialistic") telegraphy was taboo.

Western Union had other persuasive pressures. Friendly legislators received "franks"—vouchers providing free telegraph privileges—in apparently unlimited quantities. Alvin Harlow quoted a letter to a New York politician from a Western Union official:

> Dear Mr. __________:
> I enclose another book of franks, of which I have extended the limits to cover all Western Union lines. I hope they will help you make a good nomination. Please use them freely on political messages, and telegraph me when you want a fresh supply.[1]

Politicians of both major parties shared in these benefits. In 1873, Western Union's president, William Orton, told his board of directors that the company's operations were subject to government action at various levels, and that the franks had saved revenue "many times the money value of the free service."[2] The power exercised by Western Union seems to have been used ruthlessly when it came under the control of Jay Gould. His hold over railroads, telegraph, newspapers, and politicians aroused exceptional fury, expressed in a song of the 1880s:

> We'll hang Jay Gould from a sour apple tree
> And bring to grief the plotters of a base monopoly.[3]

The influence of the communications monopoly over the political situation of the era may well have been considerable. The monopoly was eventually ended by Alexander Graham Bell's telephone, which generated its own web of wires. Western Union tried to forestall this competition with patent litigation against the infant Bell company. In 1879 Bell's successful emergence from this onslaught—contrary to most expectations—caused the company's stock to leap within weeks from $50 to $995 a share. A few years later the incorporation certificate of the American Telephone and Telegraph Company (AT&T) dazzlingly foreshadowed the future in store for the new medium. Dated 1885, it empowered the company to link every city, town, and place in the United States, Canada, and Mexico "with each and every other city, town or place in said states and countries, and also by cable and other appropriate means with the rest of the known world, as may hereafter become necessary or desirable in conducting the business of this association."[4]

[1] Alvin F. Harlow, *Old Wires and New Waves* (New York: Appleton-Century, 1936), p. 337.
[2] Western Union, *Annual Report* (1873), quoted in ibid. p. 336.
[3] Harlow, p. 405.
[4] Frederick Leland Rhodes, *Beginnings of Telephony* (New York: Harper, 1929), p. 197.

By 1909, AT&T was so wealthy that it bought control of Western Union with a $30 million check, and its president, Theodore B. Vail, also became president of Western Union. But by this time, antimonopoly sentiments had made headway, and the move was prohibited by government action. By this time also, the invention of the wireless, soon followed by radio, had created additional opportunities for the dissemination of information and ideas. The erosion of monopoly control had even permitted another telegraph company to come into existence, the Postal Telegraph Company. This private corporation, not connected with the postal system, adopted its name because of its antimonopoly ring. The Postal Telegraph Company later evolved into the powerful International Telephone & Telegraph Corporation (ITT). The monopoly's collapse also saw the rise of United Press International as a news-distribution agency offering competition to the Associated Press. All these developments seemed to rule out a return to the monopolistic nightmare of the Western Union heyday.

Yet the mix of contemporary communications technologies includes one element that, in the light of the history here recounted, deserves more attention than it has received. One of the most extraordinary of the new developments is optical fiber. AT&T, a leading pioneer in this development, refers to it as "lightwave communication," because it is based on the flow of laser beams through glass fibers. A glass thread the thickness of a human hair far exceeds the more bulky and expensive coaxial cable in its message-carrying capacity. A thin, compact cord of such fibers can thus serve a home, office, or other location with telephone, television, computer, and numerous other services, some involving two-way communication. The single link could thus bring to a home "communication center" not only all the entertainment and news services provided by present television and cable systems but also the means for such added features as sight-and-sound telephone, television conferences (with documents provided via printout), television shopping, voting, banking, mail delivery, and television use of film archives, museums, and educational offerings. The possibilities involved in this scenario – the technical feasiblity of which is no longer in doubt – are so overwhelming that little attention has been paid to the fact that all these innovations could enter the home, office, or other location through a single fiber connection. Would this create an extraordinary new monopolistic possibility? To be sure, the scenario envisages a multiplicity of choices for the citizen, but it is not limitless. At some stage a preliminary process of selection would be involved – not by the home but by a "lightwave communication" company. In its possibilities for control, would it revive the possibility of a monopoly like the one Western Union enjoyed? This question must be considered in combination with similar ambiguities involved in other new developments.

Licensed Communication

The regulatory control system set up for radio and television by the Radio Act of 1927 (PL-632) and the Communications Act of 1934 (PL-416) was essentially a licensing system, requiring government permission to communicate through these media. The technical nature of the media seemed to make such an arrangement necessary, if spectrum chaos was to be avoided. Yet the system would surely have disturbed the Founding Fathers, to whom licensed communication was anathema.

It was by licensing systems that rulers of Europe sought to control the dissemination of heresies during the centuries following the invention of the printing press. Under Henry VIII the operation of a printing press required royal permission; licensed printers, blessed by royal privilege, became gatekeepers of the society. John Milton wrote his *Areopagitica,* a protest pamphlet issued without the seal of approval, against such systems. This pamphlet denounced rulers for stifling "the winds of doctrine" with licensing requirements. He helped to make this a cause célèbre for generations of thinkers, including the Founding Fathers of the United States. The term "freedom of the press," in the Bill of Rights meant precisely freedom from licensing. America's founders were determined that in the new nation no one would need government permission to communicate with the public.

But the radio and television age did launch such a system of licensing. Some lawmakers felt troubled over this, so the new legislation provided that the regulatory commission—first the Federal Radio Commission (FRC), later the Federal Communications Commission (FCC)—must not act as censor. Its power was to lie in the right to renew or not renew a license at periodic intervals. The ban on ad hoc censorship strengthened the position of licensees vis-à-vis the commissions but did not touch the basic problem. Licensed broadcasters, like licensed printers of past centuries, had become increasingly powerful gatekeepers as the regulatory commissions tended to fall under industry control and became reluctant to regulate. With television becoming the chief source of information and ideas about world events for most Americans, the gatekeeper role has assumed central political significance. For groups and individuals, access to the electorate has become dependent on access to television. The election process has come to hinge on it.

It is widely argued, with some plausibility, that the array of new technologies has eliminated the problem. Cable television's multiplicity of channels has supposedly ended channel scarcity and made deregulation a safe policy, so that the broadcast media can now be left to market forces. This argument ignores the fact that the real issue has not been a scarcity of channels but the need for a government license to communicate. Cable systems are also licensed systems. Each is a local monopoly requiring a local franchise, in which acknowledged or unacknowledged political considerations can again play a part. Cable systems may revive some of the power of local political bosses, which network broadcasting is said to have severely weakened. In any case, these systems are clearly creating a new gatekeeping echelon.

The satellites by which cable systems are fed and linked are likewise government-licensed entities and create still another such echelon. These, like the cable systems, are high-technology and capital-intensive developments. With deregulation already proceeding, both satellite and cable systems are falling increasingly under the control of companies long associated with the media monopolies—AT&T, Western Union, ITT, General Electric, Westinghouse, Warner Communications, and RCA. To be sure, the central issue is access rather than ownership. This matter should therefore be examined in the context of still another area of ambiguity and conflict—the terms and costs of access.

Selling Air Time

When in 1922 AT&T pioneered the selling of air time in the way newspaper space was sold, the idea was prominently criticized as an offensive and unseemly intrusion of advertising into the home. A long-range political impact was foreseen by few.

Programming of every sort involves political implications; it reflects and in turn reinforces prevailing cultural assumptions. The direct and indirect influence of advertisers over sponsored programming, a large subject in itself, is too complex for detailed consideration here. But politicians and political scientists have generally been most concerned about the politician's access to the broadcast media as a means of access to the electorate.

American commercial broadcasters early established a close relationship with incumbent legislators, not unlike the relationship built around the "franks" of the Western Union monopoly. Legislators have regularly received free time to "report to their constituents"—in effect, a boost toward reelection—and this has in turn given broadcasting executives ready access to legislators. This close alliance has resembled the Western Union-Associated Press alliance of earlier days. But the free time has applied only to noncampaign periods. During election campaigns, when time-seekers are often numerous and in many cases unlikely to be successful, broadcasting time has generally been available only on a for-sale basis. This system has prevailed in the United States. But in most other Western democracies, time for important campaigns has been available free, by law, with allocations made on a mathematical basis—that is, in proportion to party enrollment, to representation in a legislature, or to votes in a previous election. Most European countries have outlawed the sale of time for political messages.

Even though the time-sale method has prevailed in the United States, broadcasters have never been eager to sell time for political appeals, especially when it meant preempting time occupied by popular and profitable entertainment. Political programs generally lose part of the audience to rival stations. Equal-time requirements have resulted in lower revenue for the stations, and broadcasters have accordingly sought to discourage political time purchases. Forbidden to charge higher than commercial rates (some had, for a time, levied higher charges), they introduced other obstacles. In the Standard Rate and Data volumes of the 1930s, a special rule appears for political broadcasts—cash in advance. Presumably, it was difficult to collect from an unsuccessful candidate and perhaps even more difficult to collect from a successful candidate. Candidates often had to arrive at stations with bundles of cash in envelopes.

Even with cash in advance, campaigning candidates have not been warmly welcomed. With time often on a sold-out basis and with prices rising, candidates have gradually been squeezed into making campaign appeals in thirty- and sixty-second advertising slots. The use of longer periods has virtually vanished. The shift has made electioneering increasingly simplistic, while giving the field of politics an air of hucksterism. But a more dangerous result may be the growing role of finance in the process.

The price of a thirty-second network slot, negotiated on a slot-by-slot basis, may vary from a few hundred dollars to more than $100,000, depending on the supposed size and nature of the audience of the surrounding programming. Local rates may likewise vary widely. Commercial sponsors will pay more for larger audiences and still more for spots that reach precisely their target sales audiences. Targets may be defined demographically—for example, "women 25 through 34 years old." Sponsors try to match program audience to product market and plot their appeals accordingly. The system pushes networks and stations into eliminating or sidetracking programs that do not yield high-value advertising slots. The low status of world and national news in network planning—twenty-three early-evening minutes preliminary to the main concerns of the evening—reflects the sales-dominated atmosphere. Politicians, hoping to reach an audience, thus find themselves caught in an expensive game of social engineering. Each segment of the audience seems to have its special price tag. Inevitably, politicians turn to advertising agencies to guide them through the time-buying maze and turn to pollsters, advertising writers, sophisticated producers, and special-effects virtuosos to develop their appeal strategies. The cost mounts accordingly.

The textbook view of the evolution of American democracy is that it began with government by the few—male, white property owners who constituted most of the voting population—but that the base has steadily expanded. In the early decades of the Republic, propertyless men won the vote and helped to create the Jacksonian era. Legislation after the Civil War enfranchised blacks, although enforcing the process was long blocked by such regional devices as the poll tax, literacy tests, and the white primary—key obstacles eventually eliminated by litigation. Women were enfranchised following World War I, and subsequent wars led to a lowering of the voting age. Extending the franchise appears to mean a broadening of the democratic base. But it can be argued that the broadcast era has reversed democratization by creating effective financial barriers to political action.

Running for major office with a television campaign requires access to staggering funds. A candidate not independently wealthy must get funds from others—individual donors or, increasingly, political action committees (PACs). PACs acquired special importance through the Federal Election Campaign Act of 1974, which was offered as a "reform" act. This law made it illegal for a candidate to receive more than $1,000 from any one donor. But there has been no limit on gifts to PACs, which have also been relatively unconstrained on how they spend money. The law appeared to have only minor effects on the 1976 elections, but in 1980 it clearly played a major role. PACs were organized by many kinds of groups. Business-related PACs, with unprecedented war chests solicited from employees, stockholders, clients, and others, proved especially influential. PACs mounted their own campaigns while also making campaign donations to candidates—donations that went primarily into television and radio drives. A congressional candidate regarded as pivotal might receive $100,000 or more in gifts from PACs.

To what extent has the value of the vote been eroded by the quest for donations and the commitments, spoken and unspoken, involved in the process? Money has always played a part in political campaigns, but it has recently acquired a decisive role, narrowing voter choices to those backed by the top economic groups. A constriction rather than a diffusion of power seems to be involved. Voter apathy, as reflected in lower voter turnout, may well be related to a pervasive sense of ineffectuality. But true believers in the new media feel that these technologies will, in the long run, bring wider and more intense citizen involvement. To support this argument, they cite a number of developments that are felt to offer the average citizen a more active media role.

Public Access

One of these developments is the public access channel. At one time the FCC required major cable systems to include a provision for such channels that would give the average citizen free access on a first-come basis. A court decision invalidated the FCC requirement, but many cities continue to include such a provision in local franchises. Results of public access have been mixed. Use of these channels has at times been exhibitionistic, drab, and trivial. Catering to diverse interests, the channels have seldom won a steady audience, and their significance is thereby diminished. The result is a sort of electronic Hyde Park corner, a place to express views on any subject to little effect. If in some locations the channels have played a meaningful role, it is partly because participating groups have used for their programming another new development, known as *video*—the use of videotape as an independent medium of expression. Low-cost and extraordinarily flexible, video may well prove a surprise factor in media competition.

Videotape entered the media industry in a quite different role. Videotape recorders, introduced in the 1950s with prices of at least $40,000, offered networks an improved means for recording and rebroadcasting live television programs. The videotape recorder promptly replaced the unsatisfactory kinescope, a film made by focusing a camera on a television tube during a performance. As videotape recorders fell sharply in price and became more convenient with the advent of cassettes, recorders began to be used in schools and homes for keeping copies of programs. Finally, with the introduction of videotape cameras and editing equipment, both increasingly compact, video became an instrument of production with unique characteristics. As equipment prices continued to drop, these characteristics appeared to offer revolutionary possibilities.

Video's images can be astonishing. Unlike film images, they require no developing and no laboratories. Production does not call for special lighting or for a studio. An individual can be a production unit. Reusable and low-cost tape can be expended almost as freely as an author uses paper. The camera, comparable in cost to a good typewriter, is easy to operate. Shots can be evaluated instantly and reshot if unsatisfactory. These characteristics give a new ease and spontaneity to the production process. Tape-editing equipment brings complex special effects within reach of individuals.

The advent of small computers has further expanded video's possibilities. Suddenly all sorts of people—individually or in schools, churches, interest groups, businesses—could enter video production. Such individuals or groups made documentaries, animated films, satires, dramas, and political arguments. Television screens already in place in homes and other locations were their ultimate link with audiences. The audience could be reached through various routes through the networks, by cable systems, or by satellites. But all of the licensed distribution systems and their gatekeepers could also be bypassed. The cassette is itself a delivery system. The compact half-inch, paperback-sized cassette can be distributed like a book and marketed by mail or through retail outlets. Easy to duplicate, cassettes lend themselves to small or large editions.

Citizen groups—political, ethnic, and others—have begun using video with dramatic results to document social problems. Antinuclear and environmental groups have been especially prominent. In some cases they have found networks or cable systems ready to carry their material. In others they have distributed cassettes to local groups for community meetings or local telecasts. These possibilities may enable video to become an important dissent medium, with a role analogous to that long played by such periodicals as *The Nation* and the *New Republic*. Effective as a springboard for group discussion, video may bring a new dimension of its own to the dissent role. Of similar importance is its possible capacity to decentralize the production of images and sounds and to wrest control from major production centers. The medium has distribution problems. There are also problems relating to competing products with incompatible standards. Once such problems are resolved, however, the medium may well give an effective voice to groups that were previously unheard.

But another of the new technologies, two-way television, has been most frequently trumpeted as having this effect. Sometimes called "interactive television," it is a key element in a cable system called QUBE, introduced in Columbus, Ohio, by Warner Communications. Its subscribers are invited to vote or to express opinions via push buttons. Throughout the day, subscribers' views are solicited on a number of issues: they can help decide winners of talent shows, debates, or quizzes. Their reactions to candidates can be measured throughout a campaign. Enthusiasts assert that this system has finally given the voice of the people its rightful place in the political process. Others are skeptical, considering push-button participation almost a mockery of the idea of democracy, one that further reduces political discourse to pollster formulations. But public reaction has been favorable, and a number of cities have launched plans for similar systems.

In addition to push buttons, two-way systems can place a microphone and camera into the home communication center for occasional or specialized uses—ultimately, for two-way videophone and television conferences. In some cable systems a camera, automatically surveying homes, serves as burglar protection, responding to any intrusion and videotaping the intruder. While camera surveillance is cited as an exceptional benefit in discussions about the future of two-way television, it is also the basis for dire predictions. The equipment so introduced into the home, subject to activation from the outside, is precisely the means used in George Orwell's *1984* for official surveillance of citizens.

Critics further point out that systems like QUBE hold computerized demographic data on subscribing homes and that information issued from homes via push buttons, microphones, or cameras goes into the cable system's data base. In the process, an astonishing range of information about any subscriber—views, finances, associations, and comings and goings—can be on file. No matter how well this information may be protected by coded-access devices, privacy would seem to be endangered and the possibilities for authoritarian control, subtle or otherwise, greatly expanded.

International Politics

The conflicting tendencies discussed so far have all been examined in their implications for domestic politics. But these tendencies also have a bearing on international politics, which offers some special problems of its own. For decades, United States television served much of the world. Its English-language programming, dubbed into other languages, has been broadcast in many countries, dominating their media environments. Most American programming is received as "entertainment" but carries political implications all the more effectively because it is viewed as entertainment. Spy series have regularly been based on cold-war premises. Most police and other action series seem to imply that social problems are solved by the violent defeat of villains by heroes. Few problems not solved in this way seem to be featured.

United States programming has won this hegemony to a large extent because of its low prices. Since the cost of American programs can be recouped in the home market, they enter foreign markets with an advantage over any local product. The price charged to a foreign television system is usually a small fraction of what it would cost to produce comparable material locally. For this reason, most foreign countries do not produce filmed entertainment series. At the same time, American manufacturers or their foreign affiliates are prominent among the sponsors. American advertising agencies are active on every continent.

The political implications are subtle but far-reaching. American clothes, phrases, gestures, music, customs, and products have become a normal part of the environment on every continent. Unconscious identifications so created are a political factor not measurable by any known standard but unquestionably significant. To many viewers, what is American is not "foreign."

The extent to which exported American culture influences the United States's international relationships may be greatly augmented (or challenged) by communication satellites. The satellite began as a relay instrument, a link for television and radio networks, computer networks, and cable systems. But Arthur C. Clarke, the science-fiction writer credited with conceiving the idea of the synchronous communications satellite (one that appears to hover over a fixed location), early foresaw that its implications went far beyond the relay function. In *Holiday* magazine, in September 1959, Clarke jocularly offered ideas on "how to conquer the world without anyone noticing." He considered the means available to both the United States and the Soviet Union and pointed out that ground stations, the links between satellites and television systems, are not really necessary. The Soviet Union, for example, might put a synchronous satellite high over Asia that could reach the entire continent. If, through Soviet trade missions, it could then flood the continent with low-cost television sets designed to receive the satellite directly, ground stations could pass into disuse. The technique could also be applied to Africa and elsewhere. From the satellite would flow drama, sports, dance, newscasts, quiz programs, and variety programs—everything to enthrall nations in the way that "even ostensibly educated nations have been unable to resist." The first prize on quiz programs would always be a free trip to the Soviet Union. Before long, uncommitted nations would become committed. Which of the two superpowers first establishes such a system, wrote Clarke, "may determine whether, fifty years from now, Russian or English is the main language of mankind."[5]

What Clarke did not say was that the United States and the Soviet Union might each beam satellite programming directly to the homes of the other nation. The right to communicate to all peoples by any means available, bypassing local authority, has been a key element in United States policy and doctrine, justifying Radio Free Europe, Radio Liberty, and other international communications activities. Similar rights are presumably available to all major and minor powers.

The possibility of such a satellite confrontation may seem remote. Yet programming by direct broadcast satellite (DBS) is already being considered by major corporations, including Sears Roebuck and Co., and the subject is already

[5] Arthur C. Clarke, "Faces From the Sky," *Holiday*, September 1959, pp. 47–48.

an issue in international debate. Will DBS prove an intercultural bridge, as is sometimes suggested, or will it raise the cold war to a new fury? Will nations start targeting each other's satellites with laser beams or other disabling devices? DBS seems to have such dramatic possibilities that it casts uncertainty over the future of all other media technologies.

Conclusion

Examined in diverse ways, each of the new technologies offers conflicting potentials. A resounding diffusion of information and ideas is obviously possible. But sobering possibilities for the centralization of influence and control can also be noted. The early centralizing effect of wired telegraphy and of network broadcasting will likely be repeated in other wired systems, especially in a nationwide array of systems linked by satellite. Video, alone among new technologies, seems to offer contrary possibilities.

A key ingredient in the current media explosion has been the discovery that many viewers, in spite of decades of "free" television, are prepared to pay for television programs and services and to pay premium prices for the more spectacular sports and entertainment events, as well as for such specialties as pornography. How politics will fare in this new plethora of media fare may not be clear for some time.

With cable systems offering a growing number of channels, it seems likely that the world of politics will be represented more frequently, especially on panel, interview, and debate programs. The proceedings of the House of Representatives are now carried by cable systems and occasionally prove spellbinding to some viewers. During crises, they may develop substantial audiences. The possibility thus exists that politics, more broadly present in the media mix, will become comprehensible to a growing number of people and that increased participation will be encouraged.

Yet any political program will apparently be competing at every moment with an array of sports, movies, quizzes, and variety and game shows and with reruns of situation-comedy, spy, cowboy, and police series. The new television will be a clamorous and competitive arena that may continue to downgrade the political process. It is possible that the present era, in retrospect, will be seen as one in which bread and circuses – in the form of social security and spectacular television – provided pacification and distraction while the affairs of government became increasingly mysterious and unknown.

Television and Election Strategy

THOMAS E. PATTERSON

It was once predicted that television would shorten the presidential campaign and reduce the opportunities for Americans to see their candidates in person. Did not television permit instant communication with millions of voters from a studio, thus saving the contenders from an endless trek around the country? Never again would a candidate have to do what Harry Truman did in 1948—whistlestopping across 30,000 miles, delivering over 300 speeches to the estimated 12 million Americans who met his train at their local railroad stations.

And, indeed, the campaigns of 1952 and 1956 were relatively leisurely affairs. Neither Dwight Eisenhower nor Adlai Stevenson endured an interminable road trip. Each appeared on television for fifteen- and thirty-minute talks with voters. Television was not a comfortable medium for either man, but it was convenient.

However, there were signs in the 1950s that television and personal-appearance campaigning were not exclusive. Estes Kefauver, always an outsider, sought the presidency through the primaries, expecting through news exposure and glad-handing to build the momentum and a popular following that party leaders could not ignore. In 1952, he defeated Truman by a 55–45 margin in New Hampshire's opening primary, went on to win all but one of the twelve primaries he entered, and had the support of 45 percent of Democrats in the final Gallup Poll before the national convention. Party leaders, however, remained unimpressed by Kefauver and handed the presidential nomination to Stevenson.

Nevertheless, Kefauver's barnstorming strategy was a model that many candidates followed in the 1960s, when it became evident that television actually rewarded candidates for taking to the campaign trail. Local television stations proved highly responsive to a touring presidential candidate, often building a day's newscasts around him. And with jet travel, the logistics of chasing from one media market to the next had become unimposing. It was even possible to campaign in the Northeast one day and in the Southwest the next.

An even greater influence on candidates was their discovery that personal appearances in the nation's cities enhanced their chances of being featured on national television. With the networks' preference for visually appealing stories, a candidate increased his odds of appearing on the evening news if he spent the day among cheering throngs on the campaign trail. Candidates also learned that the networks had a rather simple definition of newsworthiness. To be in the news regularly, it was not necessary for a presidential hopeful to prepare and deliver new speeches. It was enough to travel to different cities each day.

As late as 1968, however, the barnstorming strategy was only one option available to would-be presidents. Hubert Humphrey gained the 1968 Democratic nomination by staying out of the primaries and largely ignoring television. His campaign was directed at party leaders, who still had the controlling voice in the process. Richard Rubin has suggested that, through its intensive coverage of the primaries during the 1960s, television helped legitimize primaries "as *the* democratic way to make nomination choices," and thus contributed greatly to the demand for electoral reform that followed Humphrey's nomination in 1968.[1] Whatever television's contribution, control of the nominating process did shift to the public after 1968, as an increasing number of states adopted the primary as the means of delegate selection. In 1968, only 30 percent of national convention delegates were selected in primaries. By 1980, nearly 80 percent were chosen by this method.

It is now imperative for serious contenders to seek the nomination through the primaries and to depend on television and a personal appearance strategy. An early start is usually necessary, for a great effort is required to capture the public's attention. An important result of this situation is the influence gained by journalists. Before the increased impact of television, reporters were concerned mainly with covering the general election, in which the formulas of objective journalism dictate that the candidates of the two major parties be covered more or less equally.

Objective journalism, however, is an uncertain guide to the coverage of presidential candidates during the primaries. In the nominating phase there are many candidates to cover, and reporters, unwilling to give each the same billing, must decide who will be covered heavily and who will not. The media thus became "The Great Mentioner," to use columnist Russell Baker's term. The campaign of a candidate who is ignored by the media is almost certainly futile.

Would-be presidents now spend much of their time, particularly before the primaries, impressing themselves on journalists. A prime example was Jimmy Carter in 1975, when he spent the year visiting various newsrooms. Such efforts might be thought futile, since news organizations focus their coverage on "major" candidates, that is, contenders with at least some chance of gaining the nomination. However, there is no single standard for determining which candidates are the leading contenders. Thus, a candidate's persistence in contacting reporters and his willingness to tolerate countless days on the campaign trail far in advance of the opening primary can be taken as marks of a formidable challenger.

[1] Richard Rubin, *Press, Party, and Presidency* (New York: W. W. Norton, 1981), p. 192.

It was from such impressions that R. W. Apple of the *New York Times* in October 1975 wrote that Jimmy Carter looked like an early favorite in the Iowa caucuses, which were to be the first grassroots contest of the 1976 campaign. At that time, Carter was barely visible in the national polls, but Apple's story encouraged other reporters to take Carter more seriously and thus to cover him more heavily. From then on, whatever reservations Democratic leaders might have had about him, Carter was a legitimate contender. When the networks trumpeted the Iowa caucuses as "a critical test" and covered them live, they interpreted Carter's 28 percent showing as "a clear victory." His campaign was greatly strengthened as a result.

George Bush had a similar experience with reporters in 1980. As the Iowa caucuses approached, journalists wrote about his organizational and canvassing skills, followed by predictions that he would probably run strongly in the caucuses. In fact, he did finish first among the Republican candidates, and that earned him extraordinary press coverage in the following week. This focus resulted in one of the most extraordinary transformations in popularity in the history of opinion polls. In a survey conducted a few days before the caucuses, Bush was the nomination choice of fewer than 10 percent of rank-and-file Republicans nationwide. But in a national survey taken a few days later, Bush had the backing of 28 percent of Republicans, nearly tying him with Ronald Reagan at that point in the 1980 campaign.

Parties and Television

The notion is prevalent that television has wrecked America's political parties. But the parties were not very dependable even in their heyday. Although the persistent image of the old party is that of the urban machine that could deliver the votes of both the living and the dead, America's parties never had much organization. Nearly everywhere, the party consisted of a few, mostly inactive committeemen. Nevertheless, the party was at the center of election strategy in the early 1900s. Signs of what has been called the advertising campaign strategy (one based on the mass media and candidate-centered organization) were beginning to emerge, but the earlier militaristic strategy that stressed party loyalty and canvassing still dominated.

In the 1940s and 1950s the candidates continued to assign the party a role nearly as important as that of the media. This strategy was not a testimony of the party's vitality, for by this time rising educational levels, civil service reform, declining numbers of immigrants, and government welfare programs had deprived the party of much of its reliable manpower. Rather, the continued dependence on party was an indication of the difficulty of organizing the campaign more fully on the media: "The print media, consisting of a large number of locally based dailies, did not provide an especially suitable foundation for a national campaign. Nor was television able in its early years to provide much coverage. Like the radio, television's newscasts were brief, allowing candidates little more than passing reference on the nightly news. As well, the networks in the 1950s did not have the impressive newsgathering organizations that they have today. They made less use of pictures and depended heavily on news reports gathered by print organizations, reports that placed more emphasis on news events than on newsmakers."[2]

In the early 1960s, however, network television increased its newscasts to the present thirty-minute format and greatly expanded its news-gathering capacity. Presidential candidates then had a medium suited to their needs. Because the audience was national and the medium was visual, network news became the coverage of national politics—particularly presidential politics—and national personalities. Since 1964, in fact, the networks' evening news programs have been the principal targets of campaign activity. To a considerable degree, the candidates have scheduled their appearances around the networks' deadlines and have formed strategies around assumptions of how television organizations choose their themes and stories.

This change is as fundamental as any in American elections that has occurred in the nation's history. Michael Robinson has noted that the electoral system shifted "toward a more plebiscitary process of electing leaders—in which television journalism provided a more direct link between the public and the candidates than had ever existed."[3] Although this change did not start the parties on their decline, it did reduce the candidates' need for revitalized party organizations. In the past, party canvassing was stressed on the presumption that it was necessary in order to contact voters. Candidates are now willing to trust this task to television.

This does not mean, however, that candidates find television to be a completely trustworthy intermediary. Indeed, in a sense television is quite unreliable. The issues that concern candidates are often quite different from those that interest the networks. To a large degree, reporters' issues usually do not make for good strategy, and candidates' issues typically do not make for good television.

Candidates build their campaigns on "diffuse issues," in which their differences with the opposition are often subdued or indirect. These issues include broad policy commitments, such as promises to keep the peace or to increase government efficiency. One reason why candidates focus on general issues is that they are ordinarily the ones of greatest concern to the public. Such issues also tend to unify a coalition, since they involve consensual goals. Moreover, broad appeals, despite their universal acceptability, can be the basis for distinction, through the emphasis that candidates give to them. Every candidate wants a vigorous economy, but one may dwell on the need to control inflation, while another stresses the importance of reducing unemployment.

The candidates' interest in diffuse issues is also tied to coalition building. Each candidate naturally pledges his support for those groups and interests aligned

[2] Thomas E. Patterson, *The Mass Media Election* (New York: Praeger Publishers, 1980), p. 4.

[3] Michael Robinson, "Television and American Politics, 1956–1976," *Public Interest* 48 (Summer 1977): 14.

with his party. Since each party's coalition is broad and has unique elements, one candidate's pledges usually do not conflict directly with those of his opponent. In fact, Gerald Pomper's exhaustive study of party platforms revealed that, while a majority of the planks were distinctive pledges by one party or the other, only one in ten pledges placed presidential candidates in opposing positions.

Diffuse issues, however, tend not to be the favorites of reporters. The candidates' coalitional appeals are thought to be too narrow to be of general news interest, and their broad appeals are thought to be too vague for easy use. The press likes clear-cut issues that neatly divide the candidates. Preferably, the issues are also controversial and can be stated simply, usually by reference to a shorthand label, such as "ERA" or "busing" or "SALT." The press favors such issues partly because of their conflictual nature, which makes them colorful copy. But the major reason for the interest in these divisive issues comes from the reporter's eye for contrasts.

To be sure, candidates do not totally ignore clear-cut issues. When one develops and seems advantageous, a candidate will exploit it. Clear-cut issues also seem a prominent part of the last-minute strategy of losing candidates, who search desperately for a distinguishing issue that will rescue their effort. In general, though, diffuse issues are the cornerstone of election strategy, a conclusion supported by Benjamin Page's exhaustive study of campaign issues. He found that each presidential nominee since 1932, including ideologues like Barry Goldwater and George McGovern, stressed general goals and coalition appeals more than specific disputes.[4]

Other research has documented the same tendency, while showing also that television journalists tend to downplay diffuse issues. One comparison of candidates' speeches and election news, for example, revealed a dramatic difference in these communications. Whereas diffuse issues provided 67 percent of the issue content of candidates' speeches, these issues accounted for only 26 percent of the issue content on the nightly newscasts.

The networks' extraordinary depreciation of such issues is mostly due to television's preference for issues that do not require lengthy exposition and appeal to a diverse audience. The object of the network is to broadcast news of general interest in as short a period of time as possible. Even newspapers are sometimes reluctant to make room for the hundreds of words that may be required to present the candidates' diffuse appeals in a meaningful way. With its preference for action film and brevity, television news seldom makes time for such presentations.

A second tendency in journalism makes it difficult for candidates to get their issue messages across—the reporters' concern with what is new and different in the candidates' positions. This tendency was exemplified by a story broadcast on the "CBS Evening News" in October 1980, in which correspondent Bill Plante

[4] Benjamin I. Page, *Choices and Echoes in Presidential Elections* (Chicago: University of Chicago Press, 1978), chap. 6.

enumerated positions that Ronald Reagan had either altered or, more typically, ignored since his nomination. As Plante talked, X's were drawn across Reagan's face to dramatize his apostasy. Plante suggested that Reagan had moved to the political center in order to gain election.

Had Reagan actually changed his policies? The answer is no, apparent from a reading of Reagan's standard campaign speeches in the fall of 1980. He spoke then mainly of big government, high taxes, and inadequate national defense, the same things he had been attacking for over fifteen years. His positions were those of a conservative Republican, not those of the centrist that Plante portrayed. The reason he looked so different in Plante's report was that Plante, like other journalists on the campaign trail, focused on what was new in the candidate's statements, however slight these changes might have been. The first time that a candidate announces his position on an important issue, he can expect the television news to report it. After that the position is no longer newsworthy, but small amendments are, and candidates may give the appearance of being uncommitted to their positions and manipulative of issues.

Playing the Game

Before television, candidates had a great amount of control over their news coverage, because reporters' material came largely from the candidates' prepared speeches and news releases. Election news mostly dealt with questions of policy and leadership, a tendency that Paul Lazarsfeld, Bernard Berelson, and William McPhee documented in their landmark election studies in the 1940s.[5] Election news today, however, is dominated by reports on the "horse race," and reporters establish the agenda.

One reason for the shift in focus and control is the lengthened campaign. The shorter campaigns of the past worked to maintain the candidates' control of the agenda—what they had to say was less likely to be old news. There are, however, some 300 days in current presidential campaigns, each one of which is reported by the news organizations. It is all but impossible for any candidate to control the news for an entire year. Major speeches, after all, are limited in number. The lengthening of the campaign has created new opportunities for reporters to base news selections on their own interests.

Moreover, modern campaigns involve more strategy and maneuvering than earlier ones. This change, according to Carl Leubsdorf, "has increased the need for frequent assessments by the press of what is happening in a campaign and has downgraded the importance of daily stories that report what the candidate is saying, even though many newspapers still present them. Political reporting is often like sports reporting, concentrating on winners and losers."[6]

[5] Bernard Berelson, Paul Lazarsfeld, and William McPhee, *Voting* (Chicago: University of Chicago Press, 1954), p. 236.

[6] Carl P. Leubsdorf, "The Reporter and the Presidential Candidate," *The Annals* 427 (September 1976): 6.

The nature of television journalism has also contributed to the change in election coverage. Compared with newspapers, television places greater emphasis on "why" than on "what," attempting to explain rather than to describe. This use of interpretation may be explained by the need of television for tightly structured reports. Because television depends on the spoken word, its stories must have a clear focus. If they are to be understood readily by the listening audience, they cannot be allowed to trail off like newspaper stories.

There is no one aspect of the campaign around which television correspondents can build their narratives, and almost every aspect of the campaign contributes something at one time or another. However, television journalists tend not to view a campaign primarily as a battle over the direction of national policy and leadership. They see it mostly as a strategic power struggle between the candidates. Paul Weaver has described the view of reporters: "The game is a competitive one and the players' principal activities are those of calculating and pursuing strategies designed to defeat competitors and to achieve their goals (usually election to public office). Of course, the game takes place against a backdrop of governmental institutions, public problems, policy debates, and the like, but these are noteworthy only insofar as they affect, or are used by, players in pursuit of the game's rewards."[7]

The extent of the emphasis of the media and particularly of television on the competitive "game" between the candidates has been documented in content analyses of election news. For example, about 60 percent of television election coverage and 55 percent of newspaper election coverage in 1976 was devoted to "game" topics, such as winning and losing, strategy, tactics, and logistics. Only 30 percent of television coverage and 35 percent of newspaper coverage were devoted to the campaign issues and leadership subjects.

The change to a reporter-dominated, game-centered news has had a marked impact on election strategy. Before this change, candidates built their followings in great part on substantive appeals. Now they must contend with the dynamics of game reporting. The New Hampshire primary, for example, is regarded by reporters as the most critical test of the nominating period and is covered accordingly. Michael Robinson and Karen McPherson have documented the extraordinary emphasis placed on New Hampshire by the news media, particularly by television. In the three months leading up to the 1976 primaries, over a third of all newspaper stories on the presidential election and over half of all network news stories on the campaign related to this one primary, which was often portrayed as a "make-or-break" contest for the candidates.

As a consequence, it has become almost suicidal for a candidate to ignore New Hampshire. Senator Henry Jackson believed in 1976 that he could wait until the second primary week, when the Massachusetts primary would be held, to begin his delegate quest. After all, Massachusetts had many more delegates at stake than New Hampshire, and it was more representative of the nation as a

[7] Paul Weaver, "Is Television News Biased?," *Public Interest* 26 (Winter 1972): 69.

whole in its economic profile. Jackson won in Massachusetts, but lost the battle of strategy. It was Jimmy Carter—the winner in New Hampshire—who was on the minds of voters and reporters. "The fact is," wrote reporter Jules Witcover, "that the reality in the early going of a presidential campaign is *not* the delegate count at all. The reality in the beginning stage is the psychological impact of the result—the perception by press, public, and contending politicians of what has happened."[8]

Further, the media have the capacity to make their interpretations of the early primaries stand up. They can bestow their coverage in ways that magnify the importance of a strong showing in New Hampshire. After Carter won there in 1976, his picture was on the cover of *Time* and *Newsweek*, and his story accounted for 2,600 lines of their inside pages. The second-place finisher, Morris Udall, received 100 lines; all of Carter's opponents together received only 300 lines. The network television coverage given Carter that week was about four times the amount given his typical rival. The benefits of this publicity bonanza to Carter's candidacy are incalculable.

"Momentum," a term borowed from sportscasting, is now a major strategic concern of presidential candidates. After Ronald Reagan was nominated in 1980, his advisers decided to limit reporters' access to him, because they feared he might say something that would throw his campaign off track. This had almost happened during the primaries when Reagan told reporters an Italian joke, only to find the joke in the newspaper headlines. The rush of the primaries saved him from a lengthy roasting by reporters.

Gerald Ford was less fortunate in 1976. The consensus among journalists after his second debate with Jimmy Carter was that Ford had lost because he claimed Eastern Europe was free of Soviet domination. Although a number of hours passed before this message reached the voters, its effect was dramatic, for although viewers who were interviewed within twelve hours of the second debate felt that Ford had won (53 percent to 25 percent), those interviewed later felt that Carter had won (58 percent to 29 percent). The change was clearly due to news exposure, for in their evaluation of the debate only 10 percent of the people interviewed first mentioned Ford's statement on Eastern Europe. On their own, voters failed to see in his remark the significance that the press would later attach to it. Yet over 60 percent of those interviewed later discussed his Eastern Europe statement, most indicating that they, like the reporters, saw it as a major error causing him to lose the second debate.

In the week following the debate, the momentum that Ford had been gathering since the Republican convention, and which had brought him from far back to a virtual tie with Carter in the polls, slowed and then reversed. He never fully regained the initiative. Interestingly, his claim about Eastern Europe was not taken seriously by reporters. From the beginning, Ford's remark was seen as a slip and was reported in the news simply because of its disastrous effect on his

[8] Jules Witcover, *Marathon* (New York: The Viking Press, 1977), p. 202.

momentum. Over half of all election coverage on the evening newscasts in the week after the debate dealt with Ford's blunder and how it had hurt his campaign.

Advertising and Money

There is one aspect of television where old style politics still prevails—in the use of televised political advertising. This certainly would not have been predicted when the possibility of using televised advertising extensively in presidential campaigns was first considered. Then, critics were certain that advertising would introduce a wholly new kind of politics based on imagery, illusion, and emotional appeals.

Although some presidential televised advertisements are mere puffery, most of them are just the opposite. Using arguments that contrast sharply in content and style from most commercials for advertised brands, advertisements for presidential candidates tend to have serious messages, partly because voters are intolerant of commercials that try to sell candidates as if they were soap. Larry Sabato has related the case of the consultants who created some productlike advertisements for President Ford's 1976 campaign only to have test audiences snicker when the commercials appeared on the screen.

Television viewers also distinguish between product and political advertising. Viewers are about twice as attentive to presidential commercials as they are to those for national product brands. On television only every four years, the novelty of presidential advertisements attracts attention, as does their subject matter. Most Americans feel that choosing a president deserves serious consideration. When asked in one study to describe a presidential advertisement, 56 percent of the viewers gave a rather full description of one. In market research, any product whose commercials are recalled with half this accuracy is considered to have had a successful advertising campaign.

Viewers also evaluate presidential commercials differently from product advertisements. A study by the American Association of Advertising Agencies found that people watch product advertisements mostly for entertainment and like particular advertisements largely for that value. On the other hand, research indicates that people judge political advertisements mostly on what they say, rather than how they say it. People take the choice of a president seriously enough to want to receive useful information from the advertisements. For these reasons, and the fact that advertisements are an uncensored means for the candidates to present themselves as they wish, televised political commercials have become the most favored way for candidates to impress the main ideas of their campaigns on the television audience. In 1976, diffuse issues accounted for 62 percent of the issue material in the candidates' televised commercials. This content largely echoed the themes that the candidates were sounding in speeches on the campaign trail.

Similarly, a study of advertising in the 1972 presidential campaign found it to be a forum for the presentation of the candidates' issue priorities: "Issues covered by advertising included many of the campaign's most crucial ones. Nixon's positive spots were strongly oriented toward foreign policy—emphasizing the administration's accomplishments and its commitment to an active role for the United States in world affairs. Nixon's negative spots criticized McGovern's defense policy and his welfare proposals. McGovern's positive ads stressed Vietnam disengagement and domestic policies that would benefit working and lower-middle-class Americans—particularly tax reform and jobs. His negative ads attacked Nixon's Vietnam policy and his record on taxes, jobs, and inflation."[9]

Televised commercials appear to be effective communicators of basic policies. The most comprehensive study to date of the impact of advertising found that, while presidential commercials are not very effective in image building, they contribute substantially to voters' awareness of the candidates' issue positions. The study concluded: "Although the issue material contained in spots is incomplete and oversimplified, it is also abundant. . . . Advertising also educates voters because of the powerful way it transmits its issue content. Three basic advertising strategies—simplicity, repetition, and sight-sound coordination—combine to make presidential spots good communicators."[10]

Presidential advertising has another feature that makes it attractive to candidates. It communicates to the hard-to-reach voter. To get information from the news media, people must regularly watch the evening news or read the political pages in their daily newspapers. While nearly everyone on occasion will see a newscast or glance at a newspaper, about half of America's eligible voters have no news source that they follow with regularity. Before television, these citizens were almost beyond the reach of presidential candidates.

Lengthy television programs are not the way to contact these voters. In the 1950s, Eisenhower and Stevenson depended heavily on telethons, staged conversations, and documentaries; but candidates later discovered that fifteen- and thirty-minute television broadcasts were largely ignored. By one recent estimate, only one in twenty adults bothers to watch the typical thirty-minute candidate broadcast, and a large share of these viewers are already informed about, as well as committed to, the sponsoring candidate. Televised advertisements provide the solution for reaching the less-interested citizens, for they require no steady political commitment from their audience. Since most Americans watch television for entertainment, those exposed to political commercials include a lot of people who normally do not follow closely either the newspaper or television news.

From the candidates' viewpoint, there is only one problem with televised political advertising—its expense. It is no coincidence that the 1964 presidential campaign was both the first to use advertisements heavily and the first in which

[9] Thomas E. Patterson and Robert D. McClure, *The Unseeing Eye* (New York: Putnam, 1976), pp. 104–05.
[10] Ibid., p. 117.

overall campaign spending levels skyrocketed. The costs of a national advertising campaign for presidential candidates are extraordinarily high, even though candidates are guaranteed by law the lowest prevailing advertising rates. In both 1976 and 1980, the two major party nominees allocated about half of the more than $20 million in federal campaign funds they received to their televised advertising campaigns. To the degree that money reflects strategies, presidential advertisements are at the top of the candidates' thinking.

Television and Change

Television is truly the candidates' medium, and certainly the nature of the medium has influenced their use of it. They have adapted their strategies to the particular demands of television news and advertising in order to make the medium the cornerstone of their campaign efforts. It is a mistake, however, to say that television is the main reason why election strategy now plays a more decisive role in determining who wins the presidency. Television is simply the best medium available for candidates to capitalize on changes in voters and in the electoral process that have loosened traditional constraints to the point where strategy can matter significantly.

Before the communications revolution, party leaders often found it difficult to determine which of the possible contenders for the nomination would be the best party representative. Ordinary voters now have this responsibility, and they are much less equipped for the task. In fact, voters can be overwhelmed by a large field of semianonymous presidential contenders. In such a circumstance, how a candidate concentrates his resources, whether he runs well in the early contests, and whether the field is evenly balanced or contains more candidates of one philosophy than of another can help determine which candidate will first capture the public's imagination and thus possibly the nomination.

The practices of the television networks help narrow the candidates' strategic choices and may help decide which candidates gain a significant following, but television is not the main reason why an indifferent public is asked to choose among a large field of unkown presidential contenders. More important reasons may be party reforms that made primaries the basis for nomination and changes in campaign finance laws that provide the candidates with federal monies, thus encouraging many contenders to enter the race.

Television has also gained in importance because voters must depend more heavily on the information it provides. One of the most significant political changes in recent times has been the decline in voters' partisan loyalities. Compared with the 80 percent of Americans who identified with either the Republican or the Democratic party in 1960, only slightly more than 60 percent did in 1982 and most of them said that they were weakly committed to a party. When party loyalty was stronger, the large majority of voters supported their party's nominee; once the conventions were over, there were only slight fluctuations in the candidates' support. Because of the weakening of partisanship, the electorate is now more volatile and more sensitive to the issues, personalities, and dynamics of an election, which are developed largely through the media.

Although television has contributed to the decline of partisanship, this trend owes much more to the fact that the last domestic cataclysm, and thus the last party renewal, occurred during the Great Depression of the 1930s. The aging of the issues that grew from this cataclysm has left the voters adrift and thus has made their choices more vulnerable to how well the candidates choose their strategies, or, what has become nearly the same thing, how well they use television.

Television Reporting

JOAN BIEDER

The development of new technology in television news reporting has allowed broadcast journalists to produce instant footage of almost any news event. In 1981, for example, videotape cameras were routinely covering President Reagan's departure from a hotel in Washington, D.C., when he was shot. Unedited videotape was on the air eight minutes after the event occurred.

For more routine events, the new technology has meant a new immediacy in the coverage of political campaigns and elections. The 7 P.M. news can air pictures of what the candidates did on the campaign trail at 6 P.M. On election night, long before all the polls have closed in the West, television anchormen have often been able to tell viewers what the results of national, state, and local races will be. During the political conventions, which are "live, breaking news events," the new technology allows broadcasters to take the viewers away from the podium to the floor or out of the convention halls to airports, hotels, and the streets. In the coverage of the debates, however, the new technology has had little effect. Cameras focus on the candidates, the moderator, and the questioners, much as they would have twenty or thirty years ago.

Officials at each of the television networks generally believe that the quality of political coverage is an indication of the quality of a television news organization. This belief is one of the main reasons why each of the networks continues to spend in excess of $40 million on political coverage in presidential election years. (They spend less in other election years.) This belief also explains why, since the early 1960s, the networks have maintained year-round election units that do general political research and polling all year as well as gather information on forthcoming elections, research key precincts in order to improve their election-night projections of winners, study mistakes made in previous election predictions, and devise methods to improve their records in the next election. The same belief largely accounts for the fact that the networks, which are commercial enterprises, allot hours of valuable air time to politics, particularly the week-long gavel-to-gavel coverage of the national conventions, even though the number of viewers has steadily declined.

The belief that quality political coverage implies a quality news organization had led to increased competition among the networks, a competition heightened by technological advance. Today, the three networks have about equal financial commitments to the coverage of politics. All three are equipped with advanced computer, video, and transmission technologies. Each has large producing and reporting staffs. Each can react instantaneously should new information appear first on a competing broadcast. In the coverage of any political event there is little likelihood that one network will perform conspicuously better than the other two.

Election-night Coverage

Two technological aspects of election-night coverage are particularly important. One is the way in which information is collected. The other is the way that information is displayed to the viewers.

A major advance in gathering information came in 1964 when the News Election Service (NES) was formed. NES is a consortium of the three networks, the Associated Press, and United Press International. By pooling resources from all five participants, NES developed a fast, accurate vote-counting process that gave its members the identical tabulations simultaneously. Previously, each organization had been responsible for gathering the raw-vote data individually. With NES, the networks could concentrate fewer resources on counting votes and more resources on analyzing what the data meant and why people were voting the way they were.

Because of the concern in the early 1960s that pooling the vote count would violate antitrust laws, the broadcasters and wire services obtained a waiver from the Justice Department to set up NES, with the specific understanding that the collaboration would go no further. As a result of this restriction, the networks have not attempted to pool sample or key precincts. Thus the early prediction of winners, a frequently criticized feature of election-night coverage, remains highly competitive.

In general terms, the preparation for projecting winners works in the following way. Each network, through the research and analysis by its election unit, selects precincts within a state or other relevant electoral district. The returns from these key precincts are compared by computers with past voter performances. This comparison can yield the expected performance of the electorate throughout the district.

On the basis of this information, the networks compete in reporting results in each state on election night. Each network has its own ground rules as to exactly how much material from how many key precincts has to be in the computer before predictions are made on the air. Minutes count. It is regarded as important to be both the first and right. However, in a close election, the network that makes a prediction too quickly and is wrong pays a serious price. In that case, the network that has come out second and is right has won the day, raised morale, and gained executive approval. On election night in 1980, CBS was the last network to call Reagan the winner. In this respect, CBS suffered competitively.

Executive Producer Russ Bensley headed CBS election-night coverage. In a recent interview, he spoke about that evening: "You will recall that on election night 1980 NBC called the presidential race very early in the evening while we were still plodding along waiting for our actual votes to come in from the sample precincts. It was not a triumphant evening for CBS. We were certainly pure, but we were also certainly last. . . . We knew before we went on the air at 6:30 that it was all over for Jimmy Carter because of the figures we were getting from the exit polling. . . . But our rules insist we had to wait for actual votes and call actual states before we would start adding up electoral votes, and we didn't call it until sometime after Jimmy Carter had conceded."

The exit polling that Bensley mentioned has been done since 1967 by CBS, since 1973 by NBC, and since 1980 by ABC. This technique involves interviewing a sample of voters in selected precincts just after they voted. Pollsters collect data about age, race, sex, political inclinations, and attitudes on issues. They also ask people how they voted. The networks have traditionally used this information to give "trend" reports, to explain voting behavior, and to make analytical points about population subgroups. NBC used exit polling to predict races in 1980, as they had in 1978. ABC and CBS did not. The result was that NBC, which made its projection at 8:15 P.M., was the first to call Reagan the winner. ABC predicted at 9:52 P.M., CBS at 10:32 P.M.

Lester M. Crystal, NBC senior executive producer for elections and special events, said that while NBC used exit polling, it also used key precincts and raw vote data on a county-by-county basis to project Reagan as the winner. Nevertheless, Crystal acknowledged in a recent interview that NBC did rely very heavily on voter polls for projections.

Stanford Opotowsky, head of the ABC election unit, claimed that it is misleading to call any race solely on the basis of exit polls. Opotowsky cited a recent case involving the 1981 gubernatorial race in New Jersey, in which projections based solely on exit polling backfired. The race between James Florio and Thomas Kean was extremely close. ABC and CBS did exit polling for the New York City local stations (WABC and WCBS) on election day. The conclusion that each reached independently—that James Florio was the winner—was wrong. "CBS got burned because they made a call on the basis of their exit polling," said Opotowsky. But ABC was unscathed because it did not call the election.

Warren Mitofsky, head of CBS's election and survey unit, said recently that his direct prediction of a Florio victory resulted from experiments with exit-polling questionnaires and approaches. He added, however, that it was a mistake to use the results in a broadcast. CBS, which had not used exit polling to predict races until the New Jersey race, has not yet decided whether it will use the technique in future elections.

NBC, the only network that made predictions by voter polls in the 1980 election, did not do voter polling for WNBC in the New Jersey race, because the local station decided not to spend the money. NBC's Crystal concluded that projections can be based solely on voter polls only when "the margin is going to be very wide." CBS's Bensley has suggested that using exit polls alone for projections raises a serious question: "On the basis of our exit polling, if we wanted to use that only, we could have called Reagan the winner over Carter maybe at two o'clock in the afternoon. But our feeling is we would never do that. We are taking enough heat now for calling East Coast races when the West Coast polls are still open."

The networks have been severely criticized for the effect projections made after polls have closed in the East may have on voters in the West who have not yet cast their ballots. Before the 1964 presidential election, the chairman of the Federal Communications Commission, Dean Birch, asked the three networks to make no prediction until all the polls had closed in the West. But CBS President Frank Stanton contended that early projections did not influence voters. The networks did not hold back their predictions, and they have not done so since. NBC's Crystal and CBS's Mitofsky said they have not seen any confirmation that the impact of early projections has affected significantly either voter turnout or the outcome of any races on the local, state, or national level. Nevertheless, there appears to be a perception among people who have not studied election statistics and questionnaires that the projections may have an effect.

There is now some statistical evidence to support this view. A survey by the Field Institute of California concluded that 10 percent of those who failed to vote in California said that they did so because of early network projections.[1] The institute admitted, however, that the sample of the study was too small to be definitive. A study by the University of Michigan's Center for Political Studies examined why so many people failed to vote in the 1980 election and concluded among other things that "among eligible Westerners . . . 84 percent of those who did not hear [projections or Carter's concession speech] went to the polls, compared to 64 percent of those who did hear."[2]

Concern about these issues resulted in the introduction of a series of bills in Congress in January 1981. Hearings were held on bills that would provide a common poll-closing time across the country, change the election to Sunday or Monday, or restrict the release of results from presidential elections until all polls are closed. Two other bills related to broadcasting have been introduced, but hearings had not been held on them as of the spring of 1982. S. 762 would amend the Communications Act of 1934 to prohibit the broadcasting of results or projection of results of an election until all polling places are closed. In con-

[1] Mervin Field, "Attitudes Toward Media Coverage of the November 1980 Presidential Election," Field Institute Poll (January 1981).

[2] John E. Jackson and William H. McGee III, "Election Reporting and Voter Turnout," Center for Political Studies, Institute for Social Research, University of Michigan (October 1981), p. 3.

trast, S. 1161 would specifically forbid such restrictions, but would also direct a complete investigation "to determine if the practices of the communications industry affect voter behavior."

Technological advances have also affected the way information is displayed on election night. From 1952 through 1960, the networks used manual displays to indicate the raw vote in each state—walls of boards with thumb-wheel numbers on them. Employees would climb up on scaffolding when there was a new vote total and turn the wheels, one at a time, until they had the right figure. Then a camera would focus on the new numbers. Soon after, digital display units (DDUs) came into use. An operator would sit at a console and push keys, causing the electromechanical numbers to flop over one by one until the correct vote total appeared. Still, the only way to get the totals on television screens was to point a studio camera at the board. There was a board for every race arranged in a big circle around the studio so that reporters in the studio could refer to them.

Computer displays were first used to cover the 1974 elections. The boards and studio cameras were eliminated and replaced by a computer console with a television screen. The operator could also call up a colored background over which the numbers would be superimposed. When the producer decided it was time to report on a particular state, the information would appear on the home television screen. The figures were automatically kept up-to-date, and in-studio correspondents had computer screens set into their desks.

This system, with some improvements, is essentially the same one used today. In addition to making it possible to display letters, numbers, and any color as the background, by 1976 the operator could simultaneously call up a still color photograph of the winning candidate. The device that made this possible, called the electronic still store (ESS), can display still pictures of every candidate for every race. CBS has used the device since 1976. The most recent innovation, computer-driven graphics, lets a producer turn information in the computer instantly into a visual display available for broadcast. That information may include such things as how blacks voted, how women voted, how a candidate did in this election compared to the previous one, and which states are being won by which candidates. A producer who wanted to display how blacks voted and how whites voted could use a simple trend graph, a pie chart, or a bar graph. Technologically, these displays are not difficult. The difficulty lies in buying the hardware and doing the necessary extensive programming.

At ABC and NBC, computer-driven graphics have already been integrated into election-night coverage. ABC uses a machine made by Dubner. It can create an electronic photograph by using the graph-paper principle. The information is put into a computer program, the computer instructs the machine, and the result is a "sketched" photograph.

Election-night coverage, a regularly scheduled television event, usually begins at 7:30 P.M. and can last from five to ten hours or longer, depending on the closeness of the race. But network officials say that some day technology will reduce coverage to a short, simple program. CBS's Bensley said, "My own vision of the ultimate election night is one in which every voting machine in the country is wired directly into a central computer some place, and there is a common across-the-country poll-closing time. So, at nine o'clock you push a button and all the results will print out instantly or display themselves on your screen. You go on the air, do a half hour broadcast; you go off the air, and that's your election."

Campaign Coverage

A major change in all television coverage came in the mid-1970s when the networks and most large local stations began using electronic news gathering (ENG) cameras and editing equipment rather than 16-millimeter film. The technological advance did away with time-consuming film processing. At the same time, developments in microwave transmission allowed live coverage from almost any location. Television suddenly acquired the immediacy that radio had always had.

Before ENG, all news stories from the field were shot, processed, edited, and sent or "fed" to the network via telephone lines before they could be aired. If a candidate gave a speech at noon to farmers in a small midwestern town, the film had to get to the nearest affiliate (sometimes far away) for processing, editing, and feeding. Usually, the correspondent brought the film to the local affiliate and wrote the script there. Sometimes he wrote and recorded the script in the field. The producer then took the film while the correspondent stayed with the candidate.

At the station, after the film was processed and edited, the cut story was fed via telephone lines from the local station studio to tape machines at the network. This usually occurred between 5:30 and 6:00 P.M. eastern standard time so that the story could be broadcast that night. By today's standards the process was logistically difficult and enormously time-consuming. In the 1972 presidential campaign, for example, if an event did not happen by 3:00 P.M., it could not be on the evening news. Thus the candidate who desired television coverage had to make news in the early part of the day. The half-hour evening news programs have remained the most important showcases for candidates, since they are viewed by more people than the morning news, the Sunday talk shows, or specials. Today, what a candidate or other politician says at 6:30 P.M. can be on the air at 7:00 P.M. If the event is important enough (say, a presidential statement), the president could speak at 7:00 P.M. and be on the air live, as the first item on the evening news. Processing has been eliminated. Feeding can be done from microwave trucks or via audio/video loops installed in a hotel or other location by the telephone company. The new technology means that candidate A can say something in the morning; candidate B can respond before noon; candidate A can say something in the afternoon; and candidate B can respond again. There is a chance that both exchanges will make the evening news. Now "fresher" events late in the day are more likely to get on the evening news than those in the morning.

If the technology has brought immediacy, it has taken away almost all time for reflection. A strong news judgment and a certain amount of restraint on the part of correspondents and producers are required to ensure that the new technology and intense competition do not lead them to broadcast a candidate's latest remarks rather than his or her most significant statements. In the days when film had to be processed, a reporter and producer would have about forty-five minutes to go over the script, make extra telephone calls, and think. Now, editing begins immediately at the feeding point. There is less chance to be selective and almost no time to be contemplative.

The reflective contribution of television journalists to evening news pieces may, however, be irrelevant. A 1975 study claimed that the evening newscasters pay only limited attention to major election issues and "devote most of their coverage to the trivia of political campaigning that make for flashy pictures."[3] However, it concluded, television has little effect on influencing a person's vote: "The public does not evaluate presidential candidates on their personal looks or skills as entertainer, but on their political records which the networks fail to communicate." The authors said that the medium is not the message, but that the viewer furnishes the message: "When the viewer is watching the candidate he prefers, the televised image is a good one. When watching the opposing candidate the viewer receives a poor image."[4]

Indeed, the technology that has brought more immediate coverage to news events has not changed the nature of routine campaign stories. Correspondents and producers still concentrate on what the candidates do each day. The result, some critics say, is an overemphasis on the "horse race" aspect of the campaign. Roone Arledge, president of ABC News, acknowledged this criticism in a program on his network, noting: "There's a tremendous tendency [to report the horse race aspects], and it frustrates the politicians, and I don't blame them, for us not to ever be able to get into any substantive issues the way the political people would like us to do. Because we don't have the time to do it. So what we get is impressions of competence, or impressions of niceness, or honesty, or whatever."[5]

But other technological advances have encouraged the networks to do longer stories based on the candidates and the issues. These advances have made it possible to produce issue stories without being totally dependent on good but often distracting footage. The new technology allows the networks to illustrate issues in a manner interesting to the television audience. A packaged piece on issues, for example, could use freeze frames, written-out statements on the

[3] Thomas E. Patterson and Robert D. McClure, *The Unseeing Eye* (New York: G.P. Putnam's Sons, 1976), p. 2.

[4] Ibid., p. 22.

[5] Elmer Lower, "The 1980 Elections," *Broadcast Journalism 1979–1981: The Eighth Alfred I. Dupont-Columbia University Survey*, Marvin Barrett, ed. (New York: Everest House, 1982).

screen to illustrate candidates' positions, and graphs to show how an incumbent fared in the previous election in one state compared to how polls show him doing in the same state for the current election.

Two machines have revolutionized conveying "issue" pieces in politics. The first is the character generator. Originally used to superimpose the name of a person over his picture as he talks in a television spot, the machine has become more sophisticated. It is equipped with a variety of types and is able to change colors. Changes are made electronically and instantaneously. It can print words or phrases on the screen to reinforce the thoughts the reporters are reading from their scripts. In nonpolitical stories, character generators have been particularly helpful in illustrating inaudible materials, such as the audio from the conversation recorded by the black box in the cockpit of a plane that has crashed. Similarly, an interview with a person who does not speak English or whose English is not quite understandable can be "illustrated" by the use of a character generator.

The second machine is more complicated. It is called Digital Video Effects (DVE). This machine allows a producer to alter the size and position of any picture. The DVE machine can also do rotary spins of pictures, create mirror images, give the appearance that pages of pictures are being turned, and much more. There are also computer systems in which an editor types information into a keyboard, creating cuts, fades, dissolves, edits, and controlling changes in video and audio. There are "switchers" that can put borders around any image; the size of the border can be changed, and so can the color. Using these devices, the new technology allows a person talking about an event to appear in one corner of the screen while a picture of the event is on the air.

With the new technology, stories are less dependent on moving pictures, and visuals can be created to illustrate a story that is not inherently pictorial. Thus, this technology enables television to do analytical pieces that it might not otherwise be willing to try, for fear that a viewer, confronted with a correspondent talking for a long time about a candidate's position on the issues, will tune out, mentally or literally. Before the new technology, networks had to rely on film clips to provide visual interest. This sometimes meant using footage that was only marginally related to what the correspondent was talking about, or it meant avoiding certain areas of analysis because there was nothing available to illustrate them.

In the three- to five-minute issue pieces that ran on the network during the 1980 campaign, these new techniques were used extensively. The intent was to do thoughtful journalism by taking a closer look at the issues, something day-to-day campaign coverage does not allow. The question is, Was that goal accomplished? At a recent conference on presidential election coverage, NBC anchorman Roger Mudd noted that since he was not covering the 1980 campaign, he became an "ordinary consumer of news." He said he found himself confused and that the pressure to "make it interesting" has turned coverage into a quest for entertainment over information. Mudd said: "With the quantels [DVEs] and spinning cubes there is so much coming at the viewer it's a wonder he understands anything."

The conference, "Television and the Presidential Elections," a forum held on January 29-31, 1982, was sponsored by the Institute of Politics at Harvard University and underwritten by the three networks. Academics, writers, producers, executives, and correspondents discussed where television succeeds and where it fails in covering the candidates and the campaigns in the presidential race. CBS's Bruce Morton, who was on the campaign trail in 1980, said at the same conference that reporters are better now: "There are better ways to display the information they have, and they make a conscious effort that it be understandable."

Whether producing day-to-day campaign coverage or issue pieces, the new technology is susceptible to the general criticism of gimmickry. Michael Arlen commented most effectively on the problem of technology overriding the substance in the coverage of the 1980 presidential campaign: "This is the day of the modulating engineers: the cutters, splicers, mixers, editors and so on. Listen to the hum of our modern political campaigns: the whir of tape on editing and mixing machines—forward, stop, reverse, snip, snip, splice, forward, stop, snip, whir: our new montage actuality."[6]

The engineers are the new political kingmakers, says Arlen. The only thing missing from this new technique, he notes, is "a coherent sense of the candidate. . . . It's as if the love that politicians once bore the public has been transferred to the new machines and the machines have lost sight of the one thing about these strange, complex and driven people that anyone ever really cared about: *Who they really are*."[7]

On the other hand, CBS's Senior Producer Bensley said simply: "I think a good graphic properly scripted improves the story. I think a bad graphic improperly scripted can confuse it. . . . There's nothing to say that a graphic automatically improves the story, it doesn't necessarily, but it certainly gives you the possibility of improving the story and better journalism could and should result."

While the networks have the commitment to do issue pieces and the technology to make them visually interesting, they may have to confront campaign managers who resist journalists "packaging" their candidates. Lester M. Crystal cited a case in point. In preparation for a number of issue pieces during the 1980 campaign, NBC requested an interview at length with the candidate Ronald Reagan. "'I don't know if we want to do that or not,'" Crystal recalls Lyn Nofziger saying, "'because on the night that you [NBC] decide to deal with, say, nuclear disarmament, we may want to deal with something else that night . . . but if you've already got in your hands this material, you may decide to go in a different direction than what we want to be emphasizing, so I don't know if it's

[6] Michael Arlen, "The Modulating of the Presidency," *New Yorker*, October 27, 1980, p. 174.
[7] Ibid., p. 177.

in our interest to do the interview.'" Subsequently, Reagan did the interview, but as Crystal pointed out, "its revealing as to their thinking . . . and the whole process of manipulation that goes on and that we have to deal with."

The issue of manipulation on the campaign trail is a growing concern, but it is not clear who is manipulating whom. The technology has allowed the strategists three, four, or five chances to get their candidates on the evening news during any given campaign day. They try to schedule visually attractive events and speeches that they hope will make headlines. The candidate now must be prepared to react immediately and constantly throughout the day, never quite sure which reaction will be on the evening news. Though the managers want to retain a certain image of their candidate, they schedule eight events in one day (which makes this more difficult). The press covers each event and tries to get fresh, interesting comments from the candidates.

Judy Woodruff, NBC's White House correspondent, said at the Harvard conference that television gives a "real life" image of the candidate, something newspapers cannot do. But she said the main obstacle to better coverage was that the press was trapped into the daily schedule of the candidate. Soon reporters become prisoners of that schedule, and *New Yorker* writer Elizabeth Drew then commented that many who cover political campaigns for any length of time become cynical. Robert MacNeil of WNET said that the cynicism of reporters often surfaces in the two or three sentences that close a two-minute story for the evening news.

ABC anchorman Frank Reynolds, who covered the White House during the Johnson administration, suggested another reason for the sarcastic tone of correspondents on the campaign trail: "If you follow any candidate day by day, you find it difficult not to get sarcastic," he said. "After all, what is a political campaign? Is it not an attempt to manipulate by those who run the campaigns?" Often the product of this mutual manipulation is an evening news piece that is in part an organized event and in part a reporter's choice of picture and sound, and an on-camera close-up that is all too often repetitive, written by a bored or exhausted correspondent. Candidates attempt to balance the manipulation by the press by paid television advertisements that they control. Television attempts to balance manipulation by the candidate by going beyond the day-to-day coverage.

Nominating Conventions

Convention coverage has become four nights of television programming that the networks and the politicians begin planning a year or more in advance. It is officially "live coverage of a breaking news event," but it is not the same kind of news as the story of a candidate's day; nor is it the same kind of breaking news as the winner of a Senate seat as reported on election night. Rather, it is the often slow-moving procedure of voting on the recommendations from the rules and credentials committees, accepting, rejecting, reworking the party platform, and listening to speeches. The audience has steadily declined in the past few years, even though new television technology has given coverage a faster pace. The wireless microphone has allowed correspondents to wander through their section of the convention floor free of cables. The mobile minicameras have allowed coverage outside the convention hall – the arrival and departure of candidates, as well as caucuses, demonstrations, and rallies.

If the media could depend on the National Guard being called in, as it was to quell street rioting during the 1968 Democratic National Convention in Chicago, or an upset such as George McGovern's nomination in 1972, perhaps viewers would stay tuned. But the 1976 and 1980 conventions were relatively uneventful. In 1980 both Carter and Reagan had secured the required number of committed delegates to ensure their nominations a month before the conventions. The networks, however, had already committed $14 million each to cover the conventions gavel-to-gavel, for they needed the lead time to buy additional equipment, to order construction, to secure hotel rooms, and so forth for the approximately 800 employees who would work in Detroit or New York covering the conventions. Thus, in the summer of 1980 the networks found themselves committed to expensive gavel-to-gavel coverage with not much of a story to tell.

During the 1980 Republican National Convention, sixteen network correspondents with wireless microphones worked the floor looking for stories. In an anchor booth, former President Gerald Ford and Walter Cronkite discussed the possibility of a Reagan-Ford ticket. There had been closed-door meetings touching on the topic during the day. In a short time, CBS developed a major story around the proposed ticket and the other networks began pursuing the story. At one point, Cronkite said the ticket would be Reagan and Ford. What viewers were watching in effect was news gathering on the air. Verification, usually possible in prepackaged pieces, is not always possible on stories reported as they are happening. With a great deal of air time to fill and not much news to fill it, newscasters can report wrong information.

The absence of drama in 1980 has led some network executives to contemplate cutting back convention coverage in 1984. CBS President Thomas Wyman has said that if the conventions are "coronations" in 1984, CBS will not provide gavel-to-gavel coverage. The other networks have considered the possibility of reducing coverage, but it is unlikely with the competitive element so strong that any one network will commit itself to cutting back coverage in the near future.

Political developments also need to be considered. In March 1982, the Democratic National Committee voted to change its rules so that 14 percent of the delegates to the nominating convention in 1984 would be chosen on the basis of their office or party status and without commitment to a candidate. This development could mean more political maneuvering on the floor of the convention, which might make coverage more interesting. The networks will doubtless take that into consideration when they plan their coverage.

Presidential Debates

The technology used to cover the first televised debates between presidential candidates Richard M. Nixon and John F. Kennedy in 1960 was virtually the same technology used in the 1976 and 1980 debates. It is doubtful that anyone would have given technology a second thought during the 1976 debates had not the sound system malfunctioned during one of the debates. The viewing audience saw a picture of Gerald Ford and Jimmy Carter but heard nothing for twenty-eight minutes.

An issue involving technology developed after the debate between Ronald Reagan and Jimmy Carter on October 28, 1980, just seven days before the election. Immediately after the debate concluded, ABC correspondent Ted Koppel invited viewers to call one of two telephone numbers to register their votes for the candidate they thought had won. ABC tabulated 700,000 calls and announced that Ronald Reagan had won the debate by a two-to-one majority. Koppel said frequently on the air that this telephone poll was unscientific, but many critics called the poll a major abuse of power by the network.

ABC News President Roone Arledge said of the poll, "It was made with the idea that the response would be much more limited than it was. I think had there been a 100,000 people call-in instead of 700 and however many thousand, and had it come out 51 to 49 in favor of one candidate or the other, there would have been a lot less said about its pernicious irresponsibility and all the rest." CBS News President Bill Leonard commented on the journalistic value of the ABC poll: "I think that if I had suggested that [kind of poll], professional people within my organization would have tied my hands behind my back and put a rag into my mouth and said, 'You can't do that.' "

People who may not have seen the debates heard about the ABC poll through the morning newspapers or on radio and television. ABC News seemed to have found a way, using its technological resources, to satisfy the network's competitive desire to be the first to report the winner. Two questions remain: Did the result of the telephone poll overshadow the points made by the candidates in the debate? Did the poll ultimately affect voters' balloting decisions?

Conclusion

The new technology in television has enhanced the immediacy in covering elections. Results of races are tabulated more quickly, and projected winners are announced earlier. Events on the campaign trail and reactions to them are also aired with increasing immediacy. The underlying competitiveness among the networks has intensified, and the result is a more intense use of the technology. But it is probably not correct to argue that these elements mean that the number of people carefully watching election coverage has greatly increased. Thomas E. Patterson has noted that it would be inaccurate to claim that television has made politics an everyday experience for people who have traditionally ignored it. He wrote: "Only interest in politics, and the availability of time to pursue it, can create that result."[8]

Soon, the avoidance of election coverage may prove to be nearly impossible. News has become a profit-making business. Local stations already provide up to two hours of news at dinner time, plus a half hour in the evening. Two hours of news programming are available on three of the networks in the early morning. The networks provide the half-hour evening news programs, and they broadcast one-minute news headline breaks during the day. CBS has announced plans for a news program from 2 A.M. to 5 A.M. ABC, which broadcasts "Nightline" at 11:30 P.M., has also announced a news program from 12:00 P.M. to 1:00 A.M. and another from 6:00 A.M. to 7:00 A.M. NBC has announced plans for a news program from 1:30 A.M. to 2:20 A.M. A smaller network, Independent Network News, provides a one-hour evening broadcast as well as a midday program to more than a hundred stations. If the new programs develop, viewers in New York City and other major markets could be exposed to television news for more than ten hours a day. In addition, by the summer of 1982, there will be three all-news cable programs on the air twenty-four hours a day: Ted Turner's Cable News Network I and II and ABC/Westinghouse's Satellite News.

As the news coverage continues to increase, the amount of political coverage will also increase. This will not necessarily mean that everyone will become addicted or even interested in that coverage if they do not have the prediliction to begin with, but it does suggest that it may become nearly impossible for those viewers to avoid or totally to ignore television's coverage of the elections. It also suggests that the technology that has played perhaps the key role in closing the time gap between when an event occurs and when viewers see it will continue to thrive.

[8] Thomas E. Patterson, *The Mass Media Election* (New York: Praeger Publishers, 1980), p. 66.

The Decline of Political Parties

DAVID H. EVERSON

Several themes emerge from recent commentary about American politics: the decline of political parties, the intransigence of single-issue groups, and the growing militancy of ideological groups of the left and right and their creation of political action committees (PACs). PACs and campaign consultants have pioneered in the application of communications innovations, such as direct mail, to political fund raising and campaigning. The full effects of these widely noted changes are not known precisely (nor is there full agreement on their extent), but many analysts deplore the consequences of these trends for the policymaking process in the United States. They argue that policymaking has become too fragmented to respond adequately to complex issues, such as energy and the economy. The result is that many policies are incoherent and government is often immobilized. At the heart of the problem, according to many writers, is the decline of parties, because parties have historically been the essential elements of the coalitions necessary for making coherent policies. Some suspect that the collapse of parties is virtually irreversible and therefore regard the future of American politics as bleak.

A counterview is that parties can adapt to the new political conditions and become stronger through the imaginative use of the very techniques employed in the service of candidates and causes. As evidence, one can point to the reversal of the fortunes of the Republican party, which had been crippled by Watergate. The impressive Republican gains at the state and national level in 1978 and 1980 can, in part, be traced to the imaginative use of the new weapons of politics. But that is only part of the story of Republican resurgence. The party had been able to reach a consensus on a set of ideas and to communicate them to a receptive public. The ideas were general (less government regulation, for example), but a shift in public sentiment in a conservative direction made them timely. The Democrats have been slower to respond to the changing methods of electoral politics. They have clung both to outmoded concepts of campaigning and to an exhausted set of political ideas that had been generated as a response to the Great Depression. The opportunity for party revival is there, but its realization is uncertain because fresh political ideas and effective governing are also needed. The acid test of a revived party system is whether one or both of the parties can capture the imagination and loyalty of the electorate through relevant programs and performance in governing.

American elections have changed dramatically in the past quarter-century. They have evolved from contests between rival political parties employing traditional, grass-roots methods of campaigning to skirmishes between candidate-centered organizations that hire as mercenaries highly specialized political consultants who deploy the latest hardware and techniques of mass persuasion. In this essay, the rise of technological politics and its relationship to the decline of parties will be discussed, and the potential for parties to be revitalized through the use of these techniques will be explored. The first question is: What is meant by party decline?

Party Decline, 1896–1964

The scholarly and popular writing on party decline in the United States is now extensive. Although much of it is concerned with the contemporary decline, American political parties have been gradually losing strength for some time.

Political parties as such were not envisioned by the founders of the American Republic, but they began to form shortly after its birth. Parties provided the essential structure to democratic conflict. After some false starts, vigorous two-party competition became the norm by the late 1830s. For much of the rest of the nineteenth century, the American party system was at its peak. The nineteenth-century American two-party system was marked by the following characteristics:

- Close competitiveness of two parties viewed from a national perspective.
- Exceptionally high levels of voter turnout in presidential elections.
- Stable and strong loyalty to party on the part of much of the electorate.
- Vigorous state and local party organizations.
- A militantly partisan press.
- High levels of party cohesion in Congress, especially in the late nineteenth century.

In the late nineteenth century and the early part of the twentieth century, the party system went through one of its periodic transformations, which political scientists now call a "realignment." Realignments result in fundamental shifts in the patterns of voting of groups and in the creation of new electoral coalitions. Realignments shape the nature of party competition and define the major policy issues to be addressed in the subsequent years. This particular realignment coincided with other changes in the political system to trigger a long-term decline of the parties. In the late nineteenth and early twentieth centuries, the Populists and Progressives were targeting the political parties as objects of a series of reforms designed to achieve popular democracy and to check the excesses and abuses of "party machines." Among the reforms introduced were the Australian (secret) ballot, the direct primary, initiative, referendum, and recall, and nonpartisan elections. The combined consequences of realignment and reform significantly weakened American parties. Voter turnout dropped off substantially. Two-party competition declined nationally. The Republican party became the dominant national party, controlling Congress and the presidency. The Democratic party was weakened nationally but retained its solid grip on the South. The Republican party controlled the presidency from 1896 to 1932 with the exception of the Wilson administration (1912–20). Each party had conservative and progressive wings, but the conservatives predominated in both. By 1928, there was a large unmobilized electorate made up of women, immigrants, and other nonvoters who presumably could be won over by either party.

The Depression triggered another partisan realignment, which resulted in the creation of a Democratic majority that came to be called the New Deal coalition. Voter turnout surged upward, and a new policy agenda focused on issues of government responsibility for economic security. The New Deal reversed the fortunes of the two parties, eventually establishing Democratic hegemony and checking the decline of party, but Walter Dean Burnham has argued that this was only a temporary respite. The contemporary decline seems to have emerged in full force shortly after the 1964 presidential election, reaching its nadir in the mid-1970s. Whether a party revitalization can occur again, through realignment or some other mechanism, is uncertain.

Decline of Parties since 1964

By the 1950s, a portrait of the American electorate was drawn that emphasized the absence of ideology or specific issues as political motivations for the American voter and the overwhelming importance of a sense of affiliation with party for presidential and congressional voting. "Partisan identification" was the great anchor of stability for the political system. The Democrats, as heirs to the New Deal tradition, were the majority party (in Congress and in the electorate), but the popular war hero, Dwight D. Eisenhower, was president. There was almost a bipartisan lull in national politics. Nevertheless, party identification was the single most important cue for voters.

Since the 1964 presidential election, however, there have been numerous clues that the American party system has weakened. The most obvious of these was the loosened grip of the parties on loyalties of the electorate in presidential voting. That loosened grip is indicated by the following trends:

- The substantial decline in voter turnout in national, state, and local elections.
- The major increases in the numbers of independents, especially but not exclusively among the young.
- The sharp upsurge in ticket-splitting.
- The greater instability of the electorate (often called "volatility") within and between elections.
- The increases in the expression of negative attitudes toward parties.

All of these trends suggest that party, as a cue for voting and as a motivating factor in inducing voter turnout, has receded in importance.

The decline of party loyalty means that presidential elections involve fewer voters, many of whom base their choice on the personal characteristics of the candidates as communicated via the mass media. The uncertainty of the outcome of such elections has increased substantially, and the likelihood of landslide elections has grown. Three of the last six presidential elections (in 1964, 1972, and 1980) were won by 10 percentage points or more, two by Republicans and one by a Democrat. The links between the winners of presidential elections and their fellow partisans in Congress have diminished, making it increasingly hard for presidents to govern effectively. Even a landslide presidential victory does not guarantee the winner that his party will control Congress, and even if control is not divided, presidents have problems with Congress. Jimmy Carter had a near two-to-one Democratic advantage in Congress but had great difficulties in achieving his major policy goals because he could not depend on a cohesive Democratic majority to support his initiatives. Many Democrats in Congress did not feel that Carter was responsible for their election victories, since he received fewer votes than they did in their districts. The tortuous passage of Carter's comprehensive energy proposal of 1977 is a prime example of this problem.

The emasculated condition of the parties in the electorate is not the only sign of partisan decay. The cohesion of the parties in government has undergone a long-term decline, and the recent period has been no exception. Moreover, some local party organizations have also diminished in strength. The disarray in the Chicago Democratic organization caused by the break between Mayor Jane Byrne and Richard M. Daley suggests that the last great urban party organization has been wounded, perhaps fatally. Nevertheless, a case can be made that national party organizations have been strengthened. The Republican National Committee (RNC) has worked to reinvigorate state Republican parties. There is some evidence suggesting that not all local party organizations have declined. The decline of parties, if confined to a view of the electorate, can be overstated. But on balance, it is fair to conclude that despite some gains, the parties are weaker than previously, especially in their hold on voters.

Parties Lose Their Monopoly

The decline of parties results from a loss of their near monopoly over several significant tasks that must be performed in a democratic society. Historically, parties have nominated candidates for public office, organized, financed, and conducted campaigns for office, mobilized the electorate on election day, served as a powerful cue for voters in making decisions, and played a major role in organizing the government. The performance of these functions led some observers to assert that parties were indispensable instruments of democratic government and that "the political parties created democracy and . . . modern democracy is unthinkable save in terms of parties."[1] At the base of this party

[1] E. E. Schattschneider, *Party Government* (New York: Holt, Rinehart and Winston, 1972), p. 1.

system was a vital local party organization engaged in grass-roots political activity and fueled by patronage.

Control of nominations by parties was first weakened by the widespread adoption of the direct primary in the early twentieth century. More recently, the most important nomination, that of the presidential candidate, has escaped the grip of parties as a consequence of the reforms of the late 1960s. The proliferation of primaries for delegate selection and the concomitant growth in influence of the mass media have precluded a meaningful party role in the selection of presidential candidates. One result is that the winners may represent only one faction of a bitterly divided party, as was the case with George McGovern in 1972. This may in turn cause landslide presidential defeats for the party. Or as in the case of Jimmy Carter in 1976, candidates may be nominated and elected who have few ties to the party leadership.

Candidates have quickly realized that, independently of the party, they can use the new techniques of politics to finance, conduct, and control their own campaigns. With sufficient resources, campaign consultants, including media and polling specialists, can be hired to fight the electoral wars. The strategies employed in such campaigns often serve to play down party ties. Larry J. Sabato observed: "It was difficult to know whether GOP nominee John Heinz was a Democrat or Republican in his 1976 Pennsylvania Senate race, since David Garth [Heinz's renowned media consultant] fashioned his media campaign around an anti-party theme: 'If you think Pennsylvania needs an *Independent* Senator, elect John Heinz.' One of Garth's spots actually featured a glowing 'endorsement' of Heinz's character by Jimmy Carter . . . to further confuse the voter."[2] It has become as popular to run against one's party as it has been to run for Washington political office by attacking Washington politicians.

Presidential elections represent the purest case of these trends. The competition is between rival teams of experts schooled in the most recent techniques of mass persuasion. Candidates maintain expensive polling operations that are more sophisticated than the commercial pollsters. Both primary and general-election campaigns are coordinated by the personal staff of the candidates who, in turn, hire specialists in various aspects of the campaign. Often these campaign staffs carry over into governing. Pollster Patrick Caddell, for example, was an important influence in the Carter administration.

Efforts to persuade voters are based on an understanding of the television age—the rhythms of the campaign are closely attuned to the needs of network television. The demands of making the evening news dictate the candidates' schedules and their efforts to create news. In turn, the media focus undue attention on campaign gaffes.

Voter preferences are now more volatile, even in general elections, and voters have frequently defected from their party in recent presidential elections. More voters call themselves independents. In addition, they are more likely to vote for one party in the presidential election and another party for Congress. Once

[2] Larry J. Sabato, *The Rise of Political Consultants* (New York: Basic Books, 1981), p. 289.

the election is over, the coalition that produced victory in the presidential election is often unable to produce an effective and durable governing coalition. Since winning presidential candidates have frequently gone their own way in getting elected, ad hoc (and interparty) coalitions must be forged for molding policy. Even Ronald Reagan's economic proposals in 1981 required a significant number of Democratic defections to pass in the House.

Interest Group Resurgence

The decline in parties has been paralleled by a growth in the activities of a variety of interest groups. Three species can be identified: the so-called single-issue groups, ideological groups, and public interest groups. Although there have always been groups that concentrate on a narrow range of issues (such as Prohibition), the current lore is that the number of groups passionately devoted to the pursuit of limited agendas (such as pro- or antiabortion groups) has increased substantially. In contrast, ideological groups (generally conservative or liberal) pursue a broad range of issues, but with similar intensity. Public interest organizations, such as environmental groups, presumably have objectives that do not involve immediate economic gain for their members. (Of course, no group ever claims to be against the public interest.) Interest groups of all types have taken the lead in adapting the new technologies of data gathering, data storage and manipulation, mass persuasion, and money raising to politics.

The organizational form of interest groups is the political action committees (PACs). In 1972 only 14 percent of the contributions to House and Senate general election candidates came from PACs. By 1980 the PAC share had risen to 25 percent. The number of PACs, barely 600 in 1974, surpassed 2,600 in 1981."[3] Perhaps the most visible of these PACs has been the National Conservative Political Action Committee (NCPAC). NCPAC took credit for defeating four liberal Democratic senators in 1980, spending $4.5 million on polling, television and radio advertising, and direct mail, $1.2 million of that to attack liberal Senate incumbents.

The growth of PACs and their attempts to influence elections have been spurred by three developments. The first is that the costs of political campaigning have skyrocketed, even when inflation is taken into account, because of the candidates' reliance on expensive political technology. A second factor is that public financing of presidential elections, which began in 1976, has driven interest-group dollars into congressional elections. Finally, in the wake of the landmark Supreme Court decision of *Buckley* v. *Valeo*, there has been an increase in "independent" expenditures in support of candidates (including presidential candidates). This decision allows a candidate's supporters to spend an unlimited amount to aid him, as long as they have no contact with the candidate or his campaign. Independent expenditures, mainly for conservative candidates,

[3] Nancy Lammers, ed., *Dollar Politics*, 3d ed. (Washington, D. C.: Congressional Quarterly, Inc., 1982), p. 41.

nearly tripled between 1975 and 1980. The previously mentioned NCPAC efforts are an example.

Even elected officials have gotten into the independent expenditure business. Senator Jesse Helms's own PAC, called the Congressional Club, was the second largest raiser and spender of independent funds in the 1980 elections. Elizabeth Drew has characterized this development as a "revolution in politics." Drew explained: "Helms now heads an informal group of far-right Senators . . . which meets every Wednesday. . . . This bloc . . . constitutes slightly less than half of the Senate majority, and is changing the nature and style of the Senate."[4]

Efforts to support and defeat candidates are not, of course, the sole property of conservative ideologues. Single-issue groups have also pursued their causes through electoral politics. Environmental and antiabortion groups provide illustrations. Environmental Action, since 1970, claims to have defeated twenty-four members of Congress who have appeared on its "Dirty Dozen" lists. Antiabortionists, building on their successes since 1976, entered the 1978 congressional races supporting favored candidates with PAC funds and volunteers. All of the candidates they opposed in these races lost, and the antiabortionists claimed credit for the outcomes.[5] Naturally, these efforts cost considerable sums of money. How do PACs raise their funds?

Much of the money expended by ideological and single-issue groups of the right and left is raised by computer-based direct mail, a mass mailing that simulates a personal letter by the use of computers and the development of extensive lists of potential contributors. Direct mail has long been a staple of financing for charities and various businesses, such as the solicitation of subscriptions to periodicals. The purposes and effects of direct mail are described in this manner by Larry J. Sabato: "Direct mail combines sophisticated political judgments and psychological, emotional appeals with the most advanced computer and mailing technologies. Used for two very distinct purposes (persuasion and fund raising) direct mail is considered a necessity by many candidates [and groups]. . . ."[6]

The acknowledged king of direct mail is Richard Viguerie, a conservative activist who formed a direct-mail corporation in 1965. In the 1964 Goldwater presidential campaign, Viguerie had discovered the potential for raising large sums of money from many small contributors. After that, he formed his own direct-mail business. In 1978, Viguerie raised $5.2 million for the reelection of Senator Jesse Helms. But his most successful work has been done for issues organizations. Viguerie claims among his victories for direct mail and conservative causes the defeat of the common-site picketing bill by presidential veto in 1975 and 1976. However, not all of Viguerie's candidate clients have been pleased with his methods. For example, Philip Crane, a conservative candidate

[4] Elizabeth Drew, "Jesse Helms," *New Yorker*, July 20, 1981, p. 82.

[5] William J. Crotty and Gary C. Jacobson, *American Political Parties in Decline* (Boston: Little, Brown and Company, 1980), p. 135.

[6] Sabato, p. 220.

for the Republican presidential nomination in 1980, ended his "formerly close relationship" with Viguerie and "attempted to continue direct mail fund raising from his central campaign office. . . ."[7] Crane was unhappy with the proportion of money actually raised for his campaign versus the overhead costs.

The techniques for personalizing direct mail and soliciting the contributions have become very sophisticated. The signature, the date, and even the ink used are designed to suggest intimacy. The return rate varies, but it can go over 10 percent, with an average of around 5 percent. Of course, as more groups go into the direct mail business, the returns may decline.

Although the political right has been more successful with direct mail, liberal groups use these techniques as well. One of the pioneers has been the National Committee for an Effective Congress, which has raised money for campaigns by mail since the late 1940s. At the close of the 1980 elections, liberal-oriented groups recognized the need to combat the New Right by emulating its tactics. Five new liberal organizations were created, but at midyear none was as successful in fund raising as the National Committee for an Effective Congress (and this committee could not match the efforts of conservative groups such as NCPAC). Two of these groups were also considered vehicles for the probable presidential candidacies of Edward Kennedy and Walter Mondale.

Direct mail is not a panacea for fund-raising problems. The costs are considerable. Moreover, it takes time to develop the lists of potential donors on which the appeal is based, and there is inevitable overlapping in the names on the lists of the various ideological groups. But the PACs' use of direct mail and other campaign techniques has made an impact on the parties and their methods of organizing, fund raising, and campaigning. The Republican party has studied the methods of campaign consultants and PACs and has employed the same techniques to its own ends.

Direct Mail and the Republican Revival

Writing in 1972, when the thesis of party decline was beginning to be heard, John S. Saloma III and Frederick H. Sontag argued that "instead of the demise of political parties, we conclude that in many instances broader more systematic management, financial aid program approaches are instilling new vigor into party bodies."[8] The national Republican party is a case in point. Under the leadership of former United States Senator William Brock (Republican, Tennessee), the Republican National Committee made remarkable strides toward organizational reform, modernizing the party and revitalizing it at the state level in the wake of the disastrous effects of Watergate, which were particularly felt in the 1974 elections. The Republicans adapted the new technology of

[7] Ibid., p. 250.
[8] John S. Saloma III and Frederick H. Sontag, *Parties* (New York: Alfred A. Knopf, 1972), p. 345.

politics to the tasks of candidate recruitment, political financing, and campaigning to a degree that far surpassed the efforts of the Democratic party.

Among the steps taken by the Republican National Committee (RNC) were the following:

- Creation of regional party directors (one for every two to six states).
- Creation of organizational directors in all fifty states (paid for by the RNC).
- Introduction of a program of technical assistance in the area of fund raising.
- Creation of a local elections campaign division (which involved district analysis, candidate recruitment, training and education of candidates and managers, and on-site assistance to candidates).

There have been three basic assumptions underlying the Republican approach. The first is that the party needed to be rebuilt from its base—that is, at the state and local levels. Therefore, RNC support would go to help create strong state party organizations. Second, the party could use the new technology of politics to its advantage. Third, the party could help recruit and train fresh, attractive candidates to run for office.

Ultimately, victories in state legislative elections could influence reapportionment and lead to the capture of Congress, an important goal since the Republicans realized from the Nixon experience that control of the presidency was insufficient to shift the policy direction of the national government. The RNC program has been financed by successful fund raising, utilizing direct-mail solicitations of cash contributions of less than $50. The Republicans still hold a considerable edge over the Democrats in raising and spending money. But the emphasis on smaller contributions not only gave the Republicans a financial advantage. It at once broadened their base and gave citizens a way to tie themselves more closely to and participate in the party. Over time, the national party organization changed its role, from being dependent on state and local organizations to having them become dependent on it for resources and expertise in the use of the new political technology.

But it was not just technology and fund raising that contributed to the Republican successes in 1978 and 1980. The party also had a set of ideas on which the party was basically agreed and that began to take hold in the electorate. These ideas captured the mood of a more conservative electorate and laid the groundwork for Republican triumphs in 1978 and 1980.

Republican success awakened the Democratic party to the need for more effective direct-mail fund raising, computerized voter targeting, and more extensive polling. But the Democratic party is still divided on the basic direction of its policy. No new party philosophy has come forward to replace the outmoded liberalism of the New Deal era. The Democratic party needs to reach a consensus on party programs before its efforts to match the Republicans in fund raising and organizing will provide more than a temporary solution to its problem.

The Future of the Parties

There is a prospect that the new techniques of political campaigning, if adopted by both parties, could play a role in the re-creation of the party system. But the Republican success should not obscure the fact that revitalization ultimately depends on more than organization, hardware, and short-term strategy. It also depends on restoring citizen loyalties to the parties. Such a restoration in turn depends on a widespread perception that parties are relevant to the policy concerns of citizens.

One historic way that parties have been reinvigorated has been through the process of critical realignment. In the wake of the stunning Republican successes in 1978 and 1980, there was much speculation that such a realignment was in process. If this was the case, the Republican party would become the majority party by forging a new electoral coalition. This new coalition might emerge from the ranks of a public disillusioned by big government and high taxes. The policy agenda of the 1980s then would be dominated by the issues of stronger national defense, less government regulation, and the slowing down of the growth of domestic spending. Party competition would be intensified, and voters, seeing clearly the stakes of politics, would return to the voting booths. The policy fuzziness of American parties would be replaced by sharper distinctions along liberal and conservative lines. But these changes will have to await future events. Central to a realignment along conservative and Republican lines is whether the Reagan economic policies are seen as successful.

It was just as easy to read the results of the 1980 election as another indication of the decline of parties. Voter turnout dropped again. Many voters defected from their parties. Seven percent of the electorate supported independent and third-party candidates. Voters expressed ambivalence, not clarity, about the role of big government. No large-scale movement in public opinion in the conservative direction could be detected. No major move toward reidentification with party could be discovered, much less an emerging Republican majority. The 1980 election, properly understood, was a rejection of President Carter's administration and an expression of a desire for change. It was far from certain that the hopes of the electorate for a change that would revive the economy would be realized.

Realignment will depend on the perception that Republican policies are working. From this perspective, President Reagan's initial successes with Congress were encouraging. His budget and tax-cut proposals sailed through Congress in 1981, a sharp contrast to the fate of some of President Carter's comprehensive programs. However, by the spring of 1982 there were ominous signs that Reagan's economic programs were in deep trouble. The projected budget deficits for fiscal 1983 were far above the $100 billion range. Wall Street was showing concern over the deficits and the size of administration increases in defense spending. Unemployment was approaching 10 percent, although the rate of inflation declined substantially. President Reagan could no longer count on Republican loyalists to support his programs without question, and the prospects of his party in the 1982 congressional elections looked much less favorable than they had in the afterglow of 1980. A resurgence of Democratic strength in the House, in accord with the pattern for the opposition party in off-year elections, seemed likely. No indication of a movement to the Republican party in identification by the electorate could be detected. It is too early to say definitely that a realignment "window" had been missed. Nevertheless, many indications are not favorable.

As for the Democrats, it is clear that they will try to copy the Republican formula for success. The Democratic National Committee (DNC) is emphasizing fund raising by modern techniques and providing modern services to party candidates for 1982, in reaction to the observation that many Democratic congressional candidates in 1980 were defeated by Republican technology. But it was not just technology that produced the Republican victories in 1980. It was the combination of financial resources, revived organizations, and technology that brought the Republican resurgence.

In the 1982 elections, the Democrats may make some gains, especially if the economy does not recover. A short-term Democratic revival could take place in the absence of either modernization of the party's machinery or compelling new ideas. The electorate tends to punish the party in power for poor economic conditions. But in the long run, the Democratic party faces a severe problem that no infusion of technology can solve: somehow to maintain the widespread perception that the Democratic party cares for people while changing the equally widespread perception that the programs that the party has advocated since the 1930s are no longer sufficient. It seems far easier to revive parties as campaign instruments than to translate electoral success into a mechanism for effective government. Nevertheless, that is precisely what the re-creation of a strong and competitive party system requires.

At this point, it is probable that the 1980s will see a continued weakening of the two major parties. Parties will continue to be one of many influences on the electorate, but intense issues and candidate characteristics (as perceived by the electorate) will supplant party identification as major factors in presidential voting. In turn, this will mean that the influence on elections of ideological and single-issue groups, as well as the mass media, will continue to grow. This variety of influences will lead to the creation of conditions for landslide elections and further reductions in voter turnout. The final costs of party decline are to be found in the diminished effectiveness and legitimacy of governmental action.

The future need not be so bleak. There are modest steps that parties can (and have) taken to prevent further erosion. These include restoring some influence for elected party officials in presidential nominations, modernizing and strengthening state and local party organizations, and applying the new techniques of politics to party fund raising and campaigning. Obviously, the Republicans have done more along these lines than have the Democrats. But these steps are not enough. A new code of American politics is necessary—one that sees political accountability in party rather than in individual terms.

Without such a code, candidates will continue to act primarily on the basis of individual agendas and individual chances for reelection. In addition to party responsibility, the revival of party fortunes depends on the articulation of party philosophies and delivery on party promises. In the absence of effective party government, all the "blue smoke and mirrors" of the new political technology will be insufficient to re-create the American two-party system.

Private Opinion Polls

CHARLES ROLL

It is estimated that privately commissioned opinion polls for all candidates for public office at all levels during 1980 accounted for about $20 million in campaign expenditures – and even this figure may be low. Until the recent trend toward public funding of political campaigns, private political polling was the stepchild of the survey research world. The need for it was seasonal and the relationship of pollsters with oft-defeated clients was transitory. In contrast, the rapid growth of survey research for marketing was fueled by the profit motive after its birth during the World War I era.

Publication of syndicated political poll results based on scientific sampling methods dates from the pioneer work of George Gallup, Archibald Crossley, and Elmo Roper during the mid-1930s. Since that time these public polls, whether done by polling organizations or, as recently has become more common, by newspapers or television networks, have always been designed to satisfy the professional demands of journalists, the pollsters' first clients. Journalism, in turn, cares less for the question of how the world got to where it is today than for the more elusive and exciting question of where it can expect to be tomorrow. This preoccupation with the future accounts for much of the superficiality in the treatment of published or broadcast poll results, the focus on trial heats or presidential popularity ratings. Quick assessments of opinions that result in headlines have replaced analyses of the underlying reasons for the opinions and of the dynamic factors that can change them.

The first candidate for public office to have the benefit of private polling was Mrs. Alex Miller, who in 1932 was the first woman elected secretary of state of Iowa. Her polls were conducted experimentally by her son-in-law, Dr. George Gallup, who found that she (a Democrat) had a good chance of winning in that traditionally Republican state. The first candidate for the presidential nomination with access to his own polling data was Thomas Dewey in 1940. His polls were financed by a retired industrialist, Gerard Lambert, who, after Dewey was overwhelmed at the convention by Wendell Willkie, continued his polling activity for Willkie, the first presidential candidate to have (and ignore) his own polling counsel. The first candidate to commission a poll was Jacob Javits, who in

1946 asked the Roper Organization to help him win his first electoral office—a seat in the U.S. House of Representatives.

John F. Kennedy used polls to help him become president, dignifying their use by other political candidates. Jimmy Carter was the first president, and Ronald Reagan the second, to have continuous and comprehensive private political soundings through their terms in office. Today, private political polling has evolved far beyond the rather simplistic approach of the public poll and now includes purposeful analyses and dynamic conceptualizations that do not lend themselves to news treatment. These commissioned polls can also be used politically to affect (or enhance) the impact of public poll results revealed in the media during an ongoing campaign.

Polling as Political Persuasion

Politicians and people in general cling to the "bandwagon" theory—the belief that a candidate's favorable polls encourage voters to support that candidate. There may be many reasons for voting for a candidate—some valid, others less so. But to say that voters forget their perceived self-interests, disregard their party or ideological loyalties, and overlook the candidates' personalities, attributes, and records all merely to vote for the winning candidate is neither a compelling nor a logical argument. Still, campaigns persist in leaking favorable poll data.

Pollsters frequently cite the fact that candidates shown to be behind in the early polls seldom lose ground to their front-running opponents as evidence that there is no bandwagon effect on the voters. For example, a widely reported Gallup Poll of Pennsylvania in September 1978 found Democrat Pete Flaherty twelve points ahead of Republican Dick Thornburgh (51 percent to 39 percent). But the September poll did not increase the Flaherty margin. In fact, a Gallup Poll in late October, again widely circulated, found Flaherty only four points ahead of Thornburgh (49 percent to 45 percent). The November election produced a Thornburgh victory by six points (53 percent to 47 percent).

The Gallup Poll has measured twelve presidential elections since 1936. A comparison of its published trial-heat data for September with the November election results shows that the poll-indicated losers gained an average of 5.4 points by November, while September's indicated front-runners gained only an average of 2.8 points. (Both candidates gain because the undecided percentage segment does not appear in election results.) Would the indicated losers have gained considerably more—and at the expense of the indicated front-runners—if the polls so unfavorable to them had not been published? To test for any varying effect according to the size of the margin, these twelve presidential elections were divided into three groups: (1) the four elections whose September polls indicated the widest margins between the major-party candidates (hence, theoretically, the elections in which polls would have had the most dampening effect on the trailing candidate's chances against a bandwagon-influenced electorate); (2)

the four elections whose September poll margins were close to the average; and (3) the four elections whose September polls indicated the narrowest margins.

As table 1 indicates, prospective losers by the widest margins on the average gained about three and a half times the number of points received by the underdogs in the closest contests. Most prospective winners by the widest margins gained less than one point. Only prospective winners in September's closest contests gained more than their opponents; in more one-sided races, poll-indicated losers can expect to gain considerably more than expected presidential winners.

TABLE 1

The Effect of Polls in Presidential Elections, 1936–80

	Average Gain in Points	
September Polls	*Poll-Indicated Winner*	*Poll-Indicated Loser*
Widest margins (12 to 36 points)	0.4	7.0
Moderate margins (8 to 11 points)	2.3	6.3
Narrowest margins (0 to 4 points)	5.5	2.0

Source: Compiled from Gallup Polls, 1936–80.

An examination of races in which there are more than two candidates, however, leads to a dramatically different conclusion. There can be no question that third-party candidates – no matter how promising their prospects – are seriously damaged by published polling data indicating that two candidates for one office are running significantly ahead of them. Thus, the most noted pollsters can belittle the bandwagon theory and at the same time predict that a seemingly viable third candidate's strength will dissipate by election time, when his supporters realize that he has little possibility of being elected. Curiously, pollsters detect no inconsistency in what they say.

The strength of third candidates usually does fade in the final days before an election, but without published polls it would probably not fade so drastically or so quickly. In 1968, George Wallace went from 21 percent in a mid-September Gallup Poll to 13.6 percent in the November election. Deeper, but over a longer period of time, was John Anderson's decline – from 24 percent in mid-June 1980 to 6.6 percent in the November election. Furthermore, evidence from a Senate race in New York with three strong candidates suggests that late decision-making by those who were undecided at earlier stages (and who took the trouble to vote) did not benefit the candidate known to be running third (see table 2).

Favorable polls are unhesitatingly used for raising funds for campaigns. In 1968, Richard Nixon said: "When the polls go good for me, the cash register really rings."[1] That same year, with the Gallup Poll showing Hubert Humphrey

[1] *Time Magazine*, May 31, 1968, p. 19.

TABLE 2

New York Senatorial Election, 1970

	Late September/ Early October (%)	*Late October (%)*	*Gain (Pts.)*	*November Election (%)*
James Buckley, Conservative	33	40	7	38.8
Richard Ottinger, Democrat	29	35	6	36.8
Charles Goodell, Republican	25	25	–	24.4
Undecided	13	–	–	–

Source: Survey for Political Analyses, Inc.

behind Nixon (31 percent to 43 percent), Humphrey began his presidential campaign with no money for television advertising, polling, or campaign literature and with little likelihood of attracting it. His manager was able to assemble fragmentary polling data – more favorable than the Gallup and Harris polls – and to issue a report under the ebullient heading "Humphrey on the Upswing, Gallup or Not." Humphrey's manager sent copies to editors, television anchormen, and party chairmen. News people were skeptical, but party brokers were less so, and money began to come in. More extensive polling, highly effective television advertising spots, and longer films produced for television in turn attracted more funds for use in escalating the effort. The result of this media campaign, late as it appeared, was that Humphrey came within one point of defeating Nixon.

Special-interest political action committees (PACs), with their readily available campaign funds, have increased the importance of polling. In the special promotion packets that candidates prepare for likely PAC contributors, favorable poll data are key enclosures. Years ago, the late Leonard Hall, a former Republican National chairman, wisely observed: "If no one else [does], politicians and spenders read polls. The big contributors like to know where their man stands, and, just like at the two dollar window, no one likes to put his money on a loser."[2]

Favorable polls can have other, more subtle, effects. The best newspaper and television reporters are assigned to likely winners, and their career advancement is often linked to the success of those they cover. Particularly at the lower electoral levels, perceived winners attract many more reporters than their trailing opponents. In the closing days of an unsuccessful comeback attempt in 1969, former Governor Robert Meyner of New Jersey saw his journalistic retinue significantly diminish.

Hugh Branson, former administrative assistant to Senator Howard Baker and highly experienced in statewide contests, has insisted that unfavorable polls in a campaign seriously demoralize not only the candidate, perhaps affecting his campaigning style and demeanor, but also the campaign staffers who carry out

[2] *Newsday, Weekly Magazine for Long Island*, February 17, 1968, p. 30.

the important activities of his campaign. An unfavorable poll on the eve of an election is especially damaging to an organization charged with getting out the vote on election day. This effect helps explain why, even at the end of a campaign, candidates hide unfavorable polls, leak favorable ones, and sometimes fabricate favorable polls. Thus, while unfavorable polls – published or leaked – have little direct effect on the electorate, they can have a significant indirect impact on a campaign by making it difficult to raise contributions, motivate staffers, and attract media attention.

Party loyalists – whether county chairmen, convention delegates, or the average voter – can be persuaded by poll data to select the front-runner as their party nominee. A person who votes in his party's primary is hardly likely to overlook completely the important question, Who is the strongest candidate we can put up? At the presidential level, success in primary contests is usually perceived as indicative of success in November.

Jimmy Carter entered the 1976 primaries as a little-known former governor of Georgia, with a 4 percent level of support among Democrats in the Gallup Poll. By mid-June he had garnered 53 percent in a steady rise fueled by sequential primary election victories in a number of states. By spending most of his precampaign time in Iowa, Oklahoma, New Hampshire, and Florida – the early-decision states – Carter built his strength in those states far above the strength he had at the national level. Each early victory produced a media response that increased public awareness of him, and his national support in the polls rose. As his poll ratings rose, especially after April, a bandwagon effect was produced everywhere (except California, where Jerry Brown was better known). George Bush tried this approach in 1980, but after winning the Iowa Republican caucuses, he lost in New Hampshire and his campaign came to an early end.

One of the most courageous, though foolhardy, efforts to win a presidential nomination – Nelson Rockefeller's 1968 campaign for the Republican nomination – was based solely on anticipated poll results. Entering the contest to stop Richard Nixon, the front-runner, but too late to enter any primaries, Rockefeller had to adopt a unique strategy. He decided on an active campaign of speeches and position papers intended to attract non-Republicans. But this strategy represented only the first part of the scheme. In the words of Arch Crossley, then Rockefeller's polltaker, Rockefeller "challenged Nixon to join with him and with the Republican National Committee in financing a fifty-state poll, arguing that Nixon's own performance against John F. Kennedy in 1960 had demonstrated that the strictly Republican approach could lose electoral votes because of the voting in cities and industrial areas."[3]

Failing to obtain cofunding, Rockefeller commissioned his own polls of nine key states (with a total of 226 electoral votes), the entire nation, and five key congressional districts – all to be conducted in the month before the convention. According to Rockefeller's speechwriter, his idea was that "bold solutions and

[3] Archibald and Helen Crossley, "Polling in 1968," *Public Opinion Quarterly* 33 (Spring 1969): 7.

personal attractiveness would pull him ahead of Nixon in the polls [as against likely Democratic opponents], and the poll results would be used to persuade Republican leaders and . . . convention delegates to latch on to a winner."[4]

It seemed a safe strategy when conceived. A Gallup Poll conducted in early May showed that Rockefeller had a greater advantage than Nixon over the top Democratic candidates—Hubert Humphrey, Eugene McCarthy, and Robert Kennedy. But in politics the best of plans can be disrupted by a clever opponent. Both Nixon and Rockefeller knew well in advance that final preconvention Gallup Poll interviewing was scheduled for July 20–23. On July 18, Nixon wrung an endorsement from ailing Dwight D. Eisenhower. It is highly likely that this endorsement enabled Nixon to surpass the Rockefeller margin over the Democrats in the poll. The damage was done, the Rockefeller strategy was disarmed, and the Nixon campaign workers gleefully disseminated the Gallup Poll to delegates.

Rockefeller's own polling, which was conducted and analyzed by Gallup employees working in the same neighborhoods—in most cases just down the street from—where they had completed their Gallup Poll assignments, showed Rockefeller with a greater lead than Nixon over the Democrats. But Rockefeller's poll, also distributed at the convention, had been upstaged and discredited by the "more objective" Gallup Poll that had been conducted a day or even hours before the Rockefeller poll by the same interviewers. A Harris Poll—conducted July 26–29, showing Humphrey ahead of Nixon, and Rockefeller ahead of both Humphrey and McCarthy—also failed to impress delegates dazzled by the Gallup Poll figures.

This case is replete with lessons. To use favorable polls to influence convention delegates is not always a sound strategy. To base a campaign on what future polls might show is a gigantic gamble. The polls favoring Rockefeller over Nixon were undoubtedly realistic readings; the preconvention Gallup Poll was a fluke effected by the Eisenhower endorsement. But the delegates and objective observers believed the fluke and suspected the data that contradicted it.

A final lesson from this example is the meaninglessness of poll data from surveys conducted immediately after a major event. Networks and newspapers spend much money to obtain and quickly release such data in order to exploit its timeliness. The public, however, is left with no chance to place the event in its proper context or to decide whether to disregard it.

The most brazen use of polling for persuasion purposes was contemplated by a heavy contributor to liberal causes and candidates. In the spring of 1974, as national polls were beginning to show the public belief that Nixon was guilty in the Watergate affair, but before the House Judiciary Committee had taken any steps to consider impeachment, polling in the separate congressional districts of each committee member was contemplated. There can be no question that the results in most, if not all, of the home districts would have shown strong sup-

[4] Joseph Persico, *The Imperial Rockefeller: Nelson A. Rockefeller* (New York: Simon & Schuster, 1982), p. 71.

port for impeachment. Only the most courageous committee member would not have been moved by polling so finely focused both geographically and on such an issue. The concept was overtaken by fast-moving events before the project could get off the ground.

Such targeted polling on an important subject so strongly felt would likely prove irresistible to the most responsible polltaker seeking business and the most well-meaning cause proponent seeking speeded-up action. The only antidote is the sound reflection that House (or Senate) committees are meant to represent the legislative body as a whole, and the legislative body as a whole should represent the entire nation.

Polls as Policy Tools

The real value of political polling is its use as a guidance tool in campaigns or in public administration—guidance that should not be followed slavishly but should be used to determine the problems and needs involved in the pursuit of an already-determined course.

Political beginners have used polls to discover the problems they can expect in a race. In December 1965, Howard Baker was running for the Senate twenty points behind the incumbent governor of Tennessee, Frank Clement. Baker might have been dissuaded from running by such bleak figures. Included in the report, however, was an analysis suggesting that Baker could win if the factor of Clement's state tax policies were weighed in the public opinion balance. Baker took the chance, ran, and won his first term in the Senate.

Probably no other kind of polling data are more important to a candidate than those that portray the concerns of the people. In 1966, a survey of New York State for Nelson Rockefeller's campaign for a third term as governor showed that the most important concerns of voters throughout the state, particularly of New York City residents, were crime and narcotics. A candidate urging an all-out program to combat crime would be more likely to garner support than a candidate advocating any other position tested in the poll. Closely allied to the crime issue, especially in New York City, was a program to hospitalize narcotics addicts. The antinarcotics program the governor then set forth demonstrated to the voters his concern and his intention to take action on a problem foremost in their minds. In the November election, after campaigning vigorously in New York City on this issue, he carried three of the city's five boroughs, which are usually Democratic.

Franklin Roosevelt periodically utilized polling data during his administration's later years. In 1941, Roosevelt wished to help Great Britain in its solitary fight against the Axis powers. But he did not want to get too far ahead of American public opinion, fearing a backlash that might make any aid impossible. His polltaker, Hadley Cantril, devised a question and asked it about six times during a crucial six-month period, May to October 1941. The question was: "So far as you personally are concerned, do you think President Roosevelt has gone too far in his policies of helping Britain, or not far enough?" About 70 percent of the answers gave Roosevelt leeway to pursue his goal, while no more than 22 percent disapproved his aid to Great Britain. These fairly constant readings indicated the president's ability to pursue controversial policies at a pace not upsetting to the public.

By March 1, 1944, Roosevelt was worried that the bombing of Rome would affect Catholic morale and support of the war. The question put to the American public was: "If our military leaders believe it will be necessary to bomb Rome but take every precaution to avoid damage to its religious shrines, would you approve this decision?" The results of a quick sampling showed an overwhelming majority of Catholics as well as Protestants would approve the bombing of Rome if American military leaders thought it essential. Among Catholics, 66 percent approved and 27 percent disapproved; among Protestants, 81 percent approved and 13 percent disapproved. On March 3, 1944, Rome was heavily bombed for the first time since the previous August, with railroad yards and airports—both important targets for the movement of German troops—successfully damaged.

Polling can provide a check on the claims of special interests that clothe themselves in the guise of representatives of the American public. In 1947 the Republican Congress passed the Taft-Hartley Act, which strictly regulated organized labor. Robert Taft, the Republican senator who authored the measure, ran for reelection in 1950 but seemed doomed because of the large labor vote in industrial Ohio. Nevertheless, a poll in 1949 showed that, while 69 percent of labor union members did not "think that Congress should have passed this bill," overwhelming majorities of the same union members approved of virtually every major provision of the bill when asked about each individually. Armed with this information, Taft courageously carried his campaign into unionized factories and confronted the issue squarely. Taft carried every industrial county in Ohio and defeated his challenger in a landslide, with 57.5 percent of the vote.

Polls can measure the effects of actions already taken. Nelson Rockefeller generally used them for that purpose as governor of New York. On the morning of September 13, 1971, some 1,000 state troopers and other police stormed the Attica State Correctional Facility, where about 1,200 inmates held 38 prison guards hostage. Ending a four-day rebellion, the assault resulted in the death of nine hostages and twenty-eight convicts.

Governor Rockefeller commissioned a survey to ascertain national thinking on Attica and his role in it. A significant 38 percent believed that Rockefeller was at least "somewhat" to blame for what had happened, while 43 percent believed he was not to blame. The same pattern emerged on Rockefeller's controversial refusal to go to Attica—with 24 percent approving of the decision, 27 percent opposing it, and 49 percent undecided or unaware that he had refused to go.

It was concluded at the time that Attica had a negative but not devastating effect on the governor's reputation. Events at Attica marred Rockefeller's impressive record and ultimately worked beneath the surface to diminish his strong point, the national perception of his governmental competence and his friendly, generous nature. The public already tended to see Rockefeller as isolated by great wealth and high position from a full sympathy with and understanding of the average citizen. Attica reinforced this tendency. His national and state overall ratings began an erosion that was never to reverse.

In early December 1977, the Senate was about to consider the Panama Canal treaties for approval. Howard Baker, then minority leader of the Senate, planned to make a five-day visit to Panama in order to meet with General Torrijos. Before departing, Baker wanted a reading of how his Tennessee constituents would react if he supported ratification of the treaties, as he intended to do.

True to national form, Tennessee sentiment was about two-to-one against ratification, with an inordinately high one-third of the sample unable to answer. But the survey also indicated that deeper consideration of certain aspects of the treaties would create broader treaty support. The survey report concluded: "The only question is: will sufficient consideration be given by Tennesseans to bring about this effect by the time of the next election? Certainly, media coverage of the Senate debate on the matter will provide the raw material for such consideration. And just as certainly, sentiment accepting an already ratified treaty will grow and, without untoward incidents, will, in time fall far short as a winning issue for those opposed to it."[5] This assessment proved to be accurate. There was virtually no change in candidate standings resulting from Baker's stand on the treaties. Below the surface, however, Baker's support of the treaties generated some downward movement in his public image that could have cost him electoral support had there been an equally attractive opponent (who was also in a position to capitalize on the issue) or had there been another emotional issue with Baker on the unpopular side. To combat any erosion of support that might have developed because of the Panama Canal issue, especially among the key Baker constituencies of East Tennesseans and Republicans who were concerned about it, much attention was given during the closing days of his 1978 reelection campaign to Baker's support for an amendment to the Constitution allowing prayer in public schools, most strongly supported by those same groups. Baker's support for this amendment went a long way toward defusing potential damage from the Panama Canal issue.

The 1980 Presidential Campaign

No president seems to have allowed polls to dictate actions as much as President Carter did. Patrick Caddell, Carter's polltaker, recalled that his opinion surveys had made the president aware in early 1979 that he was "in an incredibly weak situation. By June or July, when the president went to Camp David, his job rating had dropped below Nixon's job rating in the Harris Poll; the gas lines ex-

[5] Polls, Inc., *Report*, January 1978.

isted; there was a sense that things were really out of control. In part what was going on that summer was . . . the need to assert something, some kind of control."[6] Nevertheless, Carter's popularity rating in the Gallup Poll, just below thirty points, reached a subsequent high of thirty-three points, suggesting the folly of Caddell's response to unfavorable ratings—pinpointing a supposed malaise afflicting the American people's confidence.

After the early November seizure of the American embassy and personnel by Iran, Carter's Gallup Poll rating rose from thirty-two to thirty-eight points and peaked in early December at sixty-one points. An observer noted that "Carter's enthusiasm for open discussion decreased in direct proportion to his rising poll readings; he cancelled all public appearances."[7] The cautious attitude to which front-runners are susceptible had set in and the "Rose Garden strategy" was adopted.

The sixty-one points awarded the embattled president eroded to thirty-nine points by late March 1980. Caddell's polling found that most Americans had come to believe that Carter was soft in dealing with Iran and the Soviet Union. It was for this reason that Carter broke off diplomatic relations with Iran and imposed sanctions. Still, the chief executive's rating in the polls did not improve. A Harris Poll in mid-April confirmed the lack of public support for Carter's handling of the hostage situation. Then, on April 24, Carter approved the unsuccessful rescue operation in Iran.[8]

Nevertheless, the president's approval rating rose by only four points, to 43 percent, but the initial reaction of sympathy increased his support sufficiently to enable him to win six state primaries over Edward M. Kennedy by two-to-one or better. During the primary campaign against Kennedy, which was the context for these moves against Iran, the Carter polls affected not only his actions but also his advertising. Polls showing a rising militancy among Americans led Carter's media consultant to project the president as a "born-again hawk." Then, ten days before the vote in New Hampshire, Caddell discovered that voters were shifting to Kennedy. Tough radio spots were replaced by commercials describing the president as a man of peace, and a television spot was hastily produced calling him "the peacemaker" and showing him between President Sadat and Prime Minister Begin at Camp David. Carter defeated Kennedy in New Hampshire by ten points.

The change of strategy in New Hampshire produced short-range gains that turned out to be meaningless and long-term effects that could have been disastrous. Therefore, in order to get attention off of the issues, which were unfavorable to Carter, and back on the candidates, that is, on Kennedy's weaknesses, the Carter campaign produced a series of brief television adver-

[6] Jonathan Moore, *The Campaign for President: 1980 in Retrospect* (Cambridge, Mass: Ballinger Publishing Co., 1981), pp. 21, 30.

[7] David Chagall, *The New Kingmakers* (New York: Harcourt Brace Jovanovich, Inc., 1981), p. 143.

[8] Ibid., p. 163.

tisements: a housewife saying, "I don't think Kennedy has credibility"; an old woman announcing, "I just don't believe him"; a worker complaining, "He's too liberal"; a student stating, "Kennedy would be a big spender of other people's money"; and a family man declaring, "I don't trust him."[9] Carter lost the Pennsylvania primary by a margin of only 0.3 percent. But these advertisements, alluding to Chappaquiddick, made it difficult for Kennedy to campaign for Carter in November.

Richard Wirthlin, Reagan's polltaker, tested and assessed the crisis of confidence that drove the president to Camp David in the summer of 1979. He found that the crisis could be countered by speaking of an America capable of dealing with any challenge if led by strong leaders. That became the tagline on all Reagan advertising through both the primary and general-election campaigns. Wirthlin also found that people, when asked what they liked least about Ronald Reagan, mentioned most frequently his age and his not seeming to care about ordinary people. Wirthlin's antidote for these weaknesses was an in-depth view of Reagan. By not hiding his age and by portraying his genial folksiness, these concerns tended to be overcome.

But all was not perfect in the early Reagan campaign. Polls showed Reagan ahead in the national race for the Republican presidental nomination and the choice of over 50 percent of Iowa Republicans. The Iowa Republican caucus was important as a bellwether of the campaign. John Sears, then Reagan's campaign manager, decided that Reagan should not take part in the crowded debate with the other Republican contenders in Des Moines so as to avoid appearing on an equal basis with the apparent also-rans. This overconfidence led Sears to spend only $6,000 for Iowa television time, compared with $26,000 spent on behalf of Bush. A predictable reaction set in: Iowa Republicans, like any other group of snubbed voters, felt they were being taken for granted. George Bush won 31 percent of the vote, defeating Reagan, who received 26 percent. Learning their lesson, Reagan campaigners turned the tables in New Hampshire with a solidarity ploy, publicly condemning Bush for wanting to exclude the other candidates from a debate in Nashua. Reagan became the "good guy," seeking fairness and party unity, and beat Bush in New Hampshire 49.6 percent to 22.7 percent, going on virtually unhampered to the GOP nomination.

Polls for both Reagan and Carter had located the weaknesses of the opposition. Caddell found public uncertainty about what Reagan could do about inflation and unemployment. He was also seen as sometimes not knowing what he was talking about and as a possible risk as president. As for keeping America out of war, Reagan's rating would fall at least twenty points during the campaign.

Wirthlin found Carter weak in leadership qualities and in handling the important economic issues. Wirthlin wisely decided that a successful campaign required carefully building a positive image for Reagan, by emphasizing his ac-

[9] Ibid., p. 162.

complishments as governor, for example, before launching frontal criticism on the issues of Carter's performance and leadership deficiencies. This strategy was necessary because even in September as many as 40 percent of the voters said they knew little about what Ronald Reagan really stood for.

Caddell had to devise a poll-derived strategy different from Wirthlin's strategy. Caddell pointed out that Carter had negative ratings on all but two of some fifteen dimensions of presidential performance, with "handling the economy" especially weak and likely to get worse. Since Carter lacked Reagan's positive image, which Wirthlin insisted his candidate secure before attacking Carter, Caddell decided that it was necessary to take the offensive against Reagan quickly to prevent him from crossing the threshold of credibility.

Carter thus stridently attacked Reagan on three separate occasions. In Atlanta, just after the general-election campaign began, Carter charged that Reagan was "creating stirrings of hate between blacks and whites, using code words like 'states rights' and relating the Ku Klux Klan to the South."[10] Not clearly responsive to anything turned up in a Caddell poll, this charge was undoubtedly a political mistake. Later, in California, Carter began to suggest that a Reagan presidency would endanger the peace. His advertisements showed him declaring, "Peace is my passion." This was all clearly in response to the Caddell poll finding that Americans feared that Reagan would get the United States into war.

After his polls showed he was not gaining as his planners had hoped, Carter declared in Illinois, "You will determine whether America will be unified or, if I lose the election, whether America might be separated – blacks from whites, Jews from Christians, North from South, rural from urban."[11] Again, in terms of the public perception of the candidates as revealed in their polls, this campaign tactic was rashly inappropriate. Concerned about a backlash from this last display that would reinforce the public's perception of Carter as mean, Carter aides sought to explain away some of the harshness of the statement.

A more soundly based attack on Carter by the Reagan forces blossomed according to plan in the concluding days of the campaign. Reagan challenged Carter's competence and ability to govern, hammered at two-digit inflation, and emphasized his own 30 percent income-tax reduction program. Newspaper advertisements and Reagan himself, on his election eve telecast successfully turned attention back to the last four years by asking, "Are you better off now than you were four years ago?"

On the basis of the same polling data, Reagan advisers were split on the debate decision. Political adviser Lyn Nofziger "saw no movement out there, and we thought that one way to get some movement" was to debate Carter. Polltaker Wirthlin felt "the campaign had turned the corner [and] would do well." Why lay the whole campaign in which you are leading, he asked, on an event you cannot control? The candidate himself, disregarding poll data and

[10] Ibid., p. 223.
[11] Ibid., p. 239.

probably mindful of the Iowa mistake, reasoned, "If I want to succeed Jimmy Carter, I should be willing to face him one-to-one."[12] Reagan debated, gained more than Carter did from it, and won the election a week later by ten points.

Conclusion

Polling clearly affects the American elective and governing processes. One effect is on major problem-solving. Standings and ratings of public figures – published or leaked – have their greatest effect on the politicians themselves. Popularity enhances the power to persuade and to lead and the patience to endure and to follow. In constantly measuring popularity – quantifying it, certifying it, and reporting it – polls intensify the effect of public opinion on statesmen, candidates, and the media. This focus on poll data heightens the thirst for quick results in government. Because of polls, politicians are less likely to apply long-term but painful solutions to important problems.

Political leadership has also been drastically changed because of extensive polltaking. Today's political descendants of Jim Farley and Leonard Hall and party chairmen at lower levels have been displaced at the campaign strategy tables by the candidates' polltakers. Old-style political advice – subjective, arguable, derived from intuition, gut-feeling, and past experience – has given way to the objectivity and finality of cold, hard figures, vividly presented and perceived as realities in their own right. Even the president, with party leadership among his important functions, can be persuaded by polling data from the all-out leadership assault the role calls for. Thus, on June 7, 1982, the *U.S. News and World Report* revealed that Reagan aides were urging the president to curtail plans to campaign heavily for Republican congressional candidates in the fall because "prospects for a feeble economic recovery mean the President would be less effective than expected . . . and advisers do not want him linked too closely to GOP candidates apt to go down to defeat." Polls will be avidly compared to determine just where it is safe for the president to do battle. In this, party leaders will be unable to compete with the percentages.

Polls are often helpful in indicating the problems in following a certain course or in indicating that the expected problems do not exist. Sometimes, polls even suggest approaches that will help achieve unpopular goals. However, some political actions that respond to suggestive polling data prove shallow. At best, such actions may be beneficial only momentarily or, at worst, harmful.

Too often, certain facts about the polling technique are not fully appreciated by laymen who feel dependent on them. Business-seeking polltakers may even gloss over certain limitations of the polling technique. Polls pinpoint likelihoods and tendencies, not certainties. They tap into fluidities, not stabilities. And they measure approximately, not precisely. They can fairly accurately apply to the present, but they cannot project the future scientifically.

[12] Moore, pp. 238–40.

Then there are the limitations to polling inherent in the condition and interests of the American citizenry. People do not sit on the edges of their chairs awaiting the next bit of news from the White House, the statehouse, or city hall. When news is absorbed, it is in a casual, haphazard way. People thus answer poll questions on the basis of impressions more than on facts. This inexactitude does not negate the value of poll results, because these impressions can lead to sound voting decisions. It does suggest, however, one more reason why expectations from polls should not be too high and why policies should not always be based on polls.

John Sears said in 1978 that polls "are not as valuable as they used to be, and they never were as valuable as they were supposed to be. The tragic thing is that when politicians should be relying less on these things, they are relying more on them."[13] That may be true, but more information is obviously better than less. It is still better to have a poll than not to have one.

[13] *Newsweek*, November 27, 1978, p. 32.

Executive Decision-making

DORIS A. GRABER

There are three major ways in which the nature of communications in society affects executive decision-making. In the first place, communications factors determine who the decision-makers will be for particular decisions and where they are located in the governmental structure. Second, communications factors determine the nature of the data that will be brought to bear on a particular decision. Finally, communications factors are paramount in winning support for the decision and securing its adequate implementation.

Each of these factors will be examined in turn. Most of the illustrations will be drawn from decision-making in the presidency, since most of the literature about executive decision-making in American government concerns that office. However, executive decision-making is sufficiently similar at all levels of government so that much of the discussion will also apply to other levels, such as the governor's or mayor's office, legislative bodies, and administrative agencies.

The Locus of Decision-making

The identity of decision-makers depends heavily on the nature of the channels available for information flow and on the patterns established for routing information. In turn, these factors are strongly affected by changes in communications technologies.

An example from the early days of the United States will illustrate the impact of channel availability on the locus of decision-making. For many decades following America's birth as a nation, most decisions concerning American diplomacy in Europe were made by American representatives stationed there. To consult decision-makers at home would have taken many months, given the communications technology at that time. It was therefore usually impractical. For example, at the end of the Revolutionary War, it took more than five months for the American peace commissioners in London to receive their government's instructions about the important peace treaty with England. Four different copies of the treaty had been sent aboard four different sailing vessels to make sure that the text would reach its destination with the utmost speed and security. No wonder that on many lesser matters, American diplomats acted on their own without awaiting instructions.

Today, the president can attain instant voice contact with representatives abroad. He can also consult directly by telephone with political leaders at home. The normal hierarchical patterns of information flow among officials can be, and often are, easily bypassed in this manner. Thus, many important decisions or predecisions that were made in the past by lower-echelon decision-makers are now handled at top levels. The locus of decision-making has changed, with potentially major consequences for decision outcomes.

The precise nature of these changes and their impact on the quality of decisions remain a matter of controversy. At the heart of this controversy is the question whether and under what circumstances it is advantageous to centralize decision-making at top governmental levels, bypassing knowledgeable bureaucrats in the lower echelons. For instance, one can only speculate about the differences in the quality of executive decision-making that have come in the wake of summit diplomacy. The influence of the top-level negotiator on the scene has been enhanced. The resulting human hazards, ranging from jet lag to flaws in temperament and judgment, are beyond measuring at the present time. There has generally been pressure to reach decisions more quickly. The fact that the top negotiators have great authority, and can be in instant touch with their superiors or support staffs at home, has somewhat reduced the hazards of hasty decision-making.

The locus of decision-making may also be altered because of communication-induced shifts in power. A number of changes that television wrought in American politics provide examples. Political observers agree that television technology, which has allowed politicians to be seen and heard in nearly every home in the nation, has contributed heavily to the decline of political parties. Political leaders have been able to build their power without party support through skillful direct contacts with the public via television and radio. As a result, many decisions formerly made at party levels, or with an eye to pleasing the party, are now made by successful politicians with an eye to different sets of supporters.

Similarly, the shift in decision-making power away from Congress to the presidency that has been characteristic of twentieth-century presidents can be attributed in part to changes in the communications media. Senator J. William Fulbright told Congress in 1970: "Television has done as much to expand the powers of the President as would a constitutional amendment formally abolishing the co-equality of the three branches of government."[1] Recognizing its vulnerability, Congress has since that time acquired increased information resources. In 1974, for example, it created its own budget information system

[1] Quoted in Robert O. Blanchard, ed., *Congress and the News Media* (New York: Hastings House, 1974), p. 105.

through establishing the Congressional Budget Office. As a result, the ability of the president to use superior information to dominate budget decisions was sharply reduced.

Some of the changes brought about by the new technologies may lead to a redistribution of decision-making influence or even to a reorganization of the formal decision-making mechanisms, short of an actual change in the locus of decision-making. For instance, when government agencies acquired the capacity to create their own computer models, they became better able to counter the influence of lobbies on decision-making. In the past, major lobbies, such as the oil lobby, gained distinct advantages from the fact that their information collecting and processing capabilities were superior to those of the government.

Executive decision-making structures have been reorganized to put increasing emphasis on communicating with various publics. Thus the presidential office now includes media advisers and experts on polling, along with the more traditional agencies for handling daily relations with reporters. President Carter even hired a special assistant for communication to structure presidential activities so that they would project a desirable image for press coverage. The concerns of such media experts are reflected in the manner in which decisions are presented, and often in the substance of decisions.

A number of changes in the locus of decision-making spring from the use of computer technology. When computers are given a more central role in information processing, the question of the policy orientations and the affiliations of the people who design the programs and who decide what information will be stored becomes crucial. Hard political battles are likely to be fought over the privilege to control computer inputs, model building, and programming. The technical experts who program computers, build assumptions into models, and then secure the data to go into models will have a tremendous influence on the outcome of decisions. As William H. Dutton of the University of Southern California has pointed out, "information systems seem to be highly malleable political tools which are utilized to reinforce the interests of the dominant coalition within an organization."[2] If they do not serve the interests of that coalition, they are likely to be discarded or ignored.

Many users of these models will be at the mercy of the model builders' expertise, since the users do not fully understand the logics programmed into the computer. In fact, computer technology may increase the dominance of technical experts in decision-making. Esoteric debates over the adequacy of models may replace simpler arguments about the validity of human calculations made through a combination of factual learning, hypothesizing, and intuition.

Power struggles among government agencies and leaders over computer control have already proliferated. The potential losers in the fight over control of information sources are determined to protect their intellectual turf. Besides the

[2] William H. Dutton, "The Rejection of an Innovation: The Political Environment of a Computer-Based Model," *Systems, Objectives, Solutions* 1 (November 1981):179–201.

struggles over control of the available machines, there are also the usual struggles over scarce resources. Communications technologies, both software and hardware, are costly. Social and organizational costs must be added to the direct expenses. People fight over the resources needed to own and operate their own equipment. Most do not like to share facilities or use outdated machines. Solutions to the struggles over control can have major political consequences.

Resolving such struggles by providing joint access to shared resources may help bridge gaps between the contending agencies. For instance, if the Department of State and the Department of Defense were part of the same information system, collaboration might be improved. On the negative side, the reduction of information acquisition and processing centers may reduce the diversity in policy options presented to top decision-makers, thereby reducing vigorous debate and scrutiny.

The physical location of governmental decision-making has also been changed through new technologies, and more drastic changes may be imminent. The ease of assembling conferences with the aid of telephones, satellites, and closed-circuit television has made it possible to assemble widely scattered experts and officials throughout the country without incurring the money and time costs of extensive travel. In fact, the new communications technologies may make geographic concentration of most government agencies in Washington unnecessary. Despite the dispersion, it would be possible to use teleconferencing to gather government officials as rapidly, and often more rapidly than is possible when people assemble in Washington. The dispersal of facilities would also increase safety in case of war or other major disaster.

The Nature of the Information Flow

By determining the sources of information to which an executive can be linked, communications technologies determine what kinds of information will be available for consideration in decision-making. This information, in turn, affects the outcome of decisions. For example, when President Reagan offered assistance to Britain and Argentina in 1982 to settle their dispute over the Falkland Islands, telephone contacts permitted immediate access to the views of British and Argentine leaders. Even the remote Falkland Islands could be readily contacted via electronic devices. Additionally, modern surveillance technology through satellites, radar equipment, and aircraft missions provided extensive data on air, sea, and land movements of military resources. Information gained through these contacts could be immediately incorporated into decision-making.

Had this dispute occurred a hundred years earlier, much less information would have been available. Electronic surveillance of men and material and their movements was nonexistent. Instant, direct communication among widely dispersed government leaders was impossible. In 1882, President Chester A. Arthur could not have known the dispositions of the top leadership in the two countries on a day-by-day basis. Surveillance data, if available at all from human observers, would have been rudimentary and too slow to reach decision-making circles in time to be a major influence.

The ability instantly to draw on a wide array of information sources is particularly important because many high-level decisions are made by small groups. The size of the group and the fact that its members are apt to gear information input to their own political needs severely limit the amount of information readily available. This obstacle to sound decision-making can be diminished if small groups are willing to use the wider information base made accessible through modern information storage and retrieval methods and to expand it even further by using outsiders on short notice via electronic contacts. For instance, the dangers of reliance on limited channels of information could have been lessened during the Cuban crisis of 1961 if data generated by agencies other than the CIA had been readily accessible to President John F. Kennedy. Investigations into the decision-making faults involved in the Bay of Pigs fiasco have indicated that CIA projections were seriously flawed and that these flaws were obvious from other data to which the new administration had not been alerted. More advanced technology has lessened the chances of missing salient information.

The availability of new technologies does not necessarily mean that they will be used to their fullest capacity. Political and economic constraints keep many modern communications channels fully or partly closed. For instance, communications with the Soviet Union during the 1982 Falkland Islands crisis regarding Soviet intervention in the dispute were far less plentiful than would have been technically feasible. Similarly, vast amounts of information about political and economic conditions throughout the world have been excluded from decision-making because they were never placed into communication channels or because deliberate efforts were made to conceal or misrepresent them. In fact, the art and science of information suppression has also flourished, thanks to technological advances. Accordingly, the free flow of accurate information is likely to remain far below technical capacities.

When economic or political considerations lead to selective tapping of information, the policy consequences can be vast. This is well-illustrated by the debate over the impact of unbalanced coverage of European events before America's entry into World War I. During the first year of the war, 70 percent of the front-page war news published throughout the United States came from Germany's enemies and carried their perspectives to the American public. Because of political barriers to information flow, the proportion of war news received directly from Germany never exceeded 4 percent. Britain had a virtual monopoly on cable news. Hence, the German invasion of Belgium and the sinking of the passenger ship *Lusitania* by German submarines were reported almost entirely by cables channeled through Britain. Both events helped pave the way for American entry into the war against Germany. It has been argued that tapping a more balanced array of information sources might have yielded a more balanced view of the antagonists and might have kept America out of war. Whether this would have actually happened is uncertain, of course. But it is clear that the ability to control communication flows through technological or political measures carries the potential for altering decision patterns significantly.

Decision-makers have therefore been frequently tempted to suppress information sources or tap only those sources of information that support decisions that they prefer. Selective tapping has become much easier in recent decades, since modern communications technologies provide a much wider array of choices than ever before. Chief executives can search the vast information storage available from computers for information that will support their predilections. In addition, they can commission electronic searches of rapidly growing printed sources available from libraries. They can also be almost instantly in contact with experts of their choice throughout the world.

Here again, modern technology is a double-edged sword. The advantages enjoyed by incumbent executives in finding information supporting their preferred decisions are matched by corresponding advantages enjoyed by their adversaries. For instance, during the 1982 debate about the Reagan administration's plans for increasing nuclear weapons, the opponents of Reagan's policies could also draw on a wide array of knowledgeable experts to lend weight to their arguments. Modern technology permitted them to gain wide publicity for their cause. An example was an article advocating a more limited role for nuclear weapons in United States defense planning. The article, published in the influential journal *Foreign Affairs*, expounded the views of George Kennan, former ambassador to the Soviet Union; Robert S. McNamara, former secretary of defense and president of the World Bank; McGeorge Bundy, former presidential adviser; and Gerald C. Smith, former director of the Arms Control and Disarmament Agency.

President Reagan was highly concerned about the deleterious impact that wide publicity for this article, based on the views of well-known experts, might have on his policy proposals. Therefore, he asked Secretary of State Haig to make a rebuttal just prior to publication of the article. Haig did so in a hastily arranged speech at Georgetown University on April 6, 1982. As is typical in the age of instant communication, the speech made newspaper headlines throughout the country on the next day and was widely reported on televison and radio newscasts. But the opposing expert views received even wider publicity. This publicity made it unlikely that President Reagan's decisions would survive unscathed in the ensuing public and congressional debate. High-level political battles conducted in the glare of wide publicity tend to remove the mantle of generalized support for the presidency, which often protects presidential decisions from concerted attacks.

Besides improving data-collection capabilities and providing decision-makers with instant access to an ever-wider array of sources, the new communications technologies have made the handling of information vastly more sophisticated. They make it possible to store huge amounts of information and yet have them instantly available for updating or retrieval. If the storage procedures are handled efficiently so that needed information can be quickly and selectively retrieved, the benefits to overburdened decision-makers can be vast. These technologies may be particularly crucial during political crises when it has often been difficult in the past to get sufficient information quickly enough and to digest it properly. Computer searches can accomplish tasks in a matter of minutes that formerly took days and weeks or were technically impossible to perform.

Unfortunately, retrieval arrangements are often inefficient. They may fail to retrieve essential information or they may not be designed for fine screening so that nonessential information is omitted. If too much information is produced in answer to a request, the recipient may find it unmanageable. Information overload has long been a serious problem in high-level decision-making, and effective retrieval procedures can only add to this problem. If this happens, executives will be overwhelmed rather than aided by a flood of information.

Another extremely useful feature of computerized and word-processed information is the capacity for instant updates. New data can be readily incorporated into reports at the appropriate points, without the necessity for complete revisions or bothersome appendixes to hard copies. Even graphics can be constantly updated to illustrate changing trends. This capability encourages information collectors to keep files current and enables executives to work with the latest information at all times.

Modern computers are more than storage and retrieval mechanisms. They also have substantial capabilities for information analysis. Many of the complex calculations involved in diagnosing problems and decision-making can be performed efficiently, and without human biases, by properly programmed computers. In particular, machines are not susceptible to some of the frailties of human decision-making in bureaucratic settings. For instance, unlike humans, they do not lean toward "uncertainty absorption"—the practice of distorting unclear information in line with organizational goals.[3] Nor do they suffer from "groupthink" tendencies that pressure small groups toward thinking conformity, especially in a crisis atmosphere.[4]

When computers are used, it becomes possible to incorporate a large number of contingencies into the information analysis so that problems can be scrutinized from a variety of perspectives. For example, if chief executives are considering changes in tax programs, relevant information can be fed into computers to assess the weaknesses of current programs and to predict likely impacts of the proposed changes. Beyond making predictions based on a specific tax proposal, computers make it feasible to generate predictions for a multitude of tax proposals so that their likely impact can be compared on the basis of available data.

[3] The term was coined by Anthony Downs, *Inside Bureaucracy* (Boston: Little, Brown, 1967), p. 121.

[4] The term was coined by Irving Janis for the title of his book *Victims of Groupthink* (Boston: Houghton Mifflin, 1972).

Considering the fact that executive decision-making has generally been a satisficing procedure—limited to examining relatively few rather than the total possible number of options—the increased capacity may be a substantial benefit. It opens the possibility to examine all viable options, thereby increasing opportunities for choosing the most desirable outcome.

Yet many technical problems must be solved before chief executives can relegate the bulk of decision-related operations to computers. Currently, there are still too many computer failures. When computers go down at a crucial time, disaster could result because the stored information may not be available elsewhere. It is frightening to think about the consequences of disabling or destroying the government's computer capacity in wartime. More mundanely, the security of computerized information remains a major problem. Electronic eavesdropping, inspired by a variety of motives, has been common. Should governments entrust full scenarios of possible actions to computers when there are substantial risks that the information could be purloined by electronic burglars?

More progress needs to be made in computer model building before it becomes an ideal tool. An old computer adage is GIGO—garbage in, garbage out. The same principle holds for decision-making information: if the data fed into the computer are flawed by inaccuracies, or marred by omissions, or classified so that relevant and irrelevant information cannot be separated when particular problems arise, computer outputs may be worthless in varying degrees. Moreover, if those who select the data and devise the assumptions that shape their use allow particular viewpoints to influence their choices, these viewpoints will bias outputs and may dominate the decision-making process.

It is difficult to decide which contingencies should be built into a model. Even the most sophisticated current models remain crude, incorporating only a fraction of the contingencies that come to play in real life situations. The lack of success of economic models to predict even gross economic trends, despite comparatively long experience by Nobel Prize winners in building such models, inspires little confidence. Yet, in spite of such failures, the public's and even the experts' faith in the ultimate triumph of models continues.

In dealing with technological innovation, human problems are even more serious than the potential for machine failure. Professor Mitchell L. Moss of New York University has pointed out: "Our knowledge of the technology of telecommunications is far greater than our knowledge of the social and economic factors that influence the use of new telecommunication systems. Further, the cumulative effects of new communication technologies will be felt in areas and ways that we can scarcely conceive of today."[5]

For example, the functions currently performed by the president's cabinet and various high-level policymaking bodies like the National Security Council and

[5] Mitchell L. Moss, ed., *Telecommunications and Productivity* (Reading, Mass.: Addison-Wesley, 1981), pp. xii–xiii.

the Office of Policy Development could be largely absorbed by computers. While the notion of decisions made with machine precision is intriguing, serious drawbacks loom. Reducing the time spent in joint discussion and thinking could ultimately be detrimental to the human factors involved in decision-making and implementation. Personal interchange develops rapport and solidarity, a feeling of mutual concern and emotional support, and a common understanding of the rationales that justify particular decisions. Such feelings and ideas are essential to cooperation in carrying out decisions. Moreover, decisions reached in consultation with top advisers are likely to have greater legitimacy than those reached alone, with the assistance of electronic devices. It is doubtful that the scientific aura surrounding computer printouts can equal the aura of legitimacy that human support is able to lend.

Many other human problems must be resolved before the new technologies can be fully integrated into decision-making processes. Can machine intelligence ever be the equal of human intelligence in its ability to combine ethical and moral considerations with other types of social judgments? Can these important decisional criteria be quantified? What happens when people disagree with the machines? It has long been known, for instance, that politicians put great weight on scientific polls only so long as the polls confirm their feelings and inclinations. Will presidents, or governors, or mayors adopt options that seem soundest on the basis of computer printouts when they have strong preferences for different solutions? The answer is no. High-level decision-makers will not readily abdicate their power to machines or to experts whose data and recommendations are unpalatable. They know well that machine and expert testimony can be manipulated to yield information that favors particular decisions. They are aware of the possibilities of concealment and deliberate distortion. One has also to reckon with the budding rebellion against a mechanized civilization. People resent machines that usurp their jobs. They do not like to talk to recorders or confide in robots that ask predetermined questions.

The fierce political battles that delayed the spread of cable television for decades indicate the kinds of barriers that new computer technologies face. Little of the promise has been realized thus far, despite vast technical capabilities. Teleconferencing, electronic mail, and electronic storage and retrieval of documents have also been around for ten years or more. But they are still not widely used in the public sector, despite the fact that they promise substantial savings in many work situations. As Robert Warren of the University of Delaware has pointed out: "Efforts to apply innovations in telecommunications technology to functions performed by state and local governments have had a singular lack of success over the past decade. Indeed, the gap between early expectations and actual development has been monumental."[6]

[6] Ibid., p. 277.

Mobilizing Support for Executive Decisions

In democratic societies, executives must win wide public acclaim for their decisions if they wish to retain power and prestige and if they need to win elections. Many of their decisions cannot be successfully implemented without support from other officials and from the general public. Therefore, executives must mobilize support for their decisions internally, from their staffs and from other governmental bodies, and externally, from the general public and often from foreign allies.

New communications technologies have eased this task greatly. But they have also engendered serious new problems. The mass media, particularly television, have made it possible to reach a vast public in ways that require minimal literacy skills to receive media messages. A president can gain public attention fairly easily through a speech to the nation that is televised live on the majority of audio-visual channels. Franklin D. Roosevelt pioneered the use of electronic techniques with his radio fireside chats. In the 1930s, 18 million radio sets in the nation's homes put Roosevelt in touch with nearly 60 million listeners. Currently, nearly every American is within reach of television.

Satellite communication extends this outreach capability to major population centers throughout the globe. It is becoming commonplace to schedule major pronouncements by the president and cabinet members at times when they can be simultaneously viewed in Europe. For instance, the Haig speech mentioned earlier was broadcast at 9:15 A.M. eastern standard time so that it would be available for Western Europe's evening television and for newspaper coverage on the following morning. But while competition for the public's attention has been increasing, the public's willingness to grapple with complex political issues seems to be on the decline. The media's audiences feel overloaded with intellectually demanding information. Given a choice, they prefer entertainment to listening to the appeals of public leaders.

Developing technology may enhance the opportunities for political outreach. Appeals by political leaders can be put on video-cassettes or teletext or broadcast at different times on a large number of cable television channels. Messages can be tailored to fit the needs of specific audiences. However, it remains to be seen how many appropriate audiences a particular decision-maker can reach. There is also some danger that adapting the political dialogue to the concerns of special audiences may encourage socioeconomic factionalism, which might diminish the chances for a wide consensus on important public issues that cut across existing group cleavages.

When policies require public cooperation, implementation may be aided through audio-visual instruction. If only limited segments of the public are involved, cable television makes it possible to target messages to these groups. They can be told, in language appropriate to their circumstances, how policies will affect them and what they will have to do because of the policy. For instance, through cable television, members of the executive branch might inform various communities how to cooperate with an energy conservation plan or how to reap benefits under an agricultural support program.

The ability to reach the public instantly has drawbacks as well as advantages. Pressed by news-hungry journalists, executives feel forced to explain developing situations even before the proverbial dust has settled. Premature discussion often limits decision-making options and exposes executives to undeserved criticism if initial projections turn out to be incorrect. High-speed diffusion of information increases the danger of spreading false rumors and misinformation, which may hamper sound decision-making. By the time errors are corrected, it may be too late. A media report that sugar will be rationed or that government bonds will lose their tax-free status may lead to the disastrous depletion of sugar supplies or panic dumping of government bonds, even if these statements turn out to be wrong. The prospect of an instantly publicized damaging slip of the tongue or a misquote has been a nightmare for executives who face the public frequently in press conferences and other well-publicized settings.

One major new feature in telecommunications is the ability for two-way communication, which promises to be a part of nearly all cable systems. It has raised the possibility of instant plebiscites on policy issues prior to decision-making. Chief executives could submit their ideas to their constituencies and ask for instant feedback to specific policy proposals. Decisions could then be made with greater awareness of public opinion than has been possible in the past.

The merits of this technique for gauging public opinion and incorporating it into decision-making are open to question. Would people know enough about the issues in question to give informed answers? Could executives, by controlling the form of the questions and the context in which questions are asked, predetermine the answers? How likely is it that answers to such polls might be controlled and manipulated by special interest groups? How much weight should be given to the results of such polls? Should they be binding on executives? Should they absolve executives from full responsibility for the consequences of their decisions? Should other governmental organizations, such as legislatures or city councils, take poll results seriously when they were not consulted in the shaping of the questions? Additional concerns spring from the fact that interactive technologies may increase the influence of the well-educated, articulate members of society who are most likely to participate in interactive communication. These important considerations need to be widely debated before determining what role instant polling should play in executive decision-making.

A favorite technique for gaining staff support for executive decisions has been to involve officials in the decision-making process. Insofar as the new technology leads to more centralization in the chief executive's office and less interpersonal consultation about decisions, it is likely to impair the chances for rapport and zealous policy implementation. In fact, chief executives may have to make difficult trade-offs between the higher quality of decision-making that may result from computer use and the need to sustain morale. Whatever else computers can do, they will not rally support behind a chief executive or soothe the ruffled feelings of subordinates.

However, the ill-effects of depersonalized decisions may be somewhat diminished by the ability to assemble staffs more quickly and cheaply, and by the chance to present explanatory information more effectively. New communications technologies also make it easier to monitor policy implementation, evaluate progress, and devise changes if they are needed.

Conclusion

Alexander George, in his book *Presidential Decisionmaking in Foreign Policy*, outlined five procedural tasks that are essential to effective decision-making.[7] Stated briefly, these tasks involve (1) gathering sufficient information and analyzing it so that it provides an accurate diagnosis of the problem; (2) ensuring that the major values and interests affected by the policy are taken into consideration in setting policy goals; (3) identifying and analyzing a relatively wide range of options and assessing their likely costs, risks, and benefits; (4) considering problems that may arise in implementing various options; and (5) arranging for feedback to evaluate policy outcomes with an eye to remedying deficiencies.

The new communications technologies may be exceedingly helpful in accomplishing the first and third tasks—gathering and analyzing ample diagnostic information and identifying and appraising a wide range of options. Properly programmed, computers perform these functions tirelessly, swiftly, and with superhuman precision. New communications technologies are equally useful in carrying out the fourth and fifth tasks—assessing implementation problems and developing feedback that can lead to needed policy revisions. Again, the key to effectiveness is adequate computer programming and model building. However, usefulness in these latter phases depends heavily on success in the second requirement—the need to incorporate major values and interests affected by the policy into the decision-making process. Identifying such interests and building subjective politicial and human relations concerns into computer programs remains difficult, if not impossible.

Computers, primed with a wealth of factual data, can produce excellent rational decision-making models. But these data may be worthless in practice if they ignore the political context. In the past, the emphasis on designing good models, without a corresponding concern with the human factors involved in implementation, has frequently led to grief. Herein lies the Achilles' heel of modern communication technologies: they may make a science out of political decision-making, but politics is as much art as science. What is scientifically praiseworthy may be humanly unacceptable.

[7] Alexander L. George, *Presidential Decisionmaking in Foreign Policy: The Effective Use of Information and Advice* (Boulder, Colo.: Westview Press, 1980), p. 10.

The future, as usual, will involve compromises. The new technologies and machines will be coveted status symbols of progress that will make human tasks simpler and more efficient. But technology will not, and should not, be allowed to dominate decision-making when it conflicts substantially with human concerns. Executives must retain the power and will to make final decisions and the responsibility for the ultimate outcome.

Communications and Congress

STEPHEN FRANTZICH

Congress sits at the vortex of three discrete communications flows: it is the target, sender, and subject matter of communications. As the target, Congress and its members receive and sometimes solicit massive amounts of communications from constituents, interest groups, the executive branch, substantive experts, and fellow members. Members wishing to affect congressional policy choices seek substantive information to prove their points and strategic information on when, where, and how key decisions will be made.

As senders of communications, members of Congress have turned their offices into small public-relations firms promoting only one product—their own political well-being. As congressmen have increased the size of their offices and divided functions between Washington and their home district offices, they have had to find new ways to communicate effectively with their staffs and colleagues.

As the subject matter of communications, congressmen are highly self-conscious about how they and their institution are portrayed to the public. Congressmen depend on the mass media to reach large portions of their constituencies to whom they have no way of sending effective and personalized communications. Since Congress and its members compete with other political actors for attention, power, prestige, and policy outcomes, their ability to use and control communications seriously affects their success or failure.

Traditional communications patterns with the congressman as target and sender have been personal, selective, and labor intensive. Outsiders attempting to influence policy choices communicated timely information on emerging problems, possible alternatives, and the likely consequences of each choice. Congressmen sought to create an information flow that would minimally satisfy their needs to make specific decisions, rather than attempting comprehensively to study issues. As a Senate commission report noted: "A Senator is not a research coordinator. The ranges of choice in decision-making for Senators are usually narrowly constrained by political circumstances. Senators do not operate in an open decision-making world, where all relevant objective information is gathered, sifted, and the most promising options selected. On the contrary, Senators typically seek information that justifies previous positions, or at most, resolves limited finite questions within a small range."[1]

In such an environment, congressmen tended to trust the advice of their colleagues over that of experts, since the colleagues were available when decisions had to be made and were able to temper the facts with practical political information. Constituent opinions arrived only sporadically, and members had to augment fragmented information with creative intuition to assess constituent desires and possible reactions.

As congressional decisions increased in number and complexity and as the visibility of congressional behavior was enhanced by the expanding mass media, members of Congress found themselves in need of a broader range of relevant information, while they simultaneously tried to avoid an information overload. In a simpler age, it was possible for an able generalist to gather enough information through experience and study to tackle almost any problem, but the information explosion turned many experts into instant anachronisms. Congressmen observed a simultaneous increase in the demands from their constituents. The image of the congressman leisurely reading his mail and dictating responses fell by the wayside when hundreds of letters began arriving daily. The dictum "write your congressman" has always been used to legitimize representative government, but only recently have large numbers of citizens taken the opportunity seriously to express their opinions on issues and to seek out services from their members' offices. With more congressmen running for office outside of the traditional party-recruitment process and using electronic communications channels to outmaneuver their opponents, incumbents have found themselves under severe pressure to protect themselves from defeat by a new generation of challengers with their own innovative communications technology.

In facing up to the increased demands for receiving and sending communications, congressmen have not been technological trend setters. They first reacted to these increased demands by dramatically expanding their staffs and their dependence on labor-intensive methods to handle the flood of communications demands. Congress stood in the backwaters of technological change until its membership was bolstered by an influx of members who had experienced new approaches on the outside and could quiet the fears of their senior colleagues.

As the subject matter of communications, Congress has also gone through significant changes. During the nineteenth century, Congress dominated national political coverage by the media. Whether this preeminent position was the consequence or cause of congressional power during that era is less important than the fact that the era serves as a benchmark for measuring how far Congress has fallen from both power and attention. The general expansion of mass communications led to more coverage of Congress in absolute terms, but Con-

[1] U.S., Congress, Senate, Commission on the Operation of the Senate, *Techniques and Procedures for Analysis and Evaluation* (Washington, D.C.: Government Printing Office, 1977), p. 122.

gress lost out to the executive branch in terms of relative emphasis. Doris Graber has noted: "The presidency basks in the limelight of publicity at all times, while Congress is in the shadows. . . . There are several reasons. Most importantly, the presidency is a single-headed body, readily personified, filmed, and recorded. . . . Stories about the executive branch that describe what is actually done are far more memorable than reports about the laborious process of hammering out legislation."[2]

In discussing media attention to Congress, it is important to distinguish between the national (largely electronic) and local (largely print) media. The national media tend to compare Congress as an institution with the president, and Congress often appears to lack decisiveness and efficiency. Since conflict captures attention more than hard work and inspiration, much of the congressional coverage paints a rather negative picture that encourages current high levels of alienation toward government in general and Congress in particular. The national media can get away with criticizing Congress, since the congressmen need them to promote their careers and causes. If a national reporter alienates one congressman, he has 534 others to pursue.

The local reporter, on the other hand, exists in a symbiotic relationship with his local member. He must depend on him for tips and access and therefore needs the congressman as much or more than the congressman needs him. As Michael J. Robinson has pointed out, these differences in approach help explain why people simultaneously hold Congress in low esteem while extolling the member who represents them. According to Robinson, "the national media, which reach everyone with their critical coverage of the institution, and the local media, which reach constituents and accommodate members, together serve as the single best explanation for the paradox of public opinion toward Congress."[3]

Given the importance of communications to Congress, it is no surprise that individuals attempting to communicate with or about Congress, as well as the members of Congress, are affected by technological changes in communications. Although the term *electronic communication* covers a wide variety of technology from the telegram and electronic typewriter to television and computers, this analysis will focus on the latter forms. Earlier technological breakthroughs tended to be changes in degree rather than in kind, for they augmented traditional means of communication by enhancing speed and efficiency. But these changes produced a final product quite similar to that which came from the older technology. Television and the computer, however, produce a communications product that is different in its very nature. The computer allows the collection and manipulation of such massive amounts of information at such

[2] Doris Graber, *Mass Media and American Politics* (Washington, D.C.: Congressional Quarterly, 1980), pp. 208–9.

[3] Michael J. Robinson, "Three Faces of Congressional Media," in *The New Congress*, ed. Thomas Mann and Norman Ornstein (Washington, D.C.: American Enterprise Institute, 1981), p. 90.

phenomenal speeds that it allows congressmen to take on tasks once considered infeasible. Television similarly changes the context and content of communications when it visually transports the individual to a new setting.

Congress Enters the Computer Age

Less than a decade ago, the worlds of computer technology and Capitol Hill had little in common. The computer was not seen as compatible with congressional needs and engendered fears that Congress would become the captive of the machine. Today there is hardly a congressional office without at least one computer terminal, and members and staff alike cannot conceive of how they did their jobs without them.

Computers entered congressional offices for three basic purposes. Word-processing capabilities allowed offices more efficiently and creatively to manage their incoming communications. As a bibliographic research tool, the computer linked members and their staffs with the growing number of commercial and in-house data bases, bringing to Congress timely, presorted, and more complete information on emerging policy problems and potential options. As a repository for primary data, the computer allowed Congress to analyze everything from the current status of legislation to policy-outcome projections.

Although moving from the precomputer age to the present level of computerization in Congress took less than a decade, the route was neither self-evident nor simple. The House and Senate took different paths. The House first allowed members to contract with outside vendors individually, while the Senate emphasized centralized provision. The growth of computer usage in individual offices followed a predictable incremental pattern. Members with the weakest electoral bases were the first to use computers to strengthen their ability to communicate with constituents. Members coming to Congress with computer experience in the business or academic worlds also quickly embraced the new technology. Michael J. Robinson observed:

> Today's Senate office is a spaceship of electronic communications systems. . . . Since 1960 the Senate has already been through four generations of memory typewriters. . . . The modern Senate mail system, Correspondence Management System (CMS), produces up to forty letters per hour on each in-office computer terminal. CMS letters appear personalized and individually typed, of course, although they emerge mass-produced from the multi-memory bank of the central processing unit. . . . An "average" senator now has five letter processors (terminals) working off CMS; a middle sized Senate office can send 2,500 personalized letters per week to constituents. . . . Currently, the average American receives two pieces of mail every year from Congress. . . . But the new in-house correspondence systems mean more than a greater quantity of mail, and more efficient mail. The new system can also mean "targeted" mail.[4]

[4] Robinson, pp. 59–61.

As might be expected in an institution whose members value electoral security, the most widespread use of computers involves managing communications with constituents. In most offices, incoming mail is sorted into "legislative" mail (expressing opinions on issues) and "casework" mail (soliciting direct help). The legislative mail is logged for content so that the member can get an accurate mail count on each issue. All mail is coded to create profiles of the sources, which become part of a data base from which selected lists based on such characteristics as issue orientation, occupation, and geographic location can be drawn for future targeted mailings. Responses to the legislative mail are often created using appropriate selections from a set of "canned" paragraphs. Casework mail can be tracked using the computer for follow-up action. Offices go beyond simply reacting to outside communications by acquiring mailing lists (such as registered voters, members of professional associations, and ideological groups), which can be sent targeted mailings describing the congressman's positions on issues relevant to the recipients.

One staff member described their system in this way: "I began with a personal letter to each of the special interest groups we have on file. The physicians received a letter from my congressman enclosed with a reprint from the *Congressional Record* of his recent remarks on the horrors of socialized medicine. Each of these letters began, 'Knowing of your intense personal interest in any legislation affecting physicians/nurses, I thought you might be interested to see. . . .' On the average we received one response, invariably positive, for every two letters we sent—an absolutely phenomenal 50% rate of unsolicited response."[5]

While the use of word processors to monitor and create traditional written communications is now the standard operating procedure, the computer is also becoming a means of direct communication. Over two hundred congressional offices are linked by electronic mail (EM). One staff member explained the numerous advantages of EM:

> It saves time by reducing the social amenities typical on the telephone and cuts out "telephone tag" where numerous callbacks are necessary before two people can finally get together. Now it is possible to send messages in the morning and come back at my leisure and review the responses. For members from distant states whose time zone does not coincide with Washington, communications with district offices are no longer constrained by the limited "time window" when working hours overlap. Offices can develop distribution lists to send the same communication both instantaneously and simultaneously to many recipients. Many subordinates like electronic mail since it reduces the times they are put on the spot by an oral inquiry. EM gives them some thinking time to compose a more judicious response. All in all, EM is a first step in increasing the efficiency of executives who have been largely bypassed by the revolution in electronic communications and whose time is more valuable than the clerical staff toward whom most innovations have been directed.[6]

[5] William Hayden, "Confessions of a High-Tech Politico," *Washington Monthly*, May 1980, p. 45.

[6] Confidential personal interview.

Currently, EM is used primarily for intraoffice communications. The leadership and ideological groups can send whip notices, and committees can send messages to their members using EM. Some offices are using EM to communicate casework requests to a select list of executive agencies. The opinion in Congress is that such communications are more efficient and engender quicker responses from the agencies. In a pilot project, one House office has been allowed to link itself directly to constituents with home computers. Under this system, the constituent can directly communicate with the congressman via the computer. The desire to increase the use of electronic mail, however, is tempered by some real concerns about the consequences. One senior staff member expressed reservations about giving everyone access to Congress via electronic mail, since it could turn the computer into a depository for junk mail from interest groups and dissatisfied voters. On the other hand, EM could create a situation in which the only people who could communicate with congressmen are those who can afford home computers.

The computer is not only being used as a means of communicating but also as a method of access to outside information that in the past was either not available or difficult to utilize. With the information explosion, Congress, along with other segments of society, found it increasingly difficult to sort through the massive amounts of information available from outside sources. Computerization of the bibliographic sources of the Library of Congress and the provision of access to commercial bibliographic systems, such as the New York Times Information Bank, the Justice Retrieval and Inquiry System (JURIS), and the National Institutes of Health's *Medline*, allow staff members to search for information by author, topic, and often by key words. As useful as such bibliographic systems are, they still require effort and creativity on the part of the searcher, and the output is often a mass of citations that must still be sifted and organized.

Realizing the time pressure on congressional offices, the Congressional Research Service (CRS) utilizes a computer to condense the resources. A member of Congress or staff member can put himself in the communication track for Selective Dissemination of Information (SDI), which sends out new references on preselected topics. CRS also uses the computer to place its original research, *Issue Briefs*, on line to congressional offices. Offices can also monitor the *Federal Register* or the *Congressional Record*. Many offices use the *Grants* program to discover and facilitate grant requests from constituents.

While general information on issues helps congressional offices frame their responses, outside research often fails to provide the key information that a congressman wants, such as the consequences of each policy option for the people he represents. The computer facilitates complex calculations that may allow the projection of consequences through the use of simulation models. Congress uses both logic-based and data-based models in decision-making. Logic-based models predict the future through deductive reasoning. Recent debates over budgets and taxes in Congress have seen conflicting predictions by such economic models, some accepted by the Reagan administration and others supported by the Congressional Budget Office. Differing projections occur, since at the heart of these models is a set of subjective assumptions. Improved technological capability does not keep politicians from believing those models whose projections fit their preconceptions or from changing the assumptions of the model to make the projection come out "right."

Data-based or "feed forward" models base their predictions much more heavily on data from the recent past with minor adjustments for current decisions. In tax matters, the Individual Tax Estimation system uses actual data from the previous year on such things as deductions and makes a first-order projection on the consequences of changing the rules on future deductions. The Social Programs Model projects federal funding distribution under various formulas using census and past distribution data. Employing such models, the congressman can immediately determine the impact of various decisions on the whole society or its subdivisions.

Any member of Congress who wishes to affect the content of public policy needs strategic information on when and where key decisions will be made. Congress exists as a multiring circus with a rapidly increasing amount of legislation and many decision points. The Bill Status System allows a congressman or staff member instantly to retrieve information on the status of any bill and selectively to acquire relevant information, such as where the bill is in the legislative process, who introduced it, and its salient points. Member offices can flag bills of particular importance and automatically receive a status update after any action has been taken.

Once legislation reaches the House floor, the computer supports the electronic voting system. When a roll-call vote is called, members have fifteen minutes to arrive on the floor, insert their card in a voting portal, and have it recorded in the computer and displayed. Electronic voting would be a mundane administrative application, replacing a clerk and speeding up the decision-making process, if it were not for the capability of monitoring and analyzing ongoing votes. The leadership has terminals that can be programmed to sort out voting preferences of members by such variables as state, region, and seniority. If during a vote the floor managers find a member voting against the party or out of step with his state, they can approach him on the floor and use computer information in an attempt to change his vote.

The uses of the computer as a communications and analysis tool in Congress go well beyond those listed above. To a degree, Congress, especially the House, is a classic case of the "Law of the Instrument": "Give a child a hammer, and the whole world becomes a nail."[7] The variety of computer applications and proposals is expanded daily and covers the whole spectrum of congressional activity. Although it was slow to apply the new technology, Congress is now fully committed to computerization, especially as it supports constituent communication.

The consequences of introducing electronic communications supported by computers into the Congress are substantial. In John McHale's words, "the ef-

[7] Abraham Kaplan, *The Conduct of Inquiry* (San Francisco: Chandler Publishing Co., 1964), p. 28.

fects and advance in information technology have been viewed as more disruptive than any other technological impact. . . . It is possible that such impacts will change the very locus and function of power in society."[8] The power implications of computers in Congress proceed on two levels. On the institutional level, by enhancing its information sources and analyzing capacity, Congress has curbed the erosion of its power to the executive.

However, the power shifts are even more discernible on the level of individual members. Traditionally, communications patterns in Congress guaranteed that those individuals in leadership positions had more information than their colleagues. The seniority system and the specialization fostered by the committee system made Congress a bastion of "resident information." Individuals gained power and status through long periods of apprenticeship and a growing reservoir of relevant information. As the information made it increasingly difficult even for the most diligent information gatherer to keep up with any field, and as access to computerized data bases changed the ease and nature of information gathering, power began to shift to members with "access information." In Congress now, what you know and who you know are no longer as important as what kind of information you can get. Powerful experts relying on their store of resident information are no longer a match for aggressive junior members who know how to tap and use new information sources. Wilbur Mills, for example, was able to dominate decades of tax policy through an intricate knowledge of tax law, but the current tax debate is characterized by confrontations between committee chairmen and junior members haggling over consequences and referring to their respective computer printouts. Thus the general implication of computerization has been to contribute to the democratization of Congress.

But as is usually the case, the power shift is not totally one-way. Monitoring terminals on the floor of the House gives the leadership the kind of information that was not readily available in the past and makes individual members more susceptible to pressure. The ability instantly to monitor ongoing voting may also make minimum winning coalitions more likely. Floor managers have difficulty knowing how much pressure and bargaining they must bring to bear, but the communication of accurate information increases the potential for careful strategy.

The use of computers in individual offices clearly increases their efficiency in dealing with outside communications. It is certain that the volume and quality of constituent communications have increased dramatically, especially in election years. Whether the time saved will be used simply to increase the frequency and sophistication of communications or whether it will free staff to study and better analyze policy issues is yet to be determined.

The justification usually given for expending vast resources to bring Congress to the forefront of the electronic communications age is to improve the quality

[8] John McHale, *The Changing Information Environment* (Denver: Westview Press, 1976), p. 1.

of legislation, and it seems that policymakers in Congress do now have better information and a greater ability to avoid error and do their own analyses. But it is on the darker side of communicating too much information that the computer might contribute even more. In the past, a great deal of decision-making in Congress was done on the basis of "coalitions of mixed expectations." Individuals with widely varying goals came together to vote for a particular piece of legislation with minimal information on its actual consequences. As the information available to decision-makers is increased, the result may not be a legislature made up of "philosopher kings" but rather a group of individuals more prone to conflict and more able for their narrow, parochial reasons to project the consequences of all decisions.

The introduction of computerized communications in Congress has left unsolved a number of key problems. Who should have access to the data bases, and who should pay for their creation and maintenance? What are the ethical questions involved when information is gathered on individuals or when incumbents receive subsidized resources that can easily be translated into political advantage? How can the difference between the quantity and the quality of information be known and when is each to be trusted? Computerized data bases themselves can do little if anything to help answer these difficult questions.

Despite some obvious criticisms and dangers, any evaluation of the overall impact of computerized communications on Congress to date clearly falls on the positive side. Computerization has left Congress better informed and better able to select and use relevant information. Both sides of the representation equation have been improved as congressmen have learned more about their constituents' desires and have become better able to communicate with them. Relatively open access to information has helped to democratize the decision-making process and has set the stage for better policy by individuals more fully aware of the possible consequences.

Congress on Television

Unlike the adoption of computers, which engendered little serious analysis of possible consequences, the decision to bring cameras into the House chambers in 1979 involved considerable debate, lengthy hearings by numerous committees and special commissions, contracted research, pilot projects, and surveys of membership reaction. Congressmen realized that television was the most popular and trusted news source but saw the changes it had wrought in politics and stood in both awe and fear. Many of the same concerns are resurfacing as the Senate discusses the possibility of joining the House in allowing floor coverage.

Much of the rhetoric advocating television access is couched in terms of the citizens' right to know what is going on in government. Majority Leader Howard Baker (R-TN), the primary backer of the current Senate proposal, has commented that "if the Founding Fathers had access to electronic television in their time, it would have been available from the early days of the Congress as a logical extension of the public gallery."[9] But behind such democratic rhetoric lie a number of practical goals. Television holds the promise of improving Congress's image and helping to redress its power disadvantages relative to the executive. In the past, the public saw only snippets of congressional conflict and misbehavior, and fuller access to the executive branch meant that they received coverage by default. About the time television was being discussed, a series of studies emerged verifying the low esteem in which Congress was held. Representative Elliot Levitas (D-GA) said: "I do not believe that public confidence in our government will ever be restored until the public has a clear idea of just what we are doing and how we do it. Trust must be based on understanding, and understanding must spring from a clear public perception of our intentions and our action. The television camera, I believe, is a tool for providing that perception."[10] Not only was television expected to improve Congress's image but also to improve its performance. As Senator Howard Baker argued: "Turning on the cameras to let the people see us as we really are can help bring . . . an opportunity for the Senate to actually become the great deliberative body which it was thought to be when it was created, as it has sometimes been in its past, and that we would all like it to be every day."[11]

Previous experience with selective coverage of committee hearings seems to verify these assumptions. The polls have indicated that not only does the public support the televising of Congress in general but also that television coverage could improve Congress's image. Six days of live, comprehensive coverage of the House Judiciary Committee's impeachment hearings, for example, resulted in substantially improved public ratings of Congress as an institution in the Gallup Poll.[12]

Much of the impetus for allowing television cameras on the floor of Congress grew from a frustration that the president had adapted more efficiently to the electronic media and was reaping the benefits of more frequent and positive coverage. Many proponents pointed out the irony that Congress contributed to the imbalance by allowing cameras on the House floor only when the president was present. The late Senator Hubert Humphrey (D-MN) stated: "On the one hand, we cast a blurred and confusing image for the man on the street; on the other, we are regularly made victim to end-runs and upstaging by the President. We have failed to make ourselves known and understood as an institution, with a recognizable and positive identity in the public mind. And we have been slug-

[9] U.S., Congress, Senate, Committee on Rules and Administration, *Television and Radio Coverage of Proceedings in the Senate* (Washington, D.C.: Government Printing Office, 1981), p. 6.

[10] U.S., Congress, Commission on the Operation of the Senate, *Senate Communications With the Public* (Washington, D.C.: Government Printing Office, 1977), p. 107.

[11] Senate, Committee on Rules and Administration, *Television and Radio Coverage of Proceedings in the Senate*, pp. 4–5.

[12] American Institute of Public Opinion, press release, August 29, 1974.

gish in meeting the challenge of the Executive's inherent advantage in competing with us for the public eye and ear."[13]

Finally, in an attempt to build support for television, proponents pointed out that the vast majority of states and nations welcome television cameras at regular intervals to cover routine legislative business. Despite some minor inconvenience and disruption, the impact has largely been positive, and not one legislature has rescinded the right to coverage.

Opponents of television coverage in Congress predicted dire consequences for the institution and representative government in general. At first, they argued that the technical requirements for bright lights and the instrusiveness of heavy equipment would make life on the floor intolerable. With advanced technology, however, equipment considerations faded into the background. One of the most abiding criticisms projected an image of members pandering to the cameras with frequent, unnecessary, and strident speeches that would waste time and make compromise more difficult. Some opponents argued that, in order to present an acceptable and intelligent image, members would have to spend more time on the floor to avoid scenes of empty seats and that chamber procedures would have to be changed to make the flow of business seem more rational. A special fear involved the loss of the right to "revise and extend" one's remarks. Would the videotape replace the written record as the official transcript of legislative activity and intent? Would television allow members to retain their present rights of immunity for what is said on the floor?

While most of the arguments against television in the House have been more recently resuscitated for the debate in the Senate, a number of opponents have argued that notwithstanding the seeming success of House coverage, the Senate should hold fast to its current exclusion of the cameras. David Broder noted that the Senate plays a unique role as a deliberative body in the constitutional system, "a bit removed from the currents of public opinion. That is why senators have long staggered terms. And that is why Senate rules preserve a minority's, or even a single member's right to delay decision by lengthy debate."[14] Such debate and other parliamentary tactics might be extremely difficult to explain with the nation looking on. Senator Jesse Helms (R-NC) expressed a similar view: "When our Constitution was drafted, the delegates meeting in Philadelphia in the summer of 1787 met in secrecy—not because they despised the public, but because they understood the complexities of lawmaking. . . . In a representative democracy, the people govern indirectly, not directly. . . . [Televising Congress] seeks to impose upon the legislative process an aspect of direct democracy that undermines representative government . . . [and] would act as a deterrent to the exercise of individual judgement."[15]

[13] U.S., Congress, Joint Committee on Congressional Operations, *Congress and Mass Communications: An Institutional Perspective* (Washington, D.C.: Government Printing Office, 1974), p. 26.

[14] *Washington Post*, February 21, 1982.

[15] Joint Committee on Congressional Operations, *Congress and Mass Communications*, p. 58.

The debate over televising the Senate may be decided more on the basis of budget or partisan considerations than on the merits of the issue. One recent survey showed that a majority of the Senate favored some form of Senate coverage, but only about one-third were active proponents. The majority Republicans were significantly more supportive than the Democrats, perhaps revealing that opposition to innovation may be based less on ideology than on which group would reap the most benefits from the change.

The vote in the House for introducing television to the floor was 342–44, but that figure obscures a great deal of conflict over exactly how the implementation was to take place. The networks wanted to use a pool of their own technicians and cover the floor as they would any news event, having complete editorial freedom to focus their cameras wherever they wanted. Members of Congress recoiled at the possibility of embarrassing shots. The House televising system attempted to avoid unnecessary risks. In-house technicians with stationary cameras focusing only on the Speaker and the leadership tables make sure that television will only cover the official business of the chamber and not pan the chamber for reactions or undesirable images. The screens are blackened during roll-call votes so that members cannot be caught changing their votes or not voting at all. Representatives have ready access to videotape files so they can send back "news" to local stations easily at low cost. The major distribution of live coverage is through C-SPAN (Cable Satellite Public Affairs Network), which sends out the signal to over 1,500 cable systems throughout the nation with a potential audience of over 30 million individuals. C-SPAN coverage carries with it very little commentary and allows locally oriented members of the House to present an institutional image undistorted by the editorial selectivity and commentary of the national networks. The networks do have the right to choose clips from the live coverage for their news programs, but the relatively formalized content has made the frequency of such use rare.

With only a few years' experience, it is too early to write the final chapter concerning the consequences of House coverage. In one survey, significant numbers of members reported more speechmaking and floor amendments by colleagues in the months after television coverage began in the House (though none admitted that they changed their own behavior). Most congressmen used television in their offices to monitor floor action, and a majority were pleased with the impact of the coverage.[16] In addition, there has been an increase in the number of one-minute speeches made at the beginning of each day. These are timely, pointed, and well designed for evening news coverage, though not directed toward the pending legislative business.[17]

Arguing that television slowed down the legislative process, a study by Representative John Anderson's (R-IL) office concluded that "there *was* an in-

[16] Senate, Committee on Rules and Administration, *Television and Radio Coverage of Proceedings in the Senate*, p. 115.

[17] Ibid., pp. 153–54.

crease in the amount of time spent in passing legislation (up 54% per measure); an increase in the amount of time the House was in session each day (up 6%); and an increase in the number of pages in the *Congressional Record* per measure passed (up 44%)."[18]

Other members perceived a considerable impact as well. Representative Michael Barnes (D-MD) expressed another internal effect: "I have a feeling that history may conclude that Congress finally figured out what it was doing when TV came to the Chamber. It used to be that all the representative knew about the vote he was running to cast was 'if it's Tuesday, this must be fisheries management. . . .' But it's not quite so superficial anymore. It's on TV. If the member is in his office . . . he can leave the television turned on . . . and follow what's going on. . . . I think the case can be made that Congress has finally found a way to keep up with itself."[19]

The consequences of House television on the quality of congressional performance, position of power, and public image are more difficult to discern with certainty. One analyst argued that the "broadcasting of congressional sessions apparently has reduced the power of lobbyists, who now have competition in their efforts to convince the public of the rightness of their views."[20] Another observer suggested: "The greatest effect of the new media-mix on Congress as an institution has been to attract a new kind of congressman."[21] Although Senator Howard Baker, in his attempt to bring television to the Senate, has argued that the House "has made a quantum improvement in their deliberations as a result of television,"[22] there is no direct evidence that television coverage has enhanced Congress's public prestige. The C-SPAN audience, limited to cable households, is clearly small and select, and few people seem to be aware of its coverage of Congress.

Televising Congress has had neither the expected abuses and negative consequences, nor the sweeping positive effects predicted before its introduction. House members have learned to live with the cameras, and the commercial news media and the public seem only mildly interested in observing them. While the potential for a greater impact remains, no one has been able to identify one key decision clearly changed by the presence of the cameras.

Challenges of the Future

Despite the technological change that Congress absorbed during the last decade, the future holds even more challenges for Congress's attempt to maintain and enhance its position. In the past, the time required to communicate constituent

[18] Robinson, p. 68.
[19] *Washington Post*, April 17, 1979.
[20] Graber, p. 210.
[21] Robinson, p. 58.
[22] Senate, Committee on Rules and Administration, *Television and Radio Coverage of Proceedings in the Senate*, p. 26.

demands and congressional responses tempered some of the conflict. In the future, the two-way capability of cable may allow a member to poll his district on issues in the midst of a quorum call.[23] It is conceivable that some citizens might monitor floor activity on C-SPAN and then, using electronic mail or a special voting device, have a direct impact on ongoing decisions. While such a capability might give new meaning to the concept of representation, it also has the potential for creating a "have" and "have not" division of citizens on the basis of access and influence. Electronic teleconferences would allow congressmen to have a more direct and potent influence on selected groups of constituents and would also provide constituents with a new access point to their representatives.

The ability to classify, target, and communicate with subsections of one's constituency not only increases the information that constituents have but also stands as a temptation to communicate worthless information in an appealing and sophisticated manner. Through the use of polls and analyzed mail counts, more and more representatives may tell the people only what they want to hear.

Considering the negative side of change does not imply that past advances in electronic communications applications to Congress were without dramatic positive implications. Rather, such concern stems from the realization that Congress has accepted technological change largely on its own terms. Neither computers nor cameras were welcomed until it was clear that they would serve the best interests of the chamber and its members. Michael Robinson's observation that "House TV is another case study in how Congress has adapted to the media by looking out for number one, the membership"[24] applies with equal force to the ways in which computers have typically been employed.

Electronic communications have given Congress the potential for gathering more information, more quickly, and more tailored to its specific needs. At the same time, electronic communication provides citizens more access to what Congress does and what its members want people to think it does. Congress and the nation will never be the same. The consequences are clearly mixed in value and will require constant vigilance to identify and correct the most obvious misuses and dangers. As with all technology, "information technology is a malleable tool whose ultimate social meaning, content and consequences are highly subject to the influences of the specific political values and interests that inform its use."[25]

[23] Ibid., pp. 189–90.
[24] Robinson, p. 66.
[25] McHale, p. 1.

Adtech and the Washington Reporters

STEPHEN HESS

Advanced technology (Adtech) is said to be creating a communications revolution. The revolution comes in exotic forms: one-man electronic news-gathering cameras, low-power television, cable television carrying 200 channels, two-way interactive systems, subsidiary communications authorization, pagination, electronic still cameras, laser beams, satellites, and computers. According to a representative article in a journalism review, Adtech is "drastically changing how journalists do their jobs."[1] How Adtech affects reporters, particularly Washington reporters, is the subject of this essay.

When examining the mores of Washington reporters, one must guard against assuming that the findings automatically apply elsewhere. There is at least one demographic difference between reporters in Washington and those outside the capital—Washington reporters are older. While there is not a great difference between the average ages for the Washington press corps and all reporters in the United States, the significant difference is that 21 percent of Washington reporters are in their twenties, compared to 32 percent for the nation's entire journalist population. Washington is not an entry point for young journalists. It is where reporters—except those working for low-prestige, specialized publications—are sent after they have proved themselves in other places.

A characteristic of both the Washington press corps and the nation's stock of reporters is that they showed little interest in science and technology when in college. (The figure for Washington reporters who majored in these subjects is 15 percent and for the nation 7 percent.) Most Washington reporters studied the humanities and liberal arts. Journalists are among the least likely to embrace computers and advanced technology. Thus, in several ways, reporters in the nation's capital are atypical of their younger colleagues in the rest of the country.

[1] Larry Kahaner, "Hello, Sweetheart, Forget Rewrite, Get Me the Computer," *Washington Journalism Review*, December 1981, p. 16.

Still, one supposes that the reasons why Washington reporters went into journalism also apply to those who have not yet arrived in Washington. Reporting promises excitement and opportunities to observe important or unusual events and to meet important or unusual people. However, the type of investigation that is most aided by technology is only a new form of archival retrieval that substitutes the computer for thumbing through bound volumes.

Reporters do not go into journalism to sit in libraries or to examine printouts. Computer-aided research is anathema to the Washington press corps. In fact, these reporters use no documents at all (except news releases) in the preparation of nearly three-quarters of their stories. Overwhelmingly, their research tool is the interview—an average of about five per story. This technique allows reporters to meet important or unusual people. The undergirding of Washington news—more so than in the rest of the country—is what has been called "inside-dopsterism," which involves the cultivation of sources who provide information or insights that may not be available to the reporters' competitors. Personal contacts have been the measure of peer status in the Washington press corps for so long that it is unrealistic to expect them to be replaced by computer investigations. Reporters recognize the importance of the new technology, but they want their colleagues to handle it.

One recent study surveyed 38 percent of all Washington reporters covering the government for American commercial news organizations. A key finding of the study was the tremendous autonomy that had been painfully gained over time by news gatherers at the expense of owners and editors.[2] If this finding is correct, a change in how information is acquired will not happen until there is a change in the type of people who become journalists.

The Reporter's Tools

While it may be true that the tools of journalism will change in the near future, there are now relatively few such tools that were not also available to the Washington correspondents surveyed by Leo Rosten in 1936. At the most elemental level, the tape recorder increases accuracy and accountability. Reporters can have a verbatim record of interviews; their editors, if in doubt, can demand to hear the tape. (One reporter admitted that he erases his tapes every night to prevent them from being subpoenaed. But this practice equally ensures a degree of independence from his editor.) Since Washington reporters think of being unsupervised as a professional right, they may view even the tape recorder as a mixed blessing.

The Adtech equipment most often found in Washington news bureaus is the visual display terminal (VDT). Many reporters admit that they prefer VDTs to their old typewriters. Some even claim that the new machines have improved their prose style. Others, however, are so unsure of their ability as VDT

[2] Stephen Hess, *The Washington Reporters* (Washington, D.C.: The Brookings Institution, 1981).

operators that they use a typewriter to make notes and a VDT to transmit finished copy.

They also fear the possibility of a power failure or mechanical breakdown as a deadline approaches. (When the lights went out in the motel room where Andrew Glass was sending his story during the New Hampshire presidential primary, the resourceful reporter rushed to a police station that had its own generator.) All technologies have start-up problems. Computers malfunction, and new models seem to be error-prone. Often the fault can be traced to inexperienced personnel. Failures are soon surmounted in organizations that are receptive to Adtech. To date there have been no serious "accidents" in the news media, except perhaps one incident in which a coding error delivered a confidential memo from a Washington bureau to a rival newspaper. But when the first "disaster" occurs—such as a grossly inaccurate story resulting from bad computer management—the incident will be received by an already skeptical clientele.

A description of the press room of a major government department can help place the position of VDTs in mid-1982 Washington journalism. The desks of reporters for the two American wire services are at opposite ends of the room. At the extreme right is the desk of a veteran whose knowledge is highly prized by his colleagues. He sits in front of an ancient manual typewriter, which he rarely uses, preferring to call in stories to a dictationist. For him the state of the art in advanced technology is the telephone. He speaks with pride of the speed and accuracy that has served him for over two decades. His employers, wisely, put no pressure on him to change his ways. At the other end of the room is the much younger reporter for the rival wire service who has had this assignment for less than a year. The impression obtained from watching him is of a man peering into a screen. His office even relays telephone messages via the VDT. He is considered a rising star in his organization. The contrast is not between an old hack and a bright newcomer. Rather, the description of their work habits illustrates the degree to which Adtech usage may vary with generations of journalists.

What does the changeover to VDTs mean to reporters? It has not yet translated into more time for reporters to do stories, that is, into significantly later deadlines. There are expectations that this will happen when the "bugs are worked out of the system," but some studies now show that pencil editing is faster than VDT editing, although not as accurate. At least one reporter wondered whether the VDTs would mean more editing by the home office. He worried that VDTs would make it easier for editors to rewrite his copy. On the other hand, a foreign news editor for a major United States newspaper complained that the new system is producing an "information overload" that has added to the problems of his staff. There have been no signs that VDTs will change the content or subject matter of most stories. Over time the conversion to VDTs will be a complete success. Given reporters' normal resistance to change, this will not happen because of a desire or even a perceived need on their part. New technology will come into use because it has been mandated by management, though the news-industry has rarely made such demands.

Technology and Research

As research tools, rather than as aids in recording or transmitting, various Adtech systems are available to journalists. For instance, Information Bank, a subsidiary of the New York Times Company, in 1977 had a data base consisting of abstracts of articles from the *New York Times* and sixty other publications ranging from *American Banker* to *American Scholar.* Larry Kahaner has noted: "Reporters no longer have to drop their work and rush to the clip library to flesh out a story — they punch up the information on their terminal."[3]

If a general-assignments reporter in 1977 had to do an article on President Carter's strip-mining policy, he might have started by looking over an assortment of clippings that had accumulated in his top drawer and then called the Interior Department and the appropriate congressional committees. If strip mining was not his regular beat, he would have had to search widely to find the right sources and some of the people he needed to speak to would have been in meetings or otherwise engaged. It is realistic to believe that this start-up process would have taken an entire morning. However, a computer search at Information Bank would have taken less than twelve minutes. The cost would have been $12, and the exercise would have produced forty-seven inches of printout.

Yet the Information Bank manager said that while the system was widely used in government agencies and in industry, it had not caught on with reporters. No more than five or six Washington news bureaus were subscribers, and even they did not use it often. The company had put a machine in the National Press Building, where many bureaus are housed, but had to remove it after six months because of low usage. The manager concluded that reporters would not take a few hours to learn to use the system properly. When a reporter typed in "Jimmy Carter" instead of "Carter, Jimmy," the computer did not respond, and the reporter was frustrated.

Journalists who do make imaginative use of data banks usually do so for one of two reasons. In large bureaus, there are trained, full-time employees operating the equipment for the reporters. Few organizations, however, are willing to make this investment. In small bureaus, a reporter trained himself in computer use and then convinced his employer to install a system.

Not all news gatherers in the Washington press corps are resistant to Adtech. A few are exhilarated by its potential. One reporter, for example, runs his copy through a computerized spelling dictionary. "It cleans things up in a hurry," he says. (This reporter's hobby is building hifi sets.) The most sophisticated exercise in investigative journalism by a Washington bureau in 1981 used computer printouts to trace 14,268 guns seized by law-enforcement officers in street

[3] Kahaner, p. 16.

crimes. The series, "The Snub-Nosed Killer: Handguns in America," by Joseph Albright and his colleagues of the Cox Newspapers, proved that the most common characteristic of crime weapons was the short length of the barrel, thus opening an entirely new approach to how to write a law to control handguns. In another example, the Washington office of the *Chicago Sun-Times,* starting with a simple Apple II Plus and then upgrading it to more elaborate hardware, is now able to produce such data as the absentee records of members of Congress, party loyalty percentages, and congressional support for defense appropriations. One of the bureau's early findings was that a Chicago congressman had missed half of the House votes in 1980. Now, according to Patrick Oster, the bureau chief, "he's in trouble."

In Washington and elsewhere, the media have been fascinated by public opinion surveys for at least a decade. Computers, by speeding up the process, have made polls even more attractive to news organizations. This probably accounts for the proliferation of press-sponsored polls at both state and national levels. Burns W. Roper has argued that the media polls, with their "unwarranted premium on speed," turn complex issues into "oversimplified questions."[4] More polling more promptly reported could have a major impact on the political process.

Changes in Foreign Reporting

In one area of Washington journalism the advent of Adtech is producing a discernible change in the nature of reportage. The way many foreign correspondents are sending their copy back to their home offices affects the nature of the copy. In 1955 a majority of foreign correspondents in the United States filed their stories by mail. Unable to compete with the American wire services on fast-breaking events, they tended to write long analytical pieces that could survive a week in transit, thereby making a virtue out of necessity.

Now most foreign bureaus have converted to forms of almost instant communication. *Japan Economic Journal,* for instance, uses Rapicom, through which whole pages and even pictures go into a machine in Washington and come out in Tokyo as the equivalent of a xeroxed copy. Until recently the Washington bureau of Canadian Press reported through one direct telex to Toronto. Now its VDTs connect with Ottawa, Montreal, Toronto, and Vancouver. When a Canadian Press reporter was asked whether they no longer leave as many stories to the American wire services, he replied excitedly: "That's just it! We've been sharing the same building with AP for a long time. But before we never even thought of trying to compete—go head to head—with AP. Now we can actually do it on select stories." Although that is not happening on a majority of the stories produced by foreign correspondents, it is the trend.

A movement away from in-depth coverage corresponds with a tally of more

[4] Burns W. Roper, "The Press and the Polls," *Topic,* March 1982, p. 4.

stories per foreign correspondent. A survey in progress of 27 percent of the foreign press corps in Washington indicates that these reporters average nearly eight stories a week and that nearly a quarter of them write ten or more stories each week. It is likely that these prolific reporters are not doing the sort of major interpretations that were once the hallmark of foreign reporting. Rather, transmission technology puts home-office pressure on the reporters to write more. If a news organization is spending a great deal of money to maintain reporters abroad, it wants a good return on its investment, which is most easily measured in column inches. News organizations that emphasize quantity rather than quality are making a mistake. Foreign audiences are better served when experienced overseas reporters try to explain the complicated, rather than to report the obvious.

Television Reporting

Without doubt, a transmission revolution is under way. Messages arrive faster than before. Newspapers are more up-to-the-minute and television more up-to-the-second. But does that make a communications revolution? Does a transmission system that is faster and more far-flung and even cheaper make any difference in what is going to be communicated?

It might be assumed that the greatest impact of Adtech would be felt by broadcast journalists. After all, radio and television are relatively new technologies. Most network reporters today have lived through the replacement of film with tape, the introduction of minicams, advances in the use of graphics, and the arrival of satellite transmission. However, television and radio correspondents tend to take their cues as to what is news from their print counterparts, particularly from those who report for prestigious newspapers. Rather than expressing enthusiasm for the way improvements in technology have expanded story opportunities, they complain about the relative advantages of print journalists: "They can ask 15 questions before we set up the lights," or "We have an earlier break-off point than print because we need more time to produce a story for broadcast." Having to rely on machinery is worrisome: "I'm constantly concerned that the recorder will jam or that I'll run out of tape."

Yet again the age factor should be stressed. Despite television's "pretty face syndrome," which carries the expectation that most network reporters will be youthful, more network television reporters in Washington are over fifty years old than are newspaper reporters. Because of the newness of television, most of the older generation of television correspondents learned their craft at newspapers or wire services. In addition, while most reporters make job changes within the same news sector, moving from newspaper to newspaper or from television network to television network, celebrated reporters from newspapers and magazines at the Washington level are often lured to higher paying television jobs. Carl Bernstein, for example, went from the *Washington Post* to the American Broadcasting Company. Future Washington television reporters, however, are young persons now working at local stations who are unlikely to have had a great deal of newspaper training and thus might be more oriented to the possibilities of technological innovation than were their predecessors.

Clearly, cable television — where the operative phrases are "selective programming," "specialized products," and "market segmentation" — will use its advantage to produce types of news that are not otherwise available. The Cable Satellite Public Affairs Network (C-SPAN) has been offering gavel-to-gavel coverage of the House of Representatives since March 1979, and more recently has added important congressional hearings. Seeing an uncut version of the activities on Capitol Hill could have consequences, both for the legislative process and the future of certain legislators. Those who have followed the televising of the Canadian House of Commons, which began in 1977, contend that the presence of the cameras has improved parliamentary decorum and the quality of debate. In another example, a by-product of satellite technology rather than market segmentation, the Cable News Network (CNN) conducts a monthly one-hour discussion between a Soviet official or expert in Moscow and his American counterpart in Washington. The possibilities for international cross-fertilization are limited only by economics and diplomacy.

Eventually, any society — even the society of journalists — accepts the level of its technology. To dispute how drastically Adtech is changing the way reporters do their jobs may be merely a quibble over the definition of change. But there has not yet been a marked change in what is news, the substance of the end-product, which is how the media should be measured. Perhaps this time perspective is too short. As Richard L. Rubin has shown, the content of American newspapers changed at the beginning of the nineteenth century from a primary emphasis on commerce to political argumentation and again late in the century from partisanship to more "objective" journalism.[5] The introduction of new technology is one of the ingredients that forces change, while deeply ingrained press traditions act as a brake. To say that the rate of recent change has been much slower than is commonly claimed may be a modest conclusion, but it is also a necessary correction when trying to assess the continuing evolutionary role of the press as a public-policy institution.

[5] Richard L. Rubin, *Press, Party, and Presidency* (New York: W.W. Norton & Co., Inc., 1981).

Technology and the Federal System

WILLIAM H. DUTTON

Two centuries ago, the Founding Fathers debated whether a republic could effectively function in a territory as large as that of the United States. Since then, modern communication and transportation systems have relegated this early concern to a historical curiosity and have generated new issues of governance. Since World War II, radio, television, and film have been viewed as revolutionary new means for national integration, but they have also been feared as powerful instruments of government control. More recently, the rapid advance and convergence of computers and telecommunication technologies have altered the information and communication systems of national, state, and local governments.

Communications technologies are politically malleable resources. The same technologies might be used to inform or enslave a population, to create an open or a secret society, and to centralize or decentralize political control. In order to discern the role of the new technology in the federal system, it is necessary to discover who controls it and who is served by the manner in which it has been used.

This essay provides an overview of how a wide array of computer and telecommunication systems has been utilized by American governments. The basic theme that emerges is that while the impacts of the new technologies are incremental and often contradictory, their role has been importantly shaped by the officials of state and local governments in ways that have supported the vitality of the American federal system.

American federalism has evolved into a dramatically different pattern from that envisioned by the framers of the Constitution. The scope and power of the national government have been expanded over time through numerous Supreme Court decisions, the expansion and modernization of national defense, and the development of national economic, transportation, and communication systems. In this process, the functions of the national government have been increasingly blended and overlapped with those of state and local governments, thus leading scholars of American government to speak of "cooperative federalism." This pattern is illustrated by drawing an analogy to a "marble cake" or, more recently, to a "picket fence." The picket fence represents the fragmentation of government services across agencies that depend on cooperation and coordination among federal, state, and local levels. This pattern is a marked contrast to the conventional images of a neat, unitary hierarchy, suggested by an analogy to a "layered cake," which might have characterized intergovernmental relations in the nineteenth century.

Despite these expansions of the scope and significance of the federal government, state and local jurisdictions have also maintained and enhanced their role in governing the United States. In the 1980s, state and local governments have continued to increase their revenues and expenditures, despite diminishing local autonomy, an escalating dependence on federal revenues for state and local government operations, and an era of increased fiscal restraint and citizen-supported tax limitations. The continued vitality of state and local governments has been accounted for by such factors as the decentralized character of the American party system, the professionalization of state and local adminstrations, the critical role of state and local governments in the implementation of federal programs, and the attitudes of citizens and elected officials wedded to the abstract values of local variety and decentralized control. The continuing vitality of state and local governments has been underscored by the New Federalism of the Reagan administration that suggests a continued devolution of even greater responsibility to them.

Communications and Federalism

Generally, new communications technology has been viewed as a nationalizing or centralizing force. Geosynchronous communication satellites linked with expanding network and cable television and with home video recording equipment (and, in the future, with low-power television and direct-broadcast satellite facilities) are thought to have brought national leaders into the living rooms and minds of Americans as never before. Likewise, increasingly sophisticated audio, video, document, and computer telecommunications can provide access to nationwide information systems. Thus, interpreters of the communications revolution believe that the closer connection of nationwide communication networks will facilitate the substitution of more centralized, national political networks for established local communication and political ones.

Similarly, the utilization of immense computer resources by the federal government might eventually dwarf and antiquate the administrative mechanisms of state and local governments by providing information services directly to citizens. Already, the capability of the Social Security Administration to process nearly 35 million checks every month and the capability of the Internal Revenue Service to process millions of complex tax returns are astounding.

However, like the early federalists, the new electronic federalists are likely to be a mixed group. Computer and telecommunication systems might centralize influence at a national level, but they might have decentralizing impacts as well.

The growth of interactive technologies—like the telephone, audio and video conferencing, interactive cable, opinion polls, viewdata, and microcomputer systems—is expected by some radically to decentralize power to the citizens of American cities. More generally, communication scholars have often noted the dual or contradictory impacts of new inventions, like the telephone, that might contribute simultaneously both to decentralization (e.g., "urban sprawl") and to centralization (e.g., skyscrapers).

Dramatic visions of the political impacts of computers and telecommunications make useful rhetorical devices. However, the effects of technological change remain constrained by the social, political, economic, and historical contexts of American governance. If viewed as one aspect of a larger and more complex social setting, the impacts of changing technology on the federal system should be seen as marginal, subtle, often countervailing, and unlike the sweeping visions that blame national centralization or decentralization on the development of an electronic communications network. Moreover, the most critical political impacts of changing technologies might entail power shifts within as well as across governments, horizontally as well as vertically.

Intragovernmental Power Shifts

Information and communication technologies are sometimes portrayed as apolitical, in that they provide new information resources without appreciably altering the distribution of power, influence, or authority in organizations and society. However, computer and telecommunication technologies are likely to redistribute power by redistributing information and the capacity to obtain other resources. First, these technologies are likely to alter the content and flow of information. Such changes—by affecting not only who knows what but also who says what through which channels, to whom, and with what results—might affect broad perceptions as well as bureaucratic politics. Computers and telecommunications are likely to enhance the decisional effectiveness of those who control the use of information technologies. Second, information and communication technologies are resources in their own right, just as budgets, equipment, and staff are the substantive resources of political organizations. (In other words, it is an advantage to have priority access to such resources as computing staff, video conferencing facilities, and telephone services.) Third, the effective use of information and communication technologies can build a capacity to acquire other resources (such as votes, prestige, legitimacy, services, and money) that can thereby enhance the decisional effectiveness of users.

The impacts of changing communication technology might reinforce the ascendance of what some have called the new "bureaucratic machines," governments that are effectively managed but are increasingly autonomous, accountable to neither elected officials nor the general public. Research on computer technology in local government has found that the use of computer-based information systems has tended to enhance the decisional effectiveness of managers and experts trained in the use of computing. Judgmental ratings of power shifts based on intensive research in forty United States cities indicated that the overall use of computing in these cities tended marginally to increase or decrease the influence of some city officials. Generally, those "who tend most often to gain influence are the planners (the information elite), followed by the top managers and departmental heads (the bureaucrats), and the mayor and council (the politicians)."[1]

Top managers have used computing to strengthen and extend management control over government operations. Management-oriented applications—such as budgeting, accounting, personnel, and operational data systems—were among the first and most extensively automated by state and local governments. Top managers use such systems to formulate and support decisions presented to elected and appointed officials, personnel, and the public. For example, one city manager used a simple listing of city employees ranked by salary (which placed several police officers at the top level) to make and defend salary adjustments.

Some state and local governments are being increasingly populated by more professionally trained and technologically sophisticated politicians. For example, Mayor Pete Wilson of San Diego brought experts in fiscal analysis, budgeting, and management-information systems onto his management team soon after his election. According to some associates, he discovered the value of these information elites while in the state assembly.

However, some managers are neither skilled nor oriented toward the use of computer-based information systems. Old-style political appointees tend to fall within this group. For example, the on-line budget monitoring system installed in Cleveland, Ohio, in response to fiscal warning signs during the early 1970s was of little value to the appointed director of budget and management. The reason was simple—he never learned how to use the unplugged computer terminal conspicuously displayed behind his desk. In many large cities, politicians are still oriented toward moderately updated versions of "smoke-filled rooms" of political and public-relations advisers, while critical roles in the government are assumed by top managers and technical experts.

In local governments, these technical experts are the planners, analysts, builders, and custodians of urban data banks, models, and various management- and decision-support systems. By utilizing information systems to develop policy recommendations, legitimize and document the existence of problems, and identify problems that had not been generally recognized, they are the major beneficiaries of power shifts tied to computing. An unusually vivid case concerns the liberal Democratic planners of one large northern city who fed computer-based analyses to the media—analyses that supported liberal urban-developmental policies and undermined the Republican mayor's conservative positions. More

[1] James N. Danziger et al., *Computers and Politics* (New York: Columbia University Press, 1982), p. 181.

common are the planners and analysts who provide and occasionally massage models and analyses to support the position of powerful elites (as occurred with David Stockman's reputed manipulation of computer-based forecasts of the Office of Management and Budget to gain support for Reagan's proposed tax cuts and defense-spending increases).

Yet new information technology has not single-handedly bestowed power on the new managers and analysts of the information age. Rather, computers have sometimes been selectively adopted and effectively utilized by those who control organizations to reinforce their influence. Accordingly, in a few local governments that had strong elected leaders, computing has been used more to reinforce the power of those leaders than to enhance the power of top managers or analysts. In this manner, information technology has not brought about major managerial and technocratic power shifts but has only tended to reinforce the general trend of increasing influence of these roles in the public sector. The change must be accounted for by a wider array of factors than new technology. For example, when Little Rock adopted the city-manager form of government, the new manager hired a skilled data-processing manager and a professionally trained financial analyst-administrator to implement an integrated financial-management information system. This computer-based system was used to reinforce the position of the manager in controlling city departments accustomed to greater autonomy under the old mayor-council system. In such ways, the rise of a new class of professional managers and analysts who use and understand new information technologies seems to be reinforced and enhanced by changing technology.

Citizen-oriented Technology

In contrast to the government's use of computers, the diffusion of new video technologies is expected to expand public involvement in government affairs, thereby countering trends toward bureaucratic centralization. Presumably, a more attentive, informed, and active public will lead to more citizen involvement. A few demonstration projects have shown a potential for local governments and citizen groups to use cable television and to become active participants in developing and programming public access channels. Cablecasts oriented toward senior citizens in Reading, Pennsylvania, are a frequently cited example. However, state and local governments have generally not utilized cable or other video technologies. Moreover, when new video technologies have been utilized, the results have often been disappointing.

One example of such disappointing results is the cablecasting of public meetings. In the 1970s, Irvine, California, was one of the first cities to cablecast its council meetings. A telephone survey of residents conducted during a council cablecast revealed that only two out of nearly 100 respondents were watching the proceedings. (One of these viewers was to appear that night and was completing her ironing while watching in order that she would know when to leave for her scheduled agenda item!) Although few actually watched the meeting, many participants "performed" as if they were being watched; during meetings that were cablecast, disagreement was lower than during meetings that were not cablecast; also, spokespersons for various citizen and community groups tended to appear on the evenings that were cablecast. Thus, video changed the tenor of council meetings but did little to enhance citizen participation, at least in these early stages.

Of course, the dramatic images of the "push-button government" are tied to interactive technologies, especially polling systems, though anecdotal evidence does not support a significant role for such innovations. So far, interactive polling systems like QUBE of Columbus, Ohio, are primarily marketing devices of cable firms that provide entertainment rather than influence to the viewers. The only widely marketed public services on interactive cable are burglar alarms that most often send police scurrying around cities responding to false alarms set off by pets or children.

The possible effects of an interactive system became clear during one of the first one-way cablecasts of an Irvine council meeting. A staff member whispered to a councillor that a constituent had telephoned to say that if the councillor did not support the measure before the council, she would never vote for him again. The councillor voted "yea," but no more telephone calls were accepted during council meetings.

Even though public uses of video technologies do not seem to have provided closer links between the public and their state and local governments, television news and public affairs coverage might do so. Here again, however, it has not been well established that television news has increased citizens' involvement in state and local government. The number of citizens voting, especially at the state and local levels, has declined with the expansion of telecommunications, but such effects are combined with a multitude of alternative explanations for lower voter turnouts.

Research on state and local governments suggests a greater concentration of authority in professional managers and their analysts and a decline in the role of elected officials and the general public. New computer-based information systems seem to reinforce this trend, and new video and home information services are unlikely to counter and might support this general trend by legitimizing the myth of electronic democracy.

Intergovernmental Power Shifts

Intergovernmental power shifts could be of three broad types, according to the implosion, explosion, and incremental adjustment models developed by Deil Wright.[2] The new technologies could be used vertically to centralize and horizontally to consolidate agencies involved in the delivery of services that re-

[2] Deil S. Wright, *Understanding Intergovernmental Relations* (North Scituate, Massachusetts: Duxbury Press, 1978), p. 320.

quire coordination and joint action. This use would tend to move the United States toward a system in which state and local governments diminish in their power and autonomy. Alternatively, communication technology might be used vertically to decentralize and horizontally to fragment jurisdictions to an even greater degree, devolving more power and autonomy to the local jurisdictions. Finally, the new technology might have no consistent use, resulting in marginal and offsetting power shifts that would leave the same basic model of "cooperative federalism" in which there is a blending and sharing of functions and which describes intergovernmental relations in the United States today.

Logically, the impacts of new technology might depend on the degree to which the public sector utilizes vertical in contrast to horizontal communication technologies. Broadcast technologies—such as television, cable, and opinion polling—facilitate vertical communication networks. Point-to-point, interactive technologies—such as telephone, audio, video and computer conferencing, and the mail—facilitate links between individuals and groups, and can therefore support horizontal communication networks within and across organizations. The utilization of vertical technologies might support centralization, and the utilization of horizontal technologies might support decentralization. Some scholars have argued that horizontal technologies are supportive of intragroup communication and are thereby supportive of pluralistic political communications. (Of course, the telephone and other horizontal technologies can be used for vertical, superior-subordinate communications, and vice versa.)

Behaviorally, it seems that neither vertical nor horizontal technologies have a particularly successful track record in the intergovernmental sector unless they support the continued vitality of state and local units. This phenomenon can be illustrated in the case of public video conferencing. The Bell and Howell Satellite Network is an interesting attempt to develop a vertical, video communications network for a federal system. The National Telecommunications and Information Administration created a grant program to support full-motion video conferencing services to link federal agencies in Washington, D.C., to their regional agencies, as well as to state and local governments in eleven additional sites to be located around the country. The first facility was installed at L'Enfant Plaza in Washington, D.C. As of the spring of 1981, no other video conferencing facility had been built in the network, despite the willingness of Bell and Howell to provide some financial support. Currently, the system is used mainly for "asymmetrical conferences" (one-way video and two-way audio), though its level of utilization has been disappointingly low. One plausible explanation for the marginal success of this venture to date is the lack of a strong pattern of vertical communications from the federal level to various local, state, and regional agencies, though other factors, such as the cost of conferencing, offer additional explanations.

Even if this system were fully implemented and utilized, it is difficult to imagine how the federal government could effectively communicate with 78,000 jurisdictions through twelve conference rooms. But video teleconferencing services are likely to be more substantial with the introduction of video conferencing facilities, called Picturephone Meeting Service, in most major cities by American Telephone & Telegraph Co. (AT&T) over the next decade (reaching forty-three sites by 1985, according to some estimates). During AT&T's market trial of video conferencing, public agencies utilized the systems nearly as often as the private sector and mainly for interorganizational and horizontal communications. If these early patterns are indicative of later use, public video teleconferencing is likely to be substantial and is likely to have incremental effects, primarily in improving horizontal communications among state and local government agencies. This use would be consistent with historical patterns of intergovernmental communications in the United States. For example, communication among local units appears more critical to the diffusion of innovations than vertical communication from the federal level.

Vertical communications might be facilitated by state-level teleconferencing systems. Alaska seems to have successfully implemented several applications of audio and video teleconferencing through the first of NASA's series of Applied Technology Satellites, ATS-1. Its success seems to be linked not only to the lack of alternative communication channels for such remote sites but also to the system's intragovernmental character. It is primarily a state system that supports the vitality of the state government. It contrasts sharply with the centralizing model that views a national communications infrastructure to support power shifts to the national level. In other words, Alaska has used a satellite-based system with a near national potential to support a state communication system. Interestingly, officials of other states, such as California, have occasionally considered state satellite systems.

These cases may be compared with the corporate sector, in which the use of video for vertical communications via closed-circuit television, video tape cassettes, satellite conferences via the Holiday Inn and Hyatt Regency networks, and training films has already become a major activity. Geographically dispersed organizations with more unitary and hierarchical structures might be more congenial to the use of vertical broadcast communication networks.

One area in which a national communications network does seem to have a nationalizing influence is the organization of interest groups and lobbies. Computer-based mailing lists, direct-mail advertising, and telephone systems have supported the organizational efforts of a number of interest groups, including state- and local-government groups and lobbies. The 1970s seem to have been a critical stage in the growth of the seven major public interest groups, including the National League of Cities, the United States Conference of Mayors, and the International City Management Association. Various professional groups have also organized on a national scale, aided by a national communications infrastructure, including such groups as the National Association of Educational Administrators, the Urban and Regional Information Systems Associations, and the American Society for Public Administration. In such ways, national communication systems have been utilized to reinforce the positions of state and local government jurisdictions, professions, and interests.

Intergovernmental Computer Systems

State and local governments have thousands of automated applications. One study identified 264 kinds of computer applications in local governments alone. The vast majority of these applications were intradepartmental and intragovernmental systems. Generally, the fragmentation of computing systems in American governments mirrors the fragmentation of their organizational structures. Moreover, the introduction of more mini- and microcomputer applications in public organizations is likely to accentuate the fragmentation of governmental information systems. Still, a significant number of intergovernmental systems have been developed to meet reporting needs and to share files on individuals and property. Generally, intergovernmental networks must support the participating local jurisdictions if they are to attract state and local participation and attention.

Some successful computer networks look like vertical, centralizing systems but in design and practice are supportive of state and local agencies. The best example is wants and warrants and criminal-history files provided through the National Crime Information Center (NCIC) of the Federal Bureau of Investigation (FBI). The NCIC centralizes the storage of information about persons wanted for serious offenses. Many years ago, the FBI perceived an advantage in gaining centralized control over information collected by state and local law-enforcement agencies on the criminal histories and statuses of known offenders and wanted persons. But FBI goals were compromised by state and local officials who refused to relinquish control over their own criminal-information systems. The NCIC therefore evolved into a complex communications network linking intelligence files in a national center and comparable centers in many state and local police agencies. By means of these automated intelligence files, local police agencies have access to regional, state, and national files through a single inquiry. The chief users are patrol officers and detectives. The system thus supports a structurally decentralized and fragmented array of agencies. This system is relatively successful in terms of its utilization, its perceived utility, and its impacts on the performance of law-enforcement agencies.

In contrast, Uniform Crime Reports (UCR) are an effort by the same agency to collect statistical data from the same jurisdictions by type of crime. Primarily serving federal reporting needs rather than local police activities, the UCR system lacks the care, attention, and support given to police intelligence files.

State and local governments use intergovernmental information systems because these systems tend to maintain and support their own organizations. Consolidated tax billing is an area in which economies of scale save money without any perceived loss in local discretion or autonomy. Other examples of centralized systems supportive of decentralized structure are areawide police and fire dispatching and various intergovernmental intelligence systems. Once localities are committed to these information and communications technologies to achieve economies, however, the distribution of governmental power may well be affected.

Even within a single metropolitan area, interagency systems that do not serve the maintenance and enhancement needs of the participating users and agencies are problematic. A good example is provided by Rob Kling's case study of a standardized, technically sophisticated, computerized client tracking system that attempted to link over forty separate welfare and social service agencies within a single metropolitan area.[3] The system generally failed to support the activities of caseworkers, received uneven support and participation from the target agencies, and seemed to contribute to few administrative gains in efficiency. Here, and in numerous other cases, information and communication systems could not consolidate or centralize agencies that were politically and organizationally fragmented.

Ultimately, the most far-reaching impact of computers and telecommunications on the viability of state and local governments may well be the creation of an infrastructure that permits these governments to avoid staff increases and to generate revenue. In an era of tax limitations and fiscal restraint, state and local government officials seem to have turned technology to the task of saving and making money. Nearly all state and local governments of a substantial size have automated their budgeting and accounting functions, and some have instituted performance reporting systems. These systems in combination with routine record storage, search, and calculating or printing applications compose the majority of state and local information systems. These basic applications are being turned to the task of revenue generation. For example, the automation of parking and traffic tickets, overdue library books, tax assessments, billing for ambulance services, and the like is a significant generator of increased revenues that requires no public referendum.

The revenue potential of computerized government was neglected in an earlier era, when property-tax rates were adjusted to match expenditures. The efficiency of the new measures can be chilling, since small revenue increments mount quickly. A medium-sized California library recently automated circulation records and overdue book notices so that users could not check out new books without paying past fines. According to their consultant, overdue book revenues increased some $200,000 in a single year.

Computers have been turned to the task of generating revenue at the policy and management levels, as well as at the operational level. At the policy level, local governments have adopted a new generation of computer models called Fiscal Impact Budgeting Systems (FIBS), which permit officials to project the relative fiscal impacts of alternative urban-development policies. Anaheim, California, utilized such a model to negotiate several new land developments with developers. In one case, the model was useful in adding a shopping center to a development in order to generate additional public revenues.

One southern California data-processing organization has launched a system-

[3] Rob Kling, "Automated Welfare Client-Tracking and Service Integration," *Communications of the ACM* 21, no. 6 (1978): 484–93.

atic program of "enterprise accounting." In this system, revenue generated by each department and agency is monitored to create incentives for every service to "pay its own way." If revenue from a program goes down, then its budget allotment for the next year is decreased. This logic, which could lead to an incredible scenario in which citizens would be paying for public goods like police services, prompted the city's data-processing manager to quip: "Why not!"

Yet this revenue-generation role of computers must be balanced by the general finding that the impacts of computing have been far less dramatic and far more costly than anticipated. An evaluation of computing in United States cities found that although the impacts are generally positive and in line with the intentions of developers, these impacts are often marginal, mixed, and varied among local governments. Clearly, many government agencies have failed efficiently and effectively to manage computing and have therefore failed to benefit from the use of the technology. This failure is reflected at the state and federal levels by recurring issues concerning the organizational location, procurement, oversight, and management of computing and telecommunications. Concern for a more effective use of computing and telecommunications is reflected in recent state and federal efforts to "manage information."

Conclusion

This essay has marshaled evidence from several social analyses of computers and telecommunications to address the impacts of changing technology on the federal system. Considering power shifts within governmental jurisdictions and agencies largely as changes in decisional effectiveness, it seems that the new technologies have reinforced the ascendance of professional managers and information elites. This ascendance is most clearly the case with computing, which has tended to enhance the decisional effectiveness of top managers, department heads, and planning and management analysts rather than that of elected officials and the public. The use of cable and other citizen-oriented technologies has not countered the rise of the new bureaucratic machines and might have even furthered this development by the symbolic role that such innovations could play in legitimizing public institutions and processes.

Likewise, with respect to power shifts across governmental jurisdictions and agencies, changing technologies have seemed to reinforce prevailing patterns of cooperative federalism rather than to promote vertical centralization or horizontal consolidation. The use of teleconferencing systems in the public sector is limited but generally supportive of horizontal rather than vertical communication networks. The use of such systems might expand the reach of government communication networks beyond a metropolitan and regional area without lessening—and possibly enhancing—the power and autonomy of individual units. A national communications infrastructure has supported state and local interests by facilitating national organizations and lobbies that represent these governments, officials, and professions at the national level. Most government information systems are fragmented along departmental and agency lines, but the successful intergovernmental systems, such as NCIC, tend to support the needs of state and local agencies.

Finally, the effectiveness of state and local agencies has been supported by the use of computing and professional-management techniques to avoid staff and cost increases and to generate revenues. Computers and telecommunications, when well managed, seem to have made administration at all levels of the federal system somewhat more efficient and effective. Changing technology is therefore associated with some centralization and professionalism within governmental jurisdictions that have helped maintain greater autonomy and effectiveness in relationships between governmental jurisdictions.

Two centuries ago, Alexander Hamilton pointed out several important constraints on the national government within the American federal system: "It is a known fact in human nature that its affections are commonly weak in proportion to the distance or diffuseness of the object. Upon the same principle that man is more attached to his family than to his neighborhood, to his neighborhood than to the community at large, the people of each State would be apt to feel a stronger bias towards their local governments than towards the government of the Union; unless the force of that principle should be destroyed by a much better administration of the latter."[4] These constraints seem relevant today, despite the communications revolution. It is hard to imagine how the evening news and national election coverage could overcome the proximity and visibility of the routine operations of local, state, and federal agencies at the community level. Moreover, the use of computer and telecommunication technologies has tended to strengthen the administrations of state and local government agencies, even when such systems are linked with the federal level.

[4] *The Federalist*, No. 17.

The author wishes to thank Janet Fulk for her comments on an early draft of this essay.

Government Regulation in the Communications System

ITHIEL DE SOLA POOL

In 1982, the communications industry engaged in two esoteric debates in Washington that foreshadowed what may become a major public issue in the last decade of this century. One debate concerned the cable industry and the other the telephone industry. Both of them dealt with common carriage and its relation to the free market.

The issue concerning cable was referred to as "leased access." On one side, CATV lobbyists sought to slip a bill through Congress to prohibit the Federal Communications Commission (FCC) or states or local governments from requiring cable franchise holders to lease channels against their will. On the other side, Henry Geller filed a petition with the FCC for a rulemaking to require large cable systems to hold a certain percentage of their channels open to lease on a first-come, first-served basis. The industry was bitterly opposed.

The 1982 American Telephone and Telegraph (AT&T) consent decree, which ended an eight-year antitrust suit, sought to restructure the telephone industry in such a way as to make maximum use of the market and to concentrate the remaining regulated monopoly activities in the divested operating companies. These companies were to engage in no other business than local telecommunications. Underlying the decree is an assumption that will hold true only transitorily—that local switching and distribution remains a monopoly. Conversely, the decree assumed that long-distance service, customers' terminals, and enhanced communications services are now all competitive. Other assumptions of the decree are that only monopoly services should be subject to regulation, that common-carrier status implies being regulated, and that competitive activities should be governed by the market.

In fact, the consent decree does not release AT&T's long lines from common-carrier regulation, because the Department of Justice did not have the power to do so. The Communications Act of 1934 requires the FCC to regulate all electrical communications carriers in the "public interest, convenience and necessity." Since the present FCC favors deregulation, it decided in its Computer Inquiry II to carry out its obligation to regulate by forebearing from regulation of entry and rate-of-return of all carriers in the "basic" transmission business that were not dominant therein; those it would regulate by allowing the market to exercise control.[1] The FCC concluded that of all the carriers in that market only AT&T was dominant.

So AT&T alone is to remain subject to traditional regulation. The future AT&T, split by the consent decree from its local operating companies, may be able to persuade the FCC that it is no longer dominant in its long-distance business and that it should also be deregulated. Others will argue that since AT&T now controls 80 percent of the long-distance telephone traffic, as opposed to 3 percent by competitors (the other 17 percent belongs to independent telephone companies), AT&T remains dominant. Whatever the FCC concludes, the logic of the consent decree certainly implies that that will not long be the case. In any event, the issue of AT&T dominance will be debated, as will the parallel issue of the local operating companies, which will begin to face growing competition from data and even voice-carrying cable systems, cellular radio, and local microwave systems.

Common Carriage

The role of common carriage is not just a technical issue. In fact, it lies at the heart of the future of the First Amendment. The establishment of a communications system operating under the privilege that the government "shall make no law . . . abridging" its freedom was predicated on the assumption that the resources that people needed in order to exercise that right were reasonably available. One can print only if paper and presses are available; that was and is the situation. On the other hand, where essential resources for communicating are monopolized, a difficult public-policy dilemma arises—laissez-faire is not enough.

Historically, the American way of handling strategic monopolies in communications resources is the system of common carriage. The first communications common carrier was the postal system, followed by the telegraph system and the telephone system.

A common carrier is required to make its facilities available to all comers on a nondiscriminatory basis. That is the essence of the matter; there are other typical but not universal regulations. Common carriers are often required to offer service, even if they are losing money. Railroads, for example, must have permission from the Interstate Commerce Commission to drop an unprofitable line, since there is a public interest in maintaining railroad service. Also, many common carriers have their rates regulated, usually on a rate-of-return basis.

[1] Docket 20828. Rules adopted April 4, 1980.

Ever since *Munn* v. *Illinois* in 1877[2] it has been accepted that businesses affecting the public interest (usually because they are monopolies) may have their rates regulated, and most common carriers do. However, it is important to keep in mind that not all common carriers are monopolies (for example, taxis), and not all are denied the right of exit or have tariffs set under rate-of-return regulation. The only essential feature is nondiscriminatory access; many alternative common-carrier arrangements are possible.

An important requirement imposed on common carriers in communications is a corollary of the rule against discrimination—carriers may not control the content of what is sent over their facilities. Any message may be put in an envelope or sent by telegram or telephone. The carrier may not regulate that, nor, unlike a publisher, is he liable for what is said. A further usual rule is that carriers may not eavesdrop on what they carry; the seal on the envelope is inviolable, and the telephone company may not tap telephones.

A current issue concerning telephonic common carriers is their right to produce electronic yellow pages. The newspaper publishers are alarmed at the prospective loss of the 31 percent of their advertising revenue that comes from classified advertisements.[3] They have persuaded the drafters of the Communications Act rewrite bill in both the House and the Senate to include a provision barring AT&T from itself going into publishing over its common carrier network. Very likely, such a provision would be ruled unconstitutional if challenged in court. How, under the First Amendment, could Congress prohibit anyone from publishing? Such a prohibition would seem to be as flagrant a violation of the amendment as could be imagined.

If under the First Amendment, AT&T, like any other organization, may publish, there is indeed a dilemma, one that has always been inherent in the common-carrier system. The carrier has to make its facilities available on a nondiscriminatory basis to all comers, including those who compete with it or who oppose it. The U.S. Postal Service has to carry literature attacking the incumbent administration or the post office and even revolutionary literature advocating the overthrow of the very government that distributes those publications. Telegraph companies were obliged to interconnect with their competitors. As figure 1 shows, Company A could not refuse telegrams at Midville sent at Westville to Eastville via Company B even though they would prefer to have all such messages sent on their own direct line.

So, a telephone common carrier that exercised its constitutional right to publish electronic yellow pages would nonetheless be obliged to provide service and circuits for any competing publisher, and indeed to provide a quality of service no less than it gives itself. Cynics wonder whether such a law can be enforced. That it would be neither easy nor totally impossible to enforce is attested to by

[2] 94 US 113.

[3] Benjamin M. Compaine, *The Newspaper Industry in the 1980's* (White Plains, New York: Knowledge Publications, 1978), p. 74.

the fact that triple damage suits have been won by parties injured by discriminating carriers.[4] Since, in the case of publishing, a separations policy that excludes anyone from the business is probably unconstitutional, there is no alternative but strictly to enforce nondiscriminatory access in such cases.

Similar points are at issue in the cable television controversy. Cablecasters like to see themselves as broadcasters, who are not common carriers. Broadcasting law, a strange aberration, is beyond the scope of this essay, but it must be mentioned briefly. When Congress organized the broadcasting system in 1927, it believed that radio was inherently monopolistic because of the scarcity of radio spectrum. But Congress did not wish to set up broadcasting as a total monopoly common carrier. It set up a system in which a few privileged licensees in each city would own competing stations and would operate them as publishers. But in the view of the fact that no one else could broadcast, these licensees were obliged to conform to some FCC concepts of what would serve the public interest and also to give fair treatment to both sides of public issues. This regulated publishing scheme, obviously at odds with the philosophy of the First Amendment, was justified by the courts on the grounds of supposedly inherent problems of spectrum limitations.[5]

Cable systems, unlike broadcast stations, suffer no such inherent resource scarcity. The cable franchise owner does not have only one channel of his own to program (like a television licensee) but rather a monopoly over fifty or possibly one hundred channels. There are many would-be publishers in a major city that would like access to these channels. The argument for requiring channels to be available for common carriage is patent.

The cablecasters' arguments against having to lease channels is less obvious and perhaps need to be stated. The cable industry says it has no monopoly. Television programs are available over the air and increasingly will be available via STV (pay over-the-air broadcasts), direct satellite broadcasts, tape cassettes, and videodiscs. Videotex, security, and data services that cablecasters can provide compete with the same services over telephone lines. But the argument that cable operators have no monopoly is a feeble one. For top shows and sports events there is indeed severe competition. For many things that cable does best, however, such as providing an unlimited number of channels, calling the alternatives "competition" is no more persuasive than a taxi-fleet monopolist claiming to be in a competitive market if there was also a mule, a camel, and an elephant available.

There is a second and stronger argument against leased access. Cable system construction is an expensive capital investment. The risks are high. The major returns are from popular pay programming, such as Home Box Office or sports spectaculars. Returns from the lease of channels would not have been enough to

[4] The largest such case is under appeal, so the $1.8 billion MCI settlement cannot be cited as conclusive.

[5] *Red Lion Broadcasting* v. *FCC*, 395 US 367.

get the systems built. In addition, if a competitor could lease a channel at cost plus a reasonable return and broadcast a rival set of movies, he would destroy the franchisee's monopoly profits, which he needs to justify building the system.

One can appreciate the franchisee's indignation at being forced to lease one of his own channels to someone who is ruining his business. Telegraphers felt the same way. Indeed, a common-carrier requirement in the early capital-intensive phase of cablecasting might have prevented the industry's development. So there is a dilemma.

Cable systems need monopoly profits to justify their construction costs. Yet sooner or later the channels must be made available (at a price) to anyone who would publish. If not, the free market in ideas will be crushed by monopoly cable publishers who control all the programming on the cable. The American public would not stand for that. If cablecasters do not provide leased access, they will find themselves the victims of radical reform: either nationalization of the conduits, the exclusion of carriers from the content business (despite the First Amendment), or the requirement of arm's length dealing between the common-carrier franchisee and a fully separated programming subsidiary.

Both CATV and the "yellow page" issue in telephone deregulation are examples of how the changes in the structure of the communications industry result in rancorous disputes about rules of common carriage. As the industry structure changes, areas that were once monopolistic and needed rules of access may now become competitive and the rules become obsolete. At the same time, new monopolistic bottlenecks emerge. The locus and character of the need for common-carrier-type access rules are fluid.

Monopoly Bottlenecks

In making communications policy for the new technologies, one task is to examine the nature of the technology and its use so as to identify places where monopolistic bottlenecks seem to be likely and then to consider the most acceptable and minimal forms of access assurance that may be feasible in those special situations. Monopolies are of two kinds: "natural" monopolies that exist when there are decreasing costs to scale at the equilibrium price and "administered" monopolies that are established by some form of coercion. The Supreme Court has recognized this distinction in an obscure way.

The Court has made a distinction between economic monopolies, such as that of the only newspaper in a city, and monopolies like those in broadcasting. Because newspapers are only economic monopolies and no inherent fact of nature prevents anyone from starting a new one, the Court in the Tornillo case held unconstitutional a Florida law that gave candidates for office who were attacked in a newspaper the right to reply.[6] The Court distinguished newspaper cases from broadcasting cases (in which the right of reply on the air has been

[6] *Miami Herald Publishing Co.* v. *Tornillo*, 418 US 241 (1974).

upheld) because of the scarcity of radio frequencies. In fact, the Supreme Court's distinction is slightly off target. What the Court perceives as economic monopolies are in fact natural monopolies; but the monopolies that the Court thinks are technological in origin are actually the result of regulatory decisions, because spectrum scarcity is not a fact of nature but the result of political action. Monopoly in broadcasting is, indeed, not caused by the natural play of market forces, but rather created by the licensing rules that Congress has enacted.

An example of a natural communications monopoly in the early years of the century was provided by the disappearance of competitive telephone systems in American cities. At first there was often more than one telephone company in a town. Customers preferred to subscribe to the larger company so as to reach more people. Also, the large fixed costs could be distributed by that system over more customers. In this way, the migration to the larger system began. The more the migration, the greater the disparity in values offered by the two systems. Eventually the smaller system failed.

Most communications monopolies, however, are administered rather than natural. They result from the coercion of laws, regulations, cartels, or threats. Copyrights, patents, licenses, franchises, the right of eminent domain, entry regulation, standards, trade agreements, and denial of service to would-be competitors are the usual sources of communications monopolies. Some are desirable, some are undesirable from the social point of view, but all are enforced monopolies that would vanish in the absence of such enforcement. The presence of such monopolistic situations needs to be identified, and they need to be treated appropriately in the law. Communications monopolies are found most often in the channels of distribution and in the production of unique "software." Research, creative work, and publishing can be small businesses with easy entry and are highly competitive.

The channels of distribution, on the other hand, usually involve a large capital plant since universal reach to everyone and everywhere is important. Thus the Postal Service, the telephone system, and CATV systems tend to be monopolies, partly naturally but also partly reinforced by administrative actions. A CATV system is most likely a natural monopoly in that a second cable system would have to support a capital investment substantially equal to that of the first, but paid by a smaller customer base. This natural disadvantage is compounded by the fact that the new system could not get rights to some of the most popular programs and would probably not get a franchise. By law, American public utility franchises do not grant a monopoly. The city retains the right to issue a second franchise, but it almost never does so. Thus a franchise is de facto a political grant of a monopoly right to dig the streets and offer service.

Not all channels of distribution are monopolies, but many are to some degree. Local newspaper and magazine distribution is a small business with easy entry, which is why organized crime has sometimes been used to create monopolies in it. However, virtually all the new technologies use the radio spectrum (which is licensed), or else use enclosed conduits (which require franchises to utilize the public ways or eminent domain to cross private land).

The fact of such a government grant of special rights creates some degree of monopoly, but such grants are often designed to constrain the scope of that effect and to avoid creating a total monopoly. Congress, in setting up the broadcasting system, followed a policy of "localism," that is, preventing a few superstations from dominating the national air. The FCC follows a policy of "diversity," that is, ensuring that there is an oligopoly of broadcasters in every city, rather than a unique monopoly. The FCC had adopted a similar policy of "open skies." Copyrights and patents are both for fixed terms, require disclosure, and may not be used to keep a product off the market; they are intended to promote rather than to restrict access. And, as previously noted, common carriers are required to give nondiscriminatory access.

Thus, monopoly in distribution channels, while partially natural, is also administered but is rarely complete. The same is true for monopolies in content or as it is now commonly called "software." There is a natural element. Once a company has compiled a bibliography of the entire physics literature of the past twenty years or has published the comprehensive yellow pages for a city, it does not pay for another company to do the same thing. What other companies can do is to provide a somewhat differentiated service that meets the needs of some customers better than the first product. A bibliography publisher may produce an annotated bibliography of astrophysics and another publisher may produce a neighborhood yellow pages.

The natural monopoly that sometimes exists in narrow areas of almost identical software is underpinned by the grant of copyright. Indeed, without a copyright it might pay to "pirate" and publish a physics bibliography or the yellow pages, for the "pirate" would have none of the compilation costs. Copyright, however, gives a monopoly even narrower than the natural monopoly. Copyright does not protect an idea or a genre but only a particular text. With many of the new technologies, copyright, as designed for print, simply does not work. There is no effective way to enforce the present copyright laws on electrostatic reproduction or on computer programs and data. However, the industry and the legislators are scrambling to find equivalent procedures that will permit some monopoly control of intellectual products. Presumably, that effort will be a partial success, and new laws will give a property incentive to intellectual efforts.

Monopolies and Public Policy

What are the implications of all this for public policy about the new technologies? A normative policy principle could be that a competitive marketplace for communications industries is a prerequisite for a free marketplace in ideas. A corollary is that public policy should facilitate easy entry into that market. Thus, whenever a communications industry seeks a special privilege from the state that is not available to all—such as radio frequencies or franchises—it may be proper to require the recipient to sell services that rest on that privilege to all buyers on a nondiscriminatory basis. Lest there be any confusion, let it be stressed that nothing is implied here concerning regulation, licensing, rate of return, or any of the other accoutrements that often go with common carriage. For many decades before regulatory commissions were invented (and still today to an extent) the remedy for those who were discriminated against was an ordinary civil suit in the courts. The recipient of a public grant of a privilege, since he sells a service incorporating that privilege, may be required not to use it for the advantage of some citizens against others. More specifically, large and developed cable systems should be obliged as a condition of enfranchisement to offer channels for lease. No communicator of content should enjoy an administered monopoly over a major medium of communication.

There are a variety of ways to implement this requirement. The Boston franchise turns some channels over to an Access and Programming Foundation, which may lease time on its channels, as may the franchisee directly. Neither one of the organizations alone, therefore, can block a would-be user, who may possibly strike a deal with the other. A Senate bill proposes that the franchisee must reserve a certain percentage of the channels for lease. As noted previously, the carrier could be required to do any programming through an arm's length subsidiary that would have to lease channels from the carrier like anyone else.

Since the franchisee could try to block leases by charging exhorbitant rates rather than by outright refusals, consideration must be given to methods of rate regulation. To solve this by establishing commission-administered rate-of-return regulation would probably be overkill and on the record a poor scheme. The industry's resistance to it can be appreciated. There are alternatives, such as the Boston scheme, which create competition on the sellers' side as well as the buyers' side. Another alternative is compulsory arbitration if the city government that granted the franchise considers the tariff card that a cablecaster posts to be unreasonable.

Specific conclusions can also be drawn about access to future point-to-point telephone networks. There is already some competition in the long-distance portions of these, and there also will be competition in the local telephone loop. As the cost of local service goes up, large customers will seek to bypass local telephone companies for their long-distance calls by using microwave links from their roofs to toll switches or by having their own satellite dishes. There will, of course, be cries of protest from local telephone companies.

The telephone operating companies are being required to offer their services to the public on a nondiscriminatory basis. The same should be required of their competitors. Those vendors who use publicly granted facilities to bypass the local loop should also operate (insofar as they offer service to the public) on a common-carrier basis, at least as far as nondiscrimination is concerned.

With the growth of numerous competing carriers, both local and long-distance, another issue arises—whether and under what conditions the government should insist on the right and possibility for interconnection. Some of the carriers will raise objections. They will say they are using novel technologies incompatible with those of some other carriers. They will also say that they are handling highly sensitive traffic, such as funds transfers or intracompany data, and do not wish to run the risk of outsiders being able to get into their system. Such arguments are sometimes valid, but often the reason will simply be the carriers' desire to lock a group of customers out of using other carriers for some services. (Figure 1 illustrates this point.)

FIGURE 1

Obligatory Interconnection among Telegraph Companies

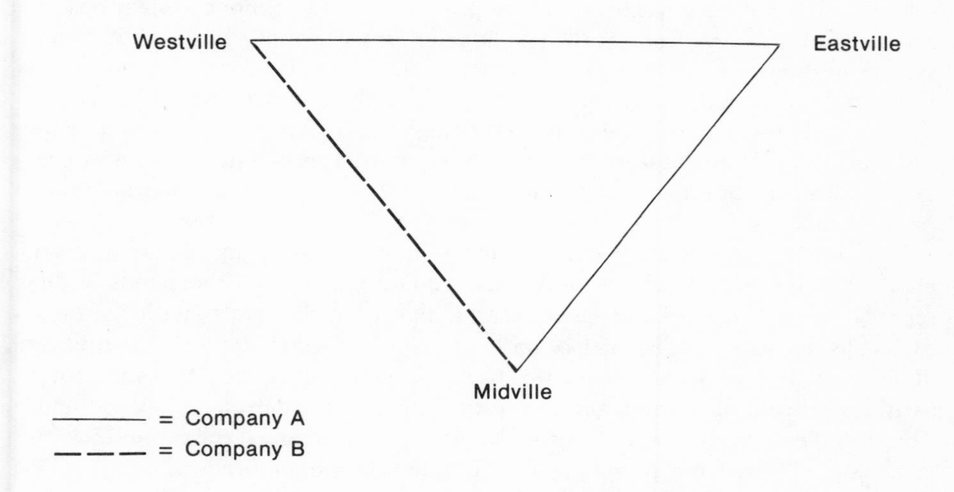

On the other side, reasons can be offered for requiring interconnection. Denial of interconnection may be used by a dominant carrier to restrict new and smaller carriers. Interconnection makes universal communication easier. It enlarges and perfects the market and thus allows competition to work more effectively. Finally, interconnection may be important for national security reasons; a highly redundant system is less vulnerable in a military situation.

Considering these conflicting factors, the best that can be said is that, in general, subject to exceptions for message security and technological innovation, government policy should facilitate interconnection. In public services that owe their existence to government-granted franchises or licenses, discrimination in interconnection should not be allowed. Government should encourage progress on common standards. For example, when the government purchases communications services, it should often require the right and technical possibility of interconnection.

A highly puzzling question is whether future technology for a universal communications system will require a central "brain" that would provide directory assistance and optimal routing, or whether interconnected partial systems will prove efficient. The *a priori* case for a central brain may be summarized as follows. A customer wants to be able to find out the location and number of anyone on the entire system. Not being able to find this information, of course, makes the system much less useful. Similarly, the system needs to know all the routes and interconnections if it is to set up optimal paths. The future telephone system will be controlled by something called "common control"—a separate management network that decides how a call that a customer makes should be set up and then establishes the links for the end-to-end circuits on the voice network. These characteristics suggest that an important monopoly element of future communications systems will be some central brain.

But that is not necessarily true. The present world telephone system has no central brain. International calls get linked from national system to national system without any supranational center. Telephone directories are produced by each city. Consequently, one cannot ask for the number of a particular individual wherever he or she may be in the world. One has to know the individual's city. It might seem that progress toward a more universal system requires a central brain that large computer memories may make possible; but perhaps not.

If communication costs go down and computing speeds go up, it may be more efficient to look for a certain individual in hundreds or even thousands of different locations, using some clever search algorithm that starts with the most plausible locations. The same sort of consideration applies to routing algorithms. It may prove more efficient to use smart algorithms that look for a satisfactory routing rather than to try to optimize by centralizing everything. That is the case at the technical level, but is is even more so if the economic efficiencies that flow from pluralism and competition are factored in.

Most likely there will be changes in the structure of networks over time. As technology changes, these changes will sometimes be in the direction of centralizing functions in fewer brain centers, and at other times in the direction of scattering functions more widely.

Clearly, government has an interest in the universality of communications and in the efficiency of interconnection, but there is no one simple means toward this that might be legislated. By research and development expenditures, by its own procurement policies, by its standards activities, and by access rules applied to enfranchised common carriers, the government can and, it is hoped, will play an important role in promoting efficiency and progress.

The Invasion of Privacy

CHRISTOPHER H. PYLE

The police state that George Orwell warned against in his novel *1984* arose from three developments indigenous to the twentieth century—the bureaucratic state, the communications revolution, and nuclear war. Orwell wrote of the country of Oceania in *1984*: "There was . . . no way of knowing whether you were being watched at any given moment. . . . It was conceivable that they watched everybody all the time. . . . You had to live—did live, from habit that became instinct—in the assumption that every sound you made was overheard, and . . . every movement scrutinized."[1] Nuclear war and its danger, Orwell feared, would cause militarized states to arm internal security bureaucracies with the technology of surveillance to produce a totalitarian society in which individuals were rendered wholly malleable by the loss of all privacy.

Of the three developments Orwell feared most, the first two have proceeded rapidly and independently since 1948. The third has yet to occur, but its likelihood has also increased insidiously, like a dark cloud that expands each time another nation joins the nuclear club. Because the danger of nuclear war and its attendant social controls grows silently, most citizens of democratic societies seem able to ignore it. Meanwhile, right-wing ideologues who seek to revive domestic surveillance are content to believe that if such a holocaust comes, Big Brother could be safely unleashed for the duration of the crisis.

During the 1970s, when fear of nuclear war with the Communist superpowers dissipated for a while, a series of exposés drastically reduced domestic intelligence in the United States. Continuing this trend, however, has not been easy, and today the suppression of domestic surveillance depends largely on a small band of beleaguered liberals who occupy strategic positions in the House of Representatives. Meanwhile, it is sobering to note that George Bush, a former head of the Central Intelligence Agency (CIA), stands but a heartbeat away from the presidency.

Equally sobering is the extent to which the United States government has ac-

[1] George Orwell, *1984* (New York: Harcourt, Brace & Co., 1949).

quired the technology of surveillance that Orwell could only imagine. Television sets do not spy on citizens as they did in *1984* (although two-way cable systems could be used for this purpose), but other equipment more than fulfills Orwell's expectations. Today, drug smugglers are flushed from the Florida Everglades by helicopter chase teams using infrared sensors that penetrate the thickest foliage to detect people by their body heat. As Orwell anticipated, television cameras patrol buildings and street corners, voice analyzers automate the tedious work of eavesdroppers, computers create Big Brother memories that never forget, and new systems of telecommunications give diverse investigative agencies the capacity to cooperate as never before. Government agencies and private corporations continue to frighten their employees with lie detector tests, while the National Security Agency (NSA), the largest and most secret spy agency in the United States, conducts massive searches of electronic communications without prior permission from the courts.[2]

As Orwell predicted, ministries of state security have found the new technology for invading privacy irresistible; indeed, they have pioneered its development. For example, much of the early research into hallucinogenic drugs was conducted by the army and the CIA, sometimes with tragic results for unsuspecting human subjects. Computers, which most Americans associate with the socially conscious International Business Machines Corporation, are equally the brainchild of the military intelligence services, which have used their wizardry to breach the privacy of foreign and domestic communications. Today no agency works harder than the NSA to obstruct the dissemination of new mathematical concepts that would permit the development of effective countermeasures to this science of privacy invasion.

Contrary to Orwell's vision, ministries of state security have not been the only, nor always the worst, privacy invaders. Equally intrusive have been televison newspeople who descend on tragedy like jackals, ask ghoulish questions, then transmit film of the grieving victims back to blow-dried newscasters who convey it with all of the sighs and clucks of village gossips. However, unlike Orwell's ministers of Truth, today's television jackals concentrate their invasions of privacy most intensely on public officials, an ironic situation that Orwell may not have anticipated but that he surely would have appreciated.

If Orwell did not anticipate the extent to which the communications revolution would strip officials of their privacy, he did foresee their efforts to use television to befuddle people's minds with "newspeak," "doublethink," and other forms of misleading language. Like Orwell's ministers of Truth, United States government spokesmen insist that the armed forces are really part of a "defense" department, that the agency of clandestine warfare is really an "intelligence" agency, and that government lawyers are really part of a "justice" department.

[2] U.S., Department of Justice, "Report on Inquiry Into CIA Related Electronic Surveillance Activities," xeroxed, 1976.

As if this were not enough, officials use the same sort of secrecy ploys used in *1984* to deprive the people of accurate information and to distort history.

Orwell understood that the primary purpose of all official efforts to debase language and undermine the reliability of information is to strip citizens of the capacity and confidence to make moral judgments about the government's use of power. His novel demonstrated in a chilling way that nothing invades privacy more than the manipulation of communications in order to destroy the ability of individuals to know truth and thereby defend themselves against psychological manipulation. But citizens are not the only victims of this manipulation. Politicians also suffer as they come to believe their own propaganda and lose the ability to distinguish between images and reality. Richard Nixon was one such politician, who in the end was destroyed by his blind faith in the power of media manipulation, secrecy, and deception.

In Orwell's world, the communications revolution strengthened the centralizing forces of an authoritarian state. For a while in the early 1970s, it looked as if the United States might suffer a similar fate, as more became known about the use of surveillance technology by J. Edgar Hoover's "Thought Police," Richard Nixon's plumbers, the NSA's eavesdroppers, and the army's political data bankers. But countervailing technologies were also at work. Chief among these was the Xerox machine, which during the 1970s made it easier to copy and leak secret information. The Nixon administration's effort to control the Pentagon Papers, the army's surveillance of civilian politics, and the FBI's programs of dirty tricks against political dissidents were all exposed through the use of Xerox machines. During the 1970s, the army's data banks were destroyed, NSA's watchlists of dissidents were discontinued, the CIA's spying on domestic politics was ended, the FBI's roundup lists were destroyed, the Watergate plumbers were sent to prison, Hoover's "Thought Police" were disbanded, and most police intelligence units were abolished. The defeat of these Orwellian activities, a major victory for political freedom, will not soon be forgotten.

However, the defeat of these activities was only a momentary advance in a much longer war against the forces that Orwell feared. The outcome of this war remains in doubt; there have been as many defeats for privacy as there have been victories. Nowhere is this more evident than in the body of law that defines the right of Americans to the privacy of their communications and the control over the government's collection and use of information about their personal lives.

Communications Privacy

The past three decades have not been kind to the privacy of electronic communications. When Orwell's countdown began, the Supreme Court was unwilling to hold that warrantless electronic searches violated the Fourth Amendment unless the eavesdroppers physically invaded their targets' property. The Court persisted in following the doublethink of Chief Justice William Howard Taft, who had declared in 1928 that electronic communications were not tangible enough to be seizable, unless, of course, they were seized on a person's property, in which case they were magically transformed and made subject to the Fourth Amendment.

During the 1960s, the Supreme Court finally came to realize how absurd it had been to tie the privacy protected by the Fourth Amendment to the technical laws of trespass. In *Katz* v. *United States* the Court even declared that the Fourth Amendment protects "persons, not places," thereby establishing a new portable personal right of privacy. What the amendment really protects, the Court seemed to say, are the reasonable expectations of privacy that people should have in certain circumstances.

But this new standard was not without its confusions. Insofar as it liberated the Fourth Amendment from heavy reliance on concepts of ownership and control, the standard constituted a positive gain for individual privacy. However, to the extent that it required proof of the subject's actual expectations, it was regressive, leaving the way open for the government to declare its intent to snoop and thereby eliminate all reasonable expectations of privacy. The Supreme Court, now dominated by Nixon appointees, has come to accept this regressive approach.

When Orwell's warning was first published, section 605 of the federal Communications Act of 1934 clearly forbade the government to "intercept and divulge" the contents of wire communications. Unwilling to accept this restraint or to work to change section 605 by legislation, successive attorneys general simply debased the statute's language. What the law really meant to say, they declared, was that the government could conduct all the nontrespassory wiretaps it desired so long as it did not divulge the contents in court or elsewhere outside the executive branch. In other words, so long as information obtained from eavesdropping was shared only within the government, no harm to privacy would be done.

By this sophistry, the "Justice" Department sought to reduce the Fourth Amendment from a principled guarantee of privacy to a technical, largely pointless, rule of criminal procedure. To these Orwellian "realists," the Bill of Rights was not a body of high moral values but an amoral prediction of what some politically shrewd judge might decide in some future case. Embracing what Oliver Wendell Holmes called the "bad man's theory of the law," they followed the tendency of all lawyers to subordinate their morality to that of their clients. Thus the law of privacy was reduced to what the surveillance agencies could not reasonably expect to get away with.

In 1968, Congress made another attempt to govern wiretapping and bugging. Title III of the Omnibus Crime Control and Safe Streets Act of that year was based on two assumptions: first, that all wiretaps are searches within the meaning of the Fourth Amendment, as the Supreme Court had ruled in *Katz* v. *United States*; and second, that the Fourth Amendment does not flatly prohibit all general searches of places, even though that was what the Framers had sought to accomplish. Searches of all telephonic and household communications are constitutional, Congress assumed, so long as they are governed by a reasonable set of authorizations.

Nineteenth-century absolutism about the "sacred privacies of life" was thus replaced with twentieth-century relativism, and the Fourth Amendment reduced to a mere counsel of moderation. Under Title III, criminal investigators are required to obtain a full-fledged judicial warrant before installing a wiretap. After the device is installed, the statute seems to say, investigators are supposed to minimize their intrusion by recording only those messages clearly associated with the purpose of their tap. However, even this requirement has been eviscerated by a 1978 Supreme Court interpretation. If the lawmakers had been serious about minimizing the effects of these general searches, they would have forbidden the investigators to use any information about other criminal activities that they happen to overhear unexpectedly. But the law's draftsmen did not forbid them. Today unsuspected persons who discuss criminal activities on a tapped telephone are as vulnerable to prosecution as the suspect himself. The government can breach their privacy without first establishing probable cause to believe that they are guilty of some criminal activity and that evidence of their crime will be found on the telephone line to be tapped.

In *1984*, claims of national security justified all breaches of privacy, for Oceania was in a perpetual state of war with other superpowers. In cold war America, claims of national security have had a similar impact. During the drafting of Title III, national security conservatives quarreled vehemently with civil libertarians over whether the president could constitutionally ignore the statute and authorize the installation of warrantless wiretaps to collect national security intelligence. The conservatives said that the president could, because Article II of the Constitution, or the "concomitants of nationality," gave him an inherent power to ignore restrictive legislation and even the Bill of Rights in order to protect whatever he might deem to be the nation's security. Civil libertarians denied that Article II gave him any such power or that the so-called concomitants of nationality belonged to the president. Accordingly, they refused to accept a provision in the bill that would have acknowledged the concept of inherent executive powers or of a national security exception to the Fourth Amendment. After lengthy debate, Congress finally avoided the issue by expressly disclaiming any legislative intent to resolve the constitutional dispute.

Johnson administration lawyers agreed to the disclaimer. However, when Richard Nixon assumed the presidency, his attorneys insisted that the provision actually constituted positive recognition by Congress that FBI agents could, as the president's lieutenants, ignore the warrant requirements of the Fourth Amendment and Title III whenever they believed that the communications to be invaded might somehow be related to national security. Not surprisingly, the bureau's definition of "national security" was Orwellian in scope.

In 1972, the Supreme Court rejected the Nixon administration's interpretation of the disclaimer. In *United States* v. *U.S. District Court*, the justices ruled that there was no inherent power or national security exception to the Fourth Amendment or to Title III for wiretaps directed against domestic political activists who are not agents of a foreign power. In so ruling, the Court separated the Fourth Amendment into its two clauses and suggested that while the reasonableness requirement of the first clause had to govern all electronic searches, the warrant requirement of the second clause might be weakened to facilitate foreign intelligence wiretaps. As in Orwell's *Animal Farm*, all have equal rights under the law, but some are more equal than others.

Two federal courts of appeal subsequently decided that prior judicial warrants for wiretaps directed at alleged foreign agents were not required at all. In the case of H. Rap Brown, a black power advocate, the court even ruled that no prior judicial review of any kind was required by the Fourth Amendment when the purpose was to gather "foreign intelligence." The court declared that the Fourth Amendment's standard of reasonableness could be satisfied in such cases by judicial review at a trial, conveniently ignoring the fact that the purpose of nearly all national security wiretaps is not to collect evidence for a criminal trial but to gather economic and political information and to obtain the means to blackmail people into becoming spies for the United States. The *Brown* decision thus gave the clandestine services of the United States a constitutional license to wiretap at will within the Fifth Circuit, regardless of the consequences to personal privacy.

When the new intelligence committees of the House and Senate undertook to draft the Foreign Intelligence Surveillance Act of 1978, they took notice of these judicial opinions and created a new system of weakened, pro-forma judicial warrants, to be administered by a specially designated national security court. The procedure prescribed by this statute is essentially a travesty of the principle of checks and balances. As a gesture to the probable cause requirement of the Fourth Amendment, the court is directed to decide whether there are grounds to believe that the target of the electronic surveillance is an agent of a foreign power. However, once the court has made this finding, it must accept on faith the executive's certification that the surveillance is rationally and substantially related to the needs of national security. On no account is the court authorized to consider the reasonableness of the proposed search on the basis of the totality of the circumstances—the kind of judgment it presumably would make when assessing an ordinary warrant request.

When this statute was enacted, some of its proponents asserted that it would undermine the appeal of broad executive claims to inherent constitutional authority to ignore both the legislation of Congress and the Fourth Amendment in order to protect the nation's security. Perhaps it will, if such a case ever reaches the Court. Meanwhile, Presidents Ford and Carter refused to renounce the Nixon claim, and President Reagan has affirmed it.

The National Security Agency has also continued its massive interceptions of international telephonic communications to and from the United States. It has done so without any judicial authorization at all—not even a pseudowarrant like that authorized by the 1978 act. NSA ignores all federal wiretap legislation largely on the theory, which it prudently keeps secret, that legitimate expectations of privacy evaporate as soon as the telephone company decides to bounce conversations off a microwave tower or satellite.[3]

In 1973, according to the Senate Select Committee on Intelligence, chaired by Senator Frank Church, the NSA had discontinued all of its "watch lists" of United States citizens whose international communications NSA agents had been instructed to intercept. However, there is a document that the Justice Department apparently did not share with the Church committee and that the Reagan administration would now like to recall and reclassify that indicates that the committee was misinformed. Watchlists or their equivalent may still exist, not only to spy on the commercial activities of selected corporations but also to investigate suspected drug smugglers, gunrunners, and terrorists.[4] Since each of these activities involves criminal activity and none is directly related to the activities of foreign intelligence, military, or diplomatic personnel, it would appear that the NSA is still engaged in the wholesale violation of Fourth Amendment rights.

Thus, despite Orwell's warnings and the exposés of the 1970s, all three branches of the federal government still strive to erode the Fourth Amendment's defenses against electronic spying. The extent of this erosion is most dramatically illustrated by positions taken on the authority of federal agents to conduct burglaries in order to install listening devices for national security purposes. According to the Nixon, Ford, and Reagan administrations, these intrusions may be authorized by the president on his authority alone. The Church committee insisted that a warrant be obtained first but did not object in principle to court-ordered burglaries. Presumably, this means that if one of the government's burglars is surprised and killed by a homeowner, the homeowner would be guilty of murder. Conversely, if the burglar killed the homeowner in the course of a struggle, the killing would not be a crime, becaues the entry had been authorized by a judge. Such is the Orwellian logic of the "Justice" Department and the legislators who are supposed to oversee it.

Informational Privacy

When Orwell wrote *1984*, intruders still seemed to pose the greatest threat to privacy because privacy was still viewed largely in physical terms. Orwell helped change this view. Big Brother was not only an eavesdropper, a Peeping Tom, and a government spy but also a keeper of records, a mind reader, and a brainwasher. The secret to Big Brother's enormous power was not only physical surveillance; his power was also based on informational control. He knew, or led people to think that he knew, as much about their personal lives as they did themselves. As a result, people lacked the capacity or courage to control Big Brother by limiting what he could know about them.

[3] Ibid., pp. 130–42.
[4] Ibid., pp. 126, 173.

Orwell understood the importance of informational privacy to individual freedom, but since he was primarily concerned with police states, he had less to say about well-meaning officials in liberal democracies who could also destroy privacy with the data they collected to administer social service programs. The idea of informational privacy, in the sense of people having some control over what others know about them, was implicit in the Fourth Amendment's guarantee against unreasonable searches and seizures. Informational privacy was also implicit in the famous 1890 *Harvard Law Review* article by Samuel Warren and Louis Brandeis that launched the tort of privacy against newspaper reporters who publish private information about the lives of private persons. The concept of informational privacy did not win widespread support, however, until the rise of internal security and social service bureaucracies in the post-World War II era, and the development of the new technology of computers and telecommunications.

In the wake of World War II, Orwell was alarmed by the extent to which returning veterans seemed to accept the impersonal, data-hungry bureaucracies of modern socialistic states. By the late 1950s, however, public trust in large organizations had declined substantially, and Americans began to question whether it was wise to entrust so much personal information to unaccountable administrators. This concern was expressed in three stages. The first period of protest occurred in the 1940s and 1950s when civil libertarians questioned the informational practices of the internal security bureaucracies. Unfortunately, knowledge of these files was effectively limited and potential critics were often intimidated.

The second stage occurred in the mid-1960s, when executive-branch officials proposed a computerized national data bank combining personal information about citizens from the records of some twenty social service agencies, including the Departments of Labor, Commerce, Agriculture, and Health, Education, and Welfare. None of the reports recommending this vast records system paid more than perfunctory attention to the concept of informational privacy, and congressional opposition killed the plan outright. Opposition to the national data bank proposal was supplemented by the appearance of an influential body of literature developing the idea of informational privacy.[5] This literature was reflected in congressional investigations of the era. In 1970, Congress passed its first informational privacy law—the Fair Credit Reporting Act. Although riddled with loopholes, the act gave individuals the right to know the substance of information about them in the files of the giant credit-reporting companies. The act ensured that individuals would be notified when adverse decisions were made on the basis of credit reports, provided for the correction of erroneous information, and required the deletion of outdated facts.

[5] The most influential works were probably Alan F. Westin, *Privacy and Freedom* (New York: Atheneum, 1967); Arthur R. Miller, *The Assault on Privacy* (Ann Arbor: University of Michigan Press, 1971); and U.S., Department of Health, Education, and Welfare, *Records, Computers, and the Rights of Citizens*, Report of the Secretary's Advisory Committee on Automated Personal Data Systems (Cambridge: MIT Press, 1973).

The third stage of concern was directed against the informational practices of the internal security bureaucracy. In 1971 the Senate Subcommittee on Constitutional Rights, led by Senator Sam J. Ervin, Jr., dismantled the army's program of domestic spying. Ervin built bipartisan support for his investigation and neutralized some of his potential cold war critics by linking the army exposé to a more far-reaching inquiry into federal data banks, computers, and the Bill of Rights. Even so, Ervin's political acumen was insufficient to convert Senator James Eastland, the right-wing chairman of the parent Judiciary Committee, and the bill to end army surveillance never reached the Senate floor.

However, the Senate hearings on army surveillance did make it politically easier for Ervin and other members of Congress to investigate the Nixon administration's misuse of confidential tax information and the political surveillance and records systems of other federal agencies, including the FBI, the CIA, and the NSA. The most successful of these investigations was conducted by the Church committee. As a direct result of that investigation, the FBI was forced to discontinue most of its domestic intelligence program, including its roundup lists of dissidents. Hoover's "Thought Police" were retired out of the bureau or reassigned to more legitimate areas of investigation.

In 1974, Senator Ervin's Subcommittee on Constitutional Rights launched the first major effort to regulate criminal justice data banks. That effort also failed to produce legislation, but the subcommittee did persuade Congress to pass the Privacy Act of 1974. The act was a product of the Watergate controversy and the consequent need of politicians of both parties to reaffirm their allegiance to the concept of privacy before the fall elections. Two alternatives were available to the legislators. They could attempt a comprehensive statute purporting to regulate all (or most) data banks of personal information, or they could draft narrower, more detailed legislation in such issue areas as banking, insurance, and arrest records. Prudence, respectful of complexity, recommended the issue-by-issue approach, while politics, driven by urgency, insisted on an omnibus statute. Thus, while work on a criminal justice data-bank bill was bogged down in a morass of technical detail, advocates of the privacy legislation took the high road, bypassed all nongovernmental and state data banks, avoided most investigative and intelligence files, and came up with an omnibus law that most members could endorse.

The result was less a privacy bill (in the sense of a law declaring what should be private or confidential) than a code of fair information practices grounded in theories of due process of law. Still, the Privacy Act established eight important principles that may someday take on constitutional significance. First, the act forbids the government to maintain any secret data banks of personal information about individuals. Second, it grants individuals the right to see and copy information about themselves, except when the information is expressly exempted from disclosure, as in the case of investigative and national security files. Third, it gives individuals the right to correct and amend their files. Fourth, it prohibits agencies from collecting any personal information that is not relevant and necessary to the accomplishment of a lawful purpose. Thus the revival of domestic intelligence files is arguably forbidden. Fifth, the law directs agencies to limit the extent to which information collected for one purpose can be shared with other agencies and used for other purposes. Sixth, it restricts the power of agencies to disclose confidential information to outsiders without the subject's consent. Seventh, it charges agencies with an affirmative duty to see that personal information that they keep on individuals remains necessary, lawful, accurate, and up-to-date. Finally, the act makes it possible for individuals to hold agencies accountable for their handling of personal information, if necessary by suing them for damages or by initiating criminal prosecutions for egregious misconduct.

Unfortunately, the Supreme Court has been far less sensitive than Congress to the dangers posed by the new technology for handling personal information. Indeed, President Nixon's appointees have been downright Orwellian. For example, in 1972, they refused to allow the innocent subjects of the army's computerized political data banks to challenge the constitutionality of that surveillance. The chilling effect on political activists caused by the existence of the files was not enough, Justice Burger ruled, to give the plaintiffs standing to sue. They had to prove that the surveillance had caused them more tangible injuries, like the loss of jobs, mortgages, or reputation. Of course, they could not prove such injuries unless they could learn what the army had done with the files, but the Nixon appointees refused to allow the plaintiffs to examine the records. Burger's ruling was a classic Catch-22 decision—"doublethink" at its best—and it effectively immunized the internal security data banks from constitutional challenge in court.

The most Orwellian of recent Supreme Court opinions have flatly refused to recognize a constitutional right of informational privacy. According to the Nixon justices, persons assume the risk, when they entrust their checks to a bank, that its officers will make copies of those checks available to government investigators on demand, even without telling them. Similarly, the justices have ruled that while persons have a legitimate right to expect that the government will not listen to their telephone calls without first obtaining a warrant, they do not have a right to expect that the the government will get a warrant before installing "pen registers," which record the numbers dialed.

There are numerous indications that the courts are waiting for Congress to exercise leadership in the development of informational rights of privacy. However, Congress has not made much progress in recent years. In 1978, the legislature did succeed in forbidding schools that received federal funds to release a student's files without the student's consent (or the consent of a parent when the student is not yet eighteen years old), and also gave students the right to see and submit corrections to their files. Congress also passed a Right to Financial Privacy Act in 1978, but federal investigative agencies defeated provisions that would have required them to obtain warrants before searching bank records. Other records systems, including insurance files, medical records, and personal records in the possession of private corporations, have escaped federal privacy legislation altogether.

Perhaps the greatest failure to expand informational privacy has occurred in the realm of arrest records, where automation has grown dramatically in the past decade. The problem posed by these files is best stated by William R. Coons, a former convict who served time at New York's Attica Correctional Facility: "Once you have a 'jacket'—a dossier with all the past details of your life, all the detrimental ones they can put together, that is—you are a criminal. The jacket does not disappear; it grows fat and follows you around wherever you go. Some day this sentence you are serving will chronologically run out, but society does not forgive, it keeps tabs. . . . "[6] In 1971, when these words were written, most criminal history records were still in file folders, and most communications among police departments were by telephone or mail. Today, many states and the federal government keep track of criminal suspects by computers and exchange these records by teletype machines.

The new technology has made law enforcement among thousands of governmental units more efficient, but it has also created a new source of systematic injustice—the "records prison." Criminals are not the only persons with criminal records. A quarter of all Americans have been arrested at one time or another for nontraffic offenses. About half of all males and 12 percent of all females will be accused of a nontraffic offense sometime in their lives. For black men living in cities, there is a 90 percent chance of being arrested at some time. And persons who have been arrested once face increased odds of being arrested again, particularly as police departments install computer terminals in squad cars.

Today, the criminal history, or "rap sheet," of the accused is central to every stage of the criminal justice process except the trial, and 90 percent of all cases are concluded without a trial. Contrary to popular impressions, traditional concepts of due process—such as the presumption of innocence, the right to confront witnesses, and the right to open proceedings—no longer characterize the criminal justice process. The system today is largely administrative, as in Orwell's Oceania. The most important decisions are made outside of court, pursuant to a presumption of guilt, without an adversary hearing and often without representation of counsel. Decisions involving prearrest investigations, postarrest investigations, plea-bargaining, sentencing, and corrections all are heavily influenced by the contents of the individual's file. The rules governing these files thus determine, to a considerable extent, the integrity of the criminal justice system and the fate of the accused.

The "records prison" created by criminal histories is not confined to the criminal justice system. Arrest and conviction records are also used extensively in employment, licensing, and even public-housing decisions, often with a disproportionate impact on black Americans. One study in the early 1970s found that 75 percent of the employment agencies in the New York City area would not accept applicants with arrest records. Convictions are an even stronger barrier to employment. State laws deny former convicts licenses to be

[6] William R. Coons, "An Attica Graduate Tells His Story," *New York Times Magazine*, October 10, 1971, p. 20.

lawyers, teachers, masseurs, fortune tellers, junk dealers, dry cleaners, barbers, plumbers, and taxi drivers.

But the unforgiving nature of the criminal records system is only part of the problem. The other part involves the inaccuracy of the records themselves. A recent inventory of state criminal history files found one state in which 70 percent of the files were inaccurate, incomplete, or misleading. Thus the "records prisons" into which many Americans are being cast are not even of their own making.

Congress, after failing in 1975 to draft a statute that would regulate all state and federal criminal histories systems, consigned the matter to its Office of Technology Assessment (OTA) for further study. The more OTA learned about the patterns of crime and the movement of criminals, the less need there appeared to be for a centralized system of criminal history records. Despite the great mobility of American society, most violent crime remains highly localized. Thus, there is less apparent need for the kind of national system that could produce Orwellian results. However, while the need for more accurate, complete, relevant, and timely records remains at all levels, the political system most capable of legislating reforms is still stymied by jurisdictional wrangles, budgetary constraints, and the antiprivacy demands of companies and professions that are determined to use criminal history files to exclude former suspects and convicts from employment.

Conclusion

It is tempting, after reviewing the weak state of informational privacy today, to blame the communications revolution for the present situation. However, the temptation should be resisted. Technology can create new opportunities for privacy invasion, manipulation, and control, but it does not by itself create the structure of power that commits those abuses. The worst abuses associated with privacy invasions in recent years—the FBI's secret programs of covert action against political dissidents—were committed by agents who used information stored in file cabinets.

The most massive invasions of communications privacy—the NSA's computerized eavesdropping on telephonic communications—are clearly a product of technological developments. However, the technology that the NSA uses against privacy could be easily turned against the eavesdroppers if the public knowledge and political will were there. Technology can also improve the quality of arrest records. Computers can be programmed to block the distribution of incomplete records and to purge outdated information systematically. The political challenge, as Orwell would surely agree, is to wrest these sytems from the exclusive control of professionals and technocrats, and to restrain these professionals and technocrats to think in larger, more humane terms.

A fully footnoted version of this essay may be obtained from the author upon request.

Media Diplomacy

PATRICIA A. KARL

The symbiotic relationship between the media and government officials in the conduct of public diplomacy has a Jekyll and Hyde quality. The actors are perceived by the public as crusaders or as culprits in a fierce competition for headlines and high ratings. Both the journalist and the diplomat are constrained by the elements of time, space, and distance; but the journalist, unlike the diplomat or head of state, has nothing to lose by promoting media diplomacy. The correspondent always gets a story, whether the foreign policy is a success or a failure. Like the correspondent, the diplomat or head of state may manipulate the media. The danger is that in an age of prime-time leaders, air-time-attempted assassinations, televised coups, and prerecorded revolutions, the constant need for a new foreign-policy script may encourage diplomatic comedies or tragedies resplendent with disinformation. Governments and the media have performed as ministers of myth information in trying to create and participate in public diplomacy.

The fall of the shah of Iran and the seizure of the United States Embassy in Tehran set the stage for one of the longest media-orchestrated foreign-policy sagas in network history. The traditional diplomat could not compete with "terrorvision" and radio revolutionaries. During the hostage crisis, debate raged within the American public and the government over the role of press coverage of the embassy takeover. For a while, half of the United States network news was preempted each night by the latest broadcast by satellite from Tehran. Critics charged that Ayatollah Khomeini and his cohorts were being given rights of what amounted to censorship that no American network would ever give to an American president or a Soviet premier. The "students" holding the hostages at the embassy were trying to pressure their own government and the United States government and public. To ensure that their programs would not be censored by any government, they installed three cameras of their own in the embassy compound, along with a dish antenna to relay signals, via satellite, through the networks in the United States and then into American homes. Part of this production included a show for viewers in which Iranian mobs shouted slogans in English (and in French for one Canadian television crew) and shook fists on cue.

If Vietnam was the living-room war, Iran was the living-room revolution. Iran established the preeminence of television in instant diplomacy. Both the United States government and public became hostages to this horrible spectacle. In Washington, President Carter and Secretary of State Cyrus Vance were talking to whoever in Tehran or Qom might be listening, not through their helpless chargé d'affaires, L. Bruce Laingen, but through press spokesman Hodding Carter. The administration did not know exactly whom in Iran it was addressing through the media and was miffed that the United States media had access to power sources in Iran that was denied to official emissaries. In Tehran, Ayatollah Khomeini became so dissatisfied with American television reporting that he eventually ran a full-page advertisement in the *New York Times* to "define [his] stance in respect to [the] embassy takeover." More recently, of course, the Iranian government has allowed American reporters back into Iran to film (and thereby confirm) Iran's victories in the Iran-Iraq war and the purported Iranian capture of 15,000 Iraqi military prisoners.

The media are increasingly a part of the process (if not the entire process) in the communications between governments and publics about international politics. A recent example of the media's ability to inform the public immediately and to preempt governments in an analysis of foreign events is the television coverage of the assassination of Egyptian President Anwar el-Sadat on October 6, 1981. The three television networks treated the American public to an almost immediate media barrage of often detailed and contradictory information about the assassination. It took hours before the American public, the Egyptian public, and foreign publics heard any word from the Egyptian government, the U.S. State Department, or President Reagan. In the United States, the print media followed the United States government line and devoted their eulogies to the "hero" legend that President Sadat's own public diplomacy had persuaded editors and reporters in the United States to create. The fact that President Sadat was a pariah in the Arab world was largely ignored by the United States print media.

Members of the government or of the media have often attempted to manipulate the public's perception of foreign-policy issues. For example, for a while the press accepted at face value the Reagan administration's "White Paper" report on El Salvador. This report apparently attempted to substantiate Secretary of State Alexander M. Haig's allegations of Soviet support for "international terrorism," though the report conflicted with a Central Intelligence Agency analysis partly exculpating Moscow. The State Department version won front-page treatment in the *New York Times*; it was two weeks later before the media—alarmed by reports that Salvadoran government forces were engaging in terrorism—began to concentrate criticism on the "White Paper." By the spring of 1982, the Reagan administration had backed itself into a public-relations corner because of its prior public support for the Duarte government and junta. Despite the fact that no parties of the left took part in the March 30, 1982, Salvadoran elections and the fact that the right-wing parties won the election (an outcome Washington did not want), the Reagan administration felt constrained to pronounce itself pleased with the results.

The United States's Central American policy was damaged earlier in March 1982 when the State Department arranged a press conference for a Nicaraguan guerrilla fighter who, the government claimed, would confirm the charge that foreign Communists were training revolutionaries to promote subversion in the Caribbean. The press conference turned into a disaster for the Reagan administration when the Nicaraguan informed television viewers that his confession had been obtained under torture in a Salvadoran prison and that, in fact, he had not been trained by the Communists at all. He was quickly ushered out of the country to spare the administration further embarrassment. Given this overt attempt to create a media event, the American public must have been amused when the State Department suggested that the United States government had been "set up" in this case.

The Reagan administration's embarrassments have not been restricted to United States policy toward Central America. The public foreign-policy debates between Secretary of Defense Caspar W. Weinberger and Secretary of State Alexander M. Haig regarding the North Atlantic Treaty Organization (NATO) strategic doctrine, for example, have alarmed and angered the United States's allies and have presented the Soviets with unearned public-relations successes. Secretary of State Haig's suggestion that United States strategic doctrine might allow for the demonstration detonation of a nuclear weapon in Europe should the Soviets attempt conventional aggression enabled Leonid Brezhnev to win over Western European public opinion with statements that the Soviet government would not consider such a policy. Secretary of Defense Weinberger then stated that there was no such contingency. The White House compounded the public confusion by stating that both the secretary of defense and the secretary of state were correct.

The United States government, of course, is not alone in having public diplomacy result in public disaster. Before Argentina invaded the Falkland Islands on April 2, 1982, British government spokesmen publicly tried to bluff the Argentine government into believing that Britain had the military capability to prevent the invasion. When the bluff was challenged by 4,000 Argentine troops, the British government's credibility was seriously undermined. This public embarrassment cost the international community the resignation of one of the world's most successful traditional diplomats, Lord Carrington, the British foreign secretary, and threatened the survival of the Thatcher government if British prestige had not been restored. The ensuing military crisis also threatened the survival of the Argentine military junta. Clearly, the public statements of both the British and the Argentine governments, by placing the prestige of both parties on the line, made it difficult for either side to negotiate a solution to the crisis.

While British and Argentine forces fought a real war over the Falklands, the British and Argentine governments fought a media war with conflicting press reports of casualties, capabilities, and damages. Both Britain and Argentina censored their war reports and attempted to manipulate media coverage of the war. Journalists reporting for both countries became almost totally dependent on their governments' information about the war. In Argentina, while the local newspapers promoted public optimism with news of victories, factions of the Argentine government were intimidating resident foreign correspondents. Reporters, including Norwegian and American journalists, were kidnapped, harassed, and threatened with death. In an attempt to redress the negative impact of these episodes, General Galtieri, head of the Argentine junta, publicly apologized to four Norwegian correspondents. One *La Prensa* journalist was also critical of the media coverage of the war: "The official and private radio stations continue adding advertisements to their news 'flashes' and war communiques as if this was a soccer game."[1]

The British also attempted to manage the war news. Almost all of the reports and photographs from the Falklands passed through British Ministry of Defense censorship. British journalists were well aware that they were being "used" by their government. Many were especially annoyed when, a day before the British landings on the East Falkland Island, Ministry of Defense spokesmen told reporters that the British military plans consisted of "hit-and-run raids," not a full-scale invasion. Newspapers in the United Kingdom faithfully printed the government's story, but a day later the British military landed an invasion force at San Carlos Bay. As one British government spokesman suggested, the government did not want to telegraph its punches.

The British government also manipulated the timing of the release of photographs and information to serve their public-relations interests. Although it took weeks for many photographs to appear in the press, the photograph of the raising of the British flag at San Carlos Bay was relayed in hours. The two dozen journalists aboard ships with the British naval task force were permitted to broadcast live to confirm British government reports of battles and losses. BBC correspondents, for example, counted the number of aircraft leaving and returning to British ships and were thus able to confirm British reports and to deny Argentine claims of the number of British aircraft damaged or lost. Indeed, when the British were not entirely successful in controlling the war news and an uncensored report appeared in *The Guardian* that the British had captured the Goose Green airstrip, a government spokesman noted that this was the "first time such a thing had happened in the two month operation," and announced that there would be an investigation of the matter.

The media, like governments, often become victims of their attempts to shape the public's image of foreign policy issues. A recent example is the story by Christopher Jones in the December 20, 1981, issue of the *New York Times Magazine*—a fabricated tale of a four-week experience with Khmer Rouge guerrillas in Cambodia. The newspaper apologized to its readers, and Executive Editor A. M. Rosenthal stated: "We do not feel that the fact the writer was a liar and a hoaxer removes our responsibility. It is our job to uncover any falsehood or er-

[1] *New York Times*, May 24, 1982.

rors." However, the public must wonder how many other false reports have been published and never discovered. Like a government pursuing the game of public diplomacy, the media may jeopardize prestige and credibility with the public and governments if "stories" become more important than substance.

Open Convenants Openly Connived

From the traditional diplomacy prescribed by de Colliere and Sir Harold Nicolson, the United States has moved to a slightly revised version of Woodrow Wilson's concept of diplomacy: open covenants openly connived. The collaboration between governments and the media has recently provided students of diplomacy and an unsuspecting public with a curious situation that may lead to a further distortion of events and issues.

In an attempt to bolster the Reagan administration's support for the Duarte regime in El Salvador and to quiet congressional and public criticism of the Salvadoran junta, President Reagan invited President Duarte to the United States for a series of public-relations exercises before the Salvadoran elections that included a congressional appearance, interviews with reporters, and appearances on several United States network news programs. President Duarte assured the United States that his government needed economic, not military, aid; and he thoughtfully disclosed that his government had dismissed approximately 600 members of the military junta for "excesses." This public-relations campaign, sponsored by the Reagan administration in an attempt to gain approval for increasing aid to the Duarte regime, neglected to mention the number of Salvadoran troops being trained in the United States, the types of weapons being used, the techniques of counterinsurgency these personnel were learning, and for what purpose these techniques would be used once the troops returned.

President Duarte's government was evidently fighting a different media battle against the press in El Salvador, as indicated by the murder of four Dutch newsmen in March 1982. The journalists were covering the rebel side of El Salvador's civil war. The Salvadoran armed forces press office treated the incident as routine and issued a veiled threat: "Journalists should not risk themselves visiting rebel camps." Surely, the United States and other countries might have been critical of a United States administration that encouraged President Duarte's access to the United States media when President Duarte's own government was discouraging media freedoms to the domestic and foreign press in El Salvador.

More than ever, selective media transmissions, like traditional diplomatic omissions, may lead to what might be called "fractured foreign policy tales" tailored to attract public and media attention. After Secretary of State Haig's accusations of Soviet support for "international terrorism," Soviet Ambassador Anatoly Dobrynin responded with an open letter to Haig, which in turn prompted President Reagan's own open letter to Leonid Brezhnev. More recently, the Defense Department's report *Soviet Military Power* drew a fast rebuttal from the Soviet government, and both accounts appeared together in the United States press. The Soviet Union is learning to use the American media effectively. During the Polish crisis, when the Soviet military maneuvers in Eastern Europe failed to impress the Polish unions as a credible threat, Moscow used both its own and the Western press to warn the Polish government and the Solidarity movement that it would intervene if Poland's economic and political crises were not brought under control.

These Soviet media maneuvers were countered when a member of the Solidarity movement arrived in New York in September 1981 to march in the Labor Day Parade and to open a public-relations office in that city. In its turn, the American Federation of Labor and Congress of Industrial Organizations (AFL-CIO), called its own workers' march in Washington "Solidarity Day." Not to be outdone by either Polish or American workers, the Soviet press added to the media melee by calling Robert Poli, representative of the Professional Air Traffic Controllers Organization (whose members were fired for striking against the government), the "Lech Walesa of the United States."

Potential adversaries are not the only actors who seek to manipulate the American press. Prime Minister Menachem Begin of Israel recently wrote a letter to President Reagan reassuring him that Israel would not attack positions in southern Lebanon unless it was provoked. The timing was interesting. Begin's letter received front-page attention in the United States a few weeks before the scheduled Israeli departure from the Sinai on April 25, 1982, and a few days after extensive United States media reports of violence and Israeli press censorship of the Arab press on the West Bank.

The American public's ability to comprehend American foreign policy on a variety of matters may also be strained by its government providing too much or too little information. The United States government's public relations concerning the issue of the MX missile, for example, must have confused the average television-news viewer or newspaper reader. There have been at least five government plans to deploy that weapon. Noting this, Hedrick Smith of the *New York Times* suggested: "In many ways the controversial MX has become a missile in search of a hole in the ground."[2] In contrast, during the public debate over the AWACS and enhancement sale to Saudi Arabia, what was not said was most significant. The publicity over this sale centered on questions of the threat of the planes to Israeli security, concerns with technology transfer, and the wisdom of selling sophisticated equipment to a moderate Arab ally in light of the fall of the shah in the Iranian revolution. Several other questions, however, were largely ignored by the media, probably much to the Reagan administration's satisfaction. Why was Richard Allen, then national security affairs adviser, chosen to wage the government's public and congressional battles on the AWACS issue? It was certainly a no-win situation for Mr. Allen. The choice did afford the Reagan administration a convenient public persuader (and a possible scapegoat) with domestic and foreign critics should the sale fail. Also largely ignored was the goverment's major reason for supporting the sale—since a large and visible American military presence in Saudi Arabia was not viable for either the American or Saudi governments, a substitute military capability

[2] Ibid., February 23, 1982.

was needed to complement the creation of the Rapid Deployment Force (RDF) in the Middle East.

The Reagan administration has, in fact, been plagued by a number of self-inflicted foreign-policy media wounds since it took office. When a secret estimation of the real defense expenditures was released to the press, Pentagon officials took polygraph tests. More recently, the leak of Secretary of State Haig's private staff notes provoked cries of foul play by administration spokesmen, although the leaks may have been intentional in order to improve the image of the secretary of state.

Dr. Jeane J. Kirkpatrick, United States ambassador to the United Nations, is well acquainted with the consequences of being caught between theory and practice. Before her UN appointment, Dr. Kirkpatrick had enunciated what would become the administration's distinction between "totalitarian" and "authoritarian" regimes. The former (which includes the Soviet Union and regimes of the left in developing countries) were tagged "repressive," while authoritarian regimes of the right were considered tolerable, if not desirable, provided they were strict anti-Communists, like the Galtieri government in Argentina. During the Falkland Islands crisis, Kirkpatrick indicated that there really was no distinction in her mind between a rightist authoritarian ally and a democratic alliance partner. This was the implicit message of her dinner appearance at the Argentine Embassy on the night of April 2, 1982, after President Reagan had been unsuccessful in trying to persuade the Argentine government not to invade the Falkland Islands on that morning.

Foreign-Policy Programming

Governments today talk not so much to each other as at each other through the media. "Theater warfare" and "diplomatic channels" have taken on new meanings in an age when communications satellites have replaced traditional means of communication. The use of the media to preempt governments may often delay normal diplomatic relations or create foreign-policy crises largely unanticipated by governments. Government misuse of the media has also led to a number of dangers that mislead domestic public opinion and foreign publics and governments.

Two current trends in public diplomacy are debasing traditional diplomatic communication. First, the recent propaganda wars between the United States and foreign governments have created a situation in which serious foreign-policy issues have been packaged as a form of entertainment both for domestic and foreign consumption. Especially in the West, the electronic media afford the listener or viewer an escape from reality. When foreign-policy issues are manufactured and events are "created" to project an image of a policy, foreign-policy crises become distorted and less real. This may lead to misperceptions of a foreign-policy question and of the actions that the United States government is taking. Second, a government's use of electronic propaganda may convey to domestic and foreign publics a false image that the government has a policy when, in fact, it does not. In short, public diplomacy has recently been a substitute for policy. Deliberate attempts at informal media penetration may lead the domestic public and foreign publics and governments to conclusions that are false, embarrassing, and difficult to correct.

The use of public diplomacy may be directed at a particular audience to promote support for or antagonism against a particular policy or action of a foreign government. However, in this age of media diplomacy, a government or media personalities cannot determine to whom the foreign-policy programming will be communicated or how it will be perceived or used by foreign governments or foreign media. The result of public diplomacy resembles that of air warfare—the target and nontarget populations become subject to the same battery of fire.

Recently, it seems that governments have been most adept at utilizing the media to promote specific policies aimed at limited audiences. The net result has been, as Marshall McLuhan had predicted, an "electronic battlefield of information and images"[3] that hinders the publics' comprehension of their own or foreign governments' definitions of an issue. Such battles also make it more difficult for the media or governments to correct their own false images or those that have been created through the domestic or foreign press.

During the hostage crisis in Iran, the captors of the United States Embassy evidently discovered, among other documents, a classified CIA report titled "Israel: Foreign Intelligence and Security Services," a forty-seven-page document issued in March 1979. Why the document was at the embassy is still unknown. The study indicates that not only have the Israelis spied on United States citizens but that they have also "blackmailed, bugged, wiretapped and offered bribes to U.S. government employees."[4] The study also contained an appraisal of Israeli intelligence agencies and their top personnel. The Iranian government decided to publish this document as a paperback book in English, and it was on sale in Tehran when William Worthy, an American journalist, purchased several copies of it. Some of the books were checked on a Lufthansa flight to New York, and others were apparently in a separate piece of luggage that accompanied the journalist upon his arrival in the United States. The checked books were confiscated by customs agents in New York who called in FBI agents. However, the other books were undetected and later formed the basis for a series of articles on the subject in the *Washington Post* in February 1982.

As a result of these stories, Israeli and United States government agencies were forced to deal with the issue during a period of already strained relations between the two nations. Clearly, the technological capabilities of the Iranian government (or any government) to mass produce a classified United States document indicate that in the future a government may be able to declassify the information of another government. This capability may create foreign-policy

[3] Marshall McLuhan, *Understanding Media: The Extensions of Man* (New York: The New American Library, 1964), p. 294.

[4] *Washington Post*, February 1, 1982.

issues between governments and/or third parties that would not be issues if the information had not been published. The publication of the CIA study surely damaged the relationship between United States and Israeli intelligence agencies and embarrassed both countries.

Recently, as well, the media were used by two American allies in crises when public diplomacy was an expedient substitute for a lack of policy. In October 1981, when a Soviet submarine was stranded in Swedish waters, the Swedish government was successful in embarrassing the Soviet Union after the crisis had been resolved by providing Swedish military and international media escorts for the Soviet submarine as it left Swedish waters. Similarly, at the time of the invasion of the Falkland Islands, when the British naval capability in the area was minimal, the British Broadcast Corporation (BBC) increased its daily broadcasts to the Falkland Islands by an hour daily. With reports that the Falkland Islanders might accept Argentine sovereignty of the islands, the British government evidently felt it necessary to bolster domestic and Falkland Island public opinions to reinforce their previous public position.

One of the most controversial attempts to manipulate the media for a foreign-policy "coup" was the United States government's television show "Let Poland Be Poland." This media extravaganza necessitated special congressional approval and featured Hollywood stars as well as world political leaders (including President Reagan) who were adept at wearing two hats (political and media). Central casting for the show was engineered by Charles Z. Wick, director of the International Communication Agency (ICA).

While President Reagan has been promoting foreign-policy information production for domestic and foreign consumption, he has been waging a different media battle in the United States, where the goal has been containment of the press. One might look, for example, at the president's proposed new executive order on national security, which will restrict the public's and the media's access to government information now protected by the Freedom of Information Act. Similarly, a directive to cabinet officials not to grant major interviews with the media may further reduce public access to government information. Actually, on foreign-policy matters the media in the United States have given President Reagan relatively soft treatment.

President Reagan's press conference on March 31, 1982, dealt with a major foreign-policy issue, nuclear arms-control negotiations with the Soviet Union. At this press conference the president tried to accomplish a number of goals. First, Reagan hoped to quell criticism that his previous televised press conferences had been during hours when the audience was limited and the president's statements could be edited before the airing of the nightly newscasts. Second, he tried to counter foreign and domestic critics who opposed his program of a nuclear buildup and arms expenditures prior to a negotiated freeze with the Soviet Union on force levels. Third, he sought to counter Soviet proposals for a "constructive dialogue" on the arms issue and proposals for a freeze on the types and levels of nuclear weapons now. Fourth, President Reagan hoped to demonstrate that he could get his facts correct on foreign-policy matters.

Later in the spring, the president continued to wage a media campaign to persuade domestic and foreign publics to support his nuclear-arms proposals. On May 7, 1982, Reagan sent a letter to Leonid Brezhnev in which he suggested a June 1982 meeting with the Soviet leader and outlined the United States position on what Reagan called Strategic Arms Reduction Talks (START). On May 9, 1982, the president publicized these proposals in a speech in Eureka, Illinois. While calling for "substantial" cuts on both sides, including a one-third reduction in land- and submarine-based missiles, the president rejected a freeze at current levels and neglected to inform his audience that his one-third reduction proposal was one-sided because the Soviets maintain a numerical superiority in vulnerable land-based missiles, while the United States retains the lead in SLBMS and strategic bombers. Nor did the president address domestic and foreign critics who have suggested that the administration's plans to build and deploy the MX missile and the B-1 bomber might indicate that the United States was attempting to create a first-strike capability against the Soviet Union.

As the president held out the "carrot" of arms-reduction negotiations with the Soviets, William P. Clark, national security affairs adviser, outlined the "stick": Reagan's new Global Strategy for dealing with the Soviet Union. This strategy is an attempt to convince a reluctant Western Europe to restrict technology transfers and credits to the Soviet Union. While the anti-Soviet rhetoric of the early period of the Reagan administration has cooled down, the ambiguous media signals about the Soviet Union remain. Adding to the public confusion and apprehension about United States policy toward the USSR in May 1982 was President Reagan's eight-page National Security Decision directive that evidently set the priorities for the use of military power in the event of a global war with the Soviet Union. While this document publicly placed the responsibility for strategic planning and priorities in the White House and attempted to resolve the internal administration bickering on strategic issues, the public remained confused because government spokesmen declined to state what, in fact, the government's geographic priorities were.

In an age of media diplomacy, statecraft may have become the hostage—if not the victim—of stagecraft. Only the media have a first-strike capability on both the national and international levels. As the United States moves from an era of advocacy and adversary journalism to one of participatory diplomacy, the traditional methods and practitioners of the media and diplomacy are being undercut and entangled. International politics is a theater in which traditional diplomacy is increasingly an ignored understudy.

In an age of front-page foreign policy, "jet-journalism," and network negotiations, the coalition of technology and foreign policy is one of necessity. Media diplomacy is conditioning the formulation and execution of foreign policy and the public's understanding of international affairs. Yet the marriage of the media and diplomacy may be an unholy alliance. In a democratic society, propaganda for domestic and foreign consumption cannot be manufactured without risking credibility and prestige with both audiences.

Strategic Intelligence

HARRY HOWE RANSOM

Strategic information is fast becoming one of the world's most precious commodities. An accelerating information and communications technology makes this so. Particularly in the case of the superpowers, which exist in a "balance-of-terror" nuclear world, a nation's most dreaded enemy today may be ill-informed leaders. Recognizing the value of information, and the broader implications of information as power, the world's major nations have thus made massive intelligence systems essential elements of governance.

As a consequence, a major feature of post-World War II international relations is an often invisible contest between methods of gathering and communicating intelligence and techniques for protecting intelligence from unwanted disclosure. The technology of modern war and of defense systems has placed an enormous demand on communications technology. The result has been communications networks of great complexity. Decision-makers can be constantly supplied with information from around the globe. They hope that this will enable them to make informed decisions. One consequence, however, is that decision-makers may become prisoners of the information system. Another consequence might be Armageddon.

The United States opted to enlarge its international role after World War II, and its informational requirements expanded rapidly. To be the "policeman of the world," the United States needed to know about events everywhere. Much of this information was available only through elaborate intelligence instruments. Other technological developments made it increasingly necessary to base decisions on military, economic, and political projections into the distant future, adding further to informational needs. As economic interdependence among nations increased, so too did requirements for economic information. All of these and other factors have produced a flood of informational input into government intelligence systems, challenging not only the communications systems but also methods of analysis, interpretation, storage, and information retrieval.

Improvements in communications technology have greatly affected policies, organizations, and programs designed to meet these requirements. Fluctuating hostility between the United States and the Soviet Union has produced a multibillion-dollar secret industry for gathering information (often by espionage), for evaluating and analyzing it, and for producing intelligence in a variety of forms for decision-makers.

This essay will describe some of these major technological developments and how they have had an impact on the gathering and communication of the major categories of intelligence information. Exemplary policy problems will be analyzed, specifically the verification of arms-control agreements and the problem of strategic warning of attack. It will be argued that information technology offers benefits in the pursuit of political objectives, but it also carries risks that can be counterproductive.

Many of the latest advances in detection and communications technology are highly secret. But an open, democratic society does not keep secrets well. This essay, based on the evidence that has become visible, is inevitably incomplete. The focus will be on strategic intelligence, or that body of information that decision-makers need at the highest level of government and that is obtained by clandestine methods.

Human Agents

Before World War II, strategic intelligence was supplied primarily by individual agents, informers, or defectors. In other words, human intelligence was the principal source of secret information, although certainly the evolution of communications technology aided human capabilities. Beginning with World War II, the spy began to be displaced by the analyst aided by the technologist. Since then, the individual spy has to some degree been displaced, or the human agent's work has been profoundly changed, by technology.

Communications have always been a critical step in the intelligence process. Valuable information that does not reach those who need to know it is patently useless. But the communications process exposes the collection agent to great danger. At the same time, the knowledge that particular information is being sought can be of crucial importance to adversaries. For this reason, the security of communications is of major concern, and for purposes of security, technology can be either an asset or a liability. Most intelligence operations are thwarted, or exposed, by the detection of secret communications. As an operational rule, then, the length and frequency of secret messages should be minimal. Indeed, agents under deepest cover are sometimes ordered not to report for years at a time. In their communications, secret agents pursue the dual aims of concealing the transmission of messages, and, even more important, of maintaining secrecy for the messages' content.

The classical way of achieving secrecy is through codes and ciphers. Computer technology has revolutionized the making and breaking of codes, yet the "one-time" pad (a unique code used once and then destroyed) maintains its inviolable secrecy. Many other classical methods of espionage remain, such as personal contacts between control officers and agents and other contacts through "live drops," "dead drops," "cut outs," and "safe houses." However, modern techniques of observation tend to increase the vulnerability of traditional methods.

Technology has vastly expanded the capabilities for human observation. Modern devices include tiny radio-controlled cameras that can photograph in the dark, radio transmitters and tape recorders the size of a deck of cards, devices for tapping a room without wires, and ultrasound techniques for "reading" window panes from a distance. Such developments engender countermeasures by the opposition.

Mechanical Information Gathering

At a higher operational level, there are technological dynamics also in the fields of electronic intelligence, radar-detection instruments, nuclear-test and missile detection, high-altitude photography, and space satellites for intelligence use. How do these affect information gathering and communications? Nearly all military activities, both in peacetime and in war, depend heavily on communications.[1] Indeed, the application of such basic strategies as deterrence, arms control, and collective security are inconceivable without intelligence and communications.

Access to the communications of one's adversaries is often the key to national security. It is hard to conceive today of an adversary planning an attack without elaborate internal communications in advance. Likewise, forewarning of such an attack neutralizes its effects; and, in fact, if an aggressor knows its adversary to be forewarned, it will probably be deterred from attacking.

Even when the content of foreign messages cannot be read or deciphered, an increasing volume of communications is often an indicator of impending action. Crucially important are communications between airborne military aircraft and ground control centers or communications among naval vessels. In wartime, certainly, and often in military exercises or maneuvers, communications security is lax.

Testing sites for missiles and rockets inevitably generate signals, messages, and other emissions that can produce tell-tale signs of great intelligence value. Scientists are inevitably in constant communication with the various research and instrument stations and headquarters, as well as with down-range testing locations. Such signals cannot be easily concealed, although security consciousness is drilled into operating teams. Security was often sought by transmitting signals at such low frequencies and with such low power that they could not be detected at great distances. Yet technology tends to catch up with such defenses and with the ability to detect weak signals. In addition, the use of

[1] Much of the technological information here is derived from Herbert Scoville, Jr., "The Technology of Surveillance," *Society* 12 (March/April 1975):58–63.

computers to single out important data has made it easier for adversaries to break message- and data-transmission security.

Espionage can become provocative and heighten conflict among nations, as shown by the case of the *U.S.S. Pueblo,* the electronic spy ship that North Korea captured in January 1968. For some types of important communications, interception from great distances is infeasible. Thus the widespread practice of using the territory of other nations for espionage purposes sometimes leads to political complications. Another problem arises when aircraft fly close to hostile borders and occasionally "lose their way," thus risking an international crisis. In some cases, too, both the United States and the Soviet Union try to operate covert espionage bases in the same third country. Sometimes a nation's intelligence can be frustrated by unforeseen events. For example, when the Iranian revolution occurred in late 1978, the United States lost important bases in northern Iran that were monitoring Soviet strategic capabilities.

A separate kind of intelligence collection utilizes the interception of electromagnetic waves from radar transmitters. In intelligence parlance this category of activity is labeled ELINT (electronic intelligence), a term once highly classified. During World War II, radar was developed for tracking hostile aircraft and missiles, and some believe that radar saved Great Britain in that war. But radar is also used for guiding antiaircraft defensive missiles, as well as for offensive missiles. Naval operations depend heavily on radar. Understandably, ELINT became a high-priority development in military intelligence agencies after World War II. Radar is useful in intelligence gathering, in part because radar beams must be constantly projected. For example, if a nation depends on radar for air defense, the system must be constantly in operation. Furthermore, training exercises must be routinely under way, all of which creates many opportunities for adversary intelligence forces to "read" the radar and make deductions. On the development frontiers, "silent radar" is a current prospect. On the other hand, the use of radar broadcasts military positions to opponents, making them vulnerable to, say, radar-seeking missiles.

Problems exist, however, with regard to radar as a rich intelligence resource. Most significant ELINT data come from reading the response of radar networks to provocative air activity. Accordingly, many international incidents have been caused by provocative acts that stimulated radar-detection activity. For example, a United States RB-47 reconnaissance aircraft was shot down while flying along the Arctic coast of the Soviet Union in 1960 and the crew was detained. The crew later admitted they were knowingly flying over Soviet territory. An incident in the Gulf of Tonkin in 1964 enabled President Lyndon Johnson to gain the authority from Congress to escalate the Vietnam war. It now is clear that the incident was precipitated by an espionage mission in which the United States was not blameless.

More recently developed than ELINT has been another form of electronic intelligence—radars for intelligence, commonly called RADINT. Using RADINT, the United States has been able to monitor launchings of Soviet long-range missile test flights. RADINT involves transmitting radio signals and is thus easily detectable. As a result, it is difficult to apply this intelligence instrument secretly. In order to observe Soviet long-range missile testing, high-powered radar units were established operating within the line-of-sight of the missile trajectory. This technique has important foreign-policy implications, because it often involves bases in other countries.

Concern with missiles, rockets, and related weapons systems, however, takes second place to the perceived information needs for the detection of nuclear tests. Several complex methods have evolved to detect such tests. Principal among these are acoustical and seismic receivers capable of detecting distant atomic tests and even of ascertaining the location, nature, and power of the weapon or explosive. Additional information can be deduced by analyzing electromagnetic waves sent out at the moment of explosion, at least for ground testing. For tests in the atmosphere, different instruments are used for collecting the debris in the air that allow precise identification of the type of explosion, its location, and other data. This capability was well developed by the early 1960s. However, since 1963, nuclear tests, other than those conducted by France and China, have been held underground. This practice thwarts detection efforts, at least as far as the collection of radioactive debris is concerned. The existence of nuclear test detection instruments has been far less provocative than other intelligence methods, since they can generally be deployed at a great distance. They do not require dangerous flights over hostile nations and can be operated either from the home base or from locations in friendly nations.

High-altitude Photography

All of the older methods of intelligence gathering are useful but have more recently been upstaged by photoreconnaissance, or IMINT, for image intelligence. IMINT has been used since World War I, but technological advances since 1960 have revolutionized it. It has become virtually impossible for any nation to hide its military or industrial activities from the United States. Secret agents have been put out of work by these developments, because high-altitude photography is now the most efficient way to obtain accurate information about troop deployments, missile sites, and military construction. Vast areas can be efficiently photographed. Cloud cover is sometimes an obstacle, but clouds are periodic in most areas of the world. Few intelligence targets are immune now from spies in the sky.

In 1960, this new capability was dramatically exposed to the public when an American U-2 reconnaissance aircraft was shot down well inside the Soviet Union and its pilot captured. U-2 flights produced miles of sharp, clear, and detailed photographs, utilizing specially developed cameras. These cameras could record 500 square miles of territory on a single frame. Until Soviet antiaircraft rockets were developed that rendered these planes obsolete for this purpose, vast areas of Soviet and Eastern European territory were filmed.

However, the U-2 was but the first of many aircraft developed for high-altitude photography. Although U-2s remain in use, they have been followed by the SR-71, known as the "Black Bird," which is capable of flying higher and faster than the U-2. More recently, the Lockheed A-11 made the SR-71 obsolete, since it is faster and more versatile for some missions.

A new era for photoreconnaissance began in 1957, when the Soviet Union orbited the first sputnik. Not only was this a profound technological revolution, but it was also the precedent for space transit of national territories at will. A satellite controlled from the Soviet Union had traversed the space over the United States and many other countries without notification to or consent from any of the nations involved. The United States filed no official complaint. When the United States launched its satellite the following year, no protest was lodged by the Soviet Union. Thus, "open skies" became a reality of international politics.

The earliest space satellites had no capability for intelligence photography. But throughout the 1960s the United States and the Soviet Union worked vigorously to develop, improve, and exploit the intelligence potential of orbiting satellites. Since the early 1960s, presidents and their national security advisers have routinely been given intelligence estimates based on extensive space intelligence. Defense officials are usually able to report quickly to the president new developments in Soviet intercontinental missiles and other military construction programs. Even so, officials on both sides of the Iron Curtain are reluctant publicly to acknowledge photoreconnaissance.

Does photography from platforms in space constitute espionage? Espionage is normally defined as the search for information that a state is trying to keep secret—it is illegal under international law. Does space reconnaissance constitute "peaceful" activity? If so, it would be in keeping with the universal principle of free access to space for peaceful purposes. The United States has been a strong advocate in the United Nations of limiting the use of outer space to nonmilitary purposes. At the same time, the United States has argued that the use of outer space for intelligence purposes is nonmilitary and consistent with the free-use principle. In the early 1960s, the Soviet Union tried to get the UN to define intelligence use of space as aggressive. As the Soviet Union's space technology improved, this posture was dropped. The pragmatic principle has seemed to be that espionage is defined as what a nation has the effective means to prevent. States do worry, nonetheless, about future capabilities of destroying space satellites. Meanwhile, the United States and the Soviet Union have ratified several treaties that concern outer space. Both have pledged not to use space for military experimentation or for other military purposes. In these treaties, photography has been neither banned nor approved; but when the Anti-Ballistic Missile Treaty and Salt I treaties were signed, the United States and the Soviet Union agreed that "national technical means" (a euphemism for IMINT) would be used for verification and more specifically pledged not to interfere with each other's information-collection methods. Patently, intelligence gathering from outer space has gained international legitimacy.

The first American spy satellite, SAMOS (satellite and missile observation system) was sent into orbit in 1961. Since then a number of more advanced systems have been developed, among them the fifty-foot-long, ten-ton LASP (low altitude surveillance platform). SAMOS contained an assortment of electronic, film, and infrared cameras. The LASP relays electronic and communications intelligence to various earthbound listening posts. In 1971, a larger and more advanced satellite was launched, a variation on the SAMOS called "Big Bird." It measures fifty feet in length, has a ten-foot diameter, and weighs over eleven tons. Big Bird's cameras, from heights exceeding 100 miles, are capable of clearly photographing objects of one square foot. Exposed film can be ejected in capsules by parachute to be collected by conventional aircraft. The satellite can transmit pictures by radio; its detection beams can penetrate ice and snow and in some cases detect submerged submarines; and through sensing devices it can indicate whether factories below are working or not.

The Soviet Union has developed its own versions of intelligence satellites, though they are believed to be somewhat less sophisticated than Big Bird. Principal among these for years has been the COSMOS. These satellites have been in orbit in significant numbers over Western countries and China since the 1960s. By ground signals, orbits can be changed in flight to direct satellites to overfly particular ground objectives.

An illustration of how "high technology spycraft" is applied in foreign- and defense-policy decisions is the Reagan administration's reaction to the recent military buildup in Nicaragua sponsored by Cuba and the Soviet Union. The administration was deeply concerned about Nicaragua's use of this military power to aid leftist rebels fighting the government of El Salvador. The administration's plans and program for containing left-wing influences in the region were being resisted by substantial segments of Congress and public opinion. To counter this resistance the administration publicized "overwhelming and irrefutable evidence" that the insurgency in El Salvador was directed from Nicaragua by Cuban and Soviet advisers.

To obtain this evidence from Nicaragua, the United States government called on an array of high-technology intelligence. Use was made of U-2 and SR-71 planes, equipped with high-resolution cameras to spot individual soldiers or tank tracks. At higher altitudes, reconnaissance satellites with heat-sensitive infrared cameras sought out camouflaged tanks or trucks moving at night. "Side-looking" radar was used to peer through clouds to detect other ground activity. Expert imagery interpreters then approximated the military strength of Nicaragua.

Additionally, electronic intelligence was collected by United States naval destroyers off the Nicaraguan Pacific coast. They tracked fishing vessels that might have been plying arms from Nicaragua to guerrillas in El Salvador and also eavesdropped on clandestine radio transmitters that allegedly served as Sandinista command posts for Salvadoran rebels. In addition, CIA agents on the ground engaged in a more traditional spycraft, gathering information from local informers. Technology would appear to have strengthened the hand of an administration trying to persuade Congress and the public to support its foreign policy. But technology does not always solve the problem of interpreting the evidence properly or applying it effectively to make decisions. Herbert Scoville has written: "At last we have available a technological intelligence collection tool which is recognized as legal and, therefore, nonprovocative. Since such reconnaissance is capable of satisfying a wide variety of information needs, it should reduce the justification for intelligence collection by more provocative methods."[2]

The argument can be made that technology has improved the ability of nations to collect intelligence by less risky and provocative methods than in the past. It has also been argued that agents on the ground, risking their own lives and sometimes creating suspicion within nations, have become less necessary. But this is not always the case, for technology over the past several decades has prompted aircraft and naval missions—such as the U-2 and the *Pueblo*—that have resulted in incidents heightening international tensions. Mutual acceptance of spying from space could quickly evaporate if one side made a technological breakthrough.

Although great advances have been made in intelligence capabilities, particularly by combining multispectral sensors, microelectronics, and rapid, high-volume communication, it can be assumed that the science of detection and reconnaissance is still in its infancy. High on the research agenda is the ability to see into the ocean, so that submarine forces can be more reliably detected and plotted. Moreover, the capacity to transmit large quantities of data rapidly and accurately to the ground from outer space still needs to be perfected. And the need is constant and unending to develop countermeasures to thwart adversaries in their intelligence missions.

Verification and Technology

The Strategic Arms Limitation Treaty (SALT II) was signed by Jimmy Carter and Leonid Brezhnev in Vienna in June 1979. Its purposes were to reduce United States and Soviet missile launchers from 2,400 to 2,250, place strict ceilings on multiple-warhead missiles, limit the number of warheads per missile, and restrict each side to the deployment of only one "new-type" of intercontinental missile. Political support for this treaty in the United States evaporated prior to debate on it in the Senate. Contributing to the collapse of this important treaty was the behavior of the Soviet Union. After the Soviets invaded Afghanistan, President Carter withdrew the treaty from Senate consideration in the face of powerful opponents who felt that the Soviet Union would gain more from it than the United States. Many of the treaty's opponents were concerned about verification. Even with all of the advances in intelligence technology, could the United States be sure that the Soviet Union would not cheat?

[2] Ibid., p. 63.

The pivotal element in any major arms-control agreement is the degree of confidence held by each side that the other will abide by the agreement. Indeed, today's spiralling arms race that could destroy modern civilization is the product of mutual distrust. Small wonder, then, that verification has been a major issue. Some treaty opponents hypothesized that the Soviet Union might cheat on the SALT II strategic weapons ceilings in various ways: by secretly deploying new types of weapons; by exceeding the allowable number of weapons to be deployed; or by converting weapons from tactical to strategic uses. Those who favored SALT II ratification and some components of the intelligence community argued that such treaty violations could be detected by intelligence methods.

Introducing a new strategic weapons system involves at least five stages spread over many years: research, development, testing, production, and deployment. In order to conceal this process, the Soviet Union would have to hide all five stages. The likelihood that such activity could be concealed from United States intelligence seems small. Line-of-sight radars, over-the-horizon radars that can penetrate deep within the Soviet Union, early-warning space satellites, infrared sensors, photographic reconnaissance, and other secret means would likely detect efforts to cheat. Granted, some methods of violating the treaty are more difficult to monitor than others, but the risk seems small and the Soviet gain from such cheating even smaller.

All of this led President Carter to declare on April 25, 1979: "We are confident that no significant violation of the treaty could take place without the United States detecting it."[3] Speaking to the American Newspaper Publishers Association, Carter explained that his confidence was based on the size and nature of activities to be monitored and "the many effective and sophisticated intelligence collection systems which we in America possess." He noted that nuclear submarines take several years to construct and assemble; missile silos are enormous and their supporting structures are clearly visible; intercontinental bombers are manufactured at few plants and require large runways. The fact that American reconnaissance satellites photograph the entire Soviet Union on a regular basis with ever more sophisticated cameras made Carter confident that little activity could go undetected. For many years, the president said, "we have monitored Soviet strategic forces and Soviet compliance with the SALT agreements with a high degree of confidence. The overall capability remains. It was certainly not lost with our observation stations in Iran, which was only one of many intelligence sources that we use to follow Soviet strategic activities."

If, for example, the Russians attempted to deploy additional intercontinental missiles under camouflage or at night, United States orbiting satellites equipped with multispectral sensors could penetrate the camouflage. They could also observe activity at night. Infrared sensors are reliable for detecting underground missile silos. Small-scale violations might go undetected, but intelligence profes-

[3] U.S., Department of State, *Salt II: The Path of Security and Peace*, Current Policy Paper No. 66, April 1979, p. 3.

sionals have confidence that significant efforts to cheat would be detected. Whenever suspicions are aroused by satellites routinely in synchronous orbit over the Soviet Union, "close-look" cameras can be ordered to rephotograph the area to provide more refined detail. Doubtless, public knowledge and confidence lag considerably behind these capabilities, which are protected by heavy secrecy.

Gradations of confidence exist with regard to verification. At the highest level of confidence is the ability to detect violations that might seriously upset the strategic balance. Verification capabilities of minor violations are somewhat shaky, but SALT II proponents consider such small-scale cheating to be insignificant. Finally, a few areas involve such weapons as cruise missiles, where verification problems may be substantial. These areas will have to be dealt with in future arms-control negotiations, but it can be assumed that intelligence techniques will continue to improve. Doubtless the battle between detection measures and countermeasures will continue.

Undeniably, confidence in verification is essential if future arms-limitation or reduction agreements are to gain the support needed for Senate ratification. The American constitutional system permits senators representing a small minority of the people to block ratification of any treaty. Thus, a convincing ability to verify Soviet compliance with any arms treaty is a prerequisite to Senate approval. In the words of Les Aspin, one of the best-informed congressmen on the subject, "the much-touted problems of verification are more imaginary than real. The multiple and duplicative methods of detection at the disposal of the U.S. are sufficient to reveal any cheating on a scale adequate to threaten this country militarily. . . . It is in the future that verification problems might become critical."[4] It is perhaps inevitable that the technology of concealment will always have to be balanced against the technologies for intelligence detection and communication.

Early Warning Systems

Never far from the president's side, in the White House or when traveling, is the field-grade officer who carries a thick black leather briefcase. Inside this case, which has been nicknamed the "football," are sealed authenticator envelopes, containing codes called "release messages." Once transmitted by the president through the White House Communications Agency to the Pentagon, these coded messages constitute authority to fire some combination of the nation's thousands of strategic nuclear warheads against preselected targets. Not only does this system place an enormous round-the-clock burden on the president, but it also makes him the potential prisoner of the highly complex intelligence and communications apparatus.

[4] "The Verification of the SALT II Agreement," *Scientific American* 240 (February 1979): 45.

On November 10, 1979, the U.S. Department of Defense announced that on the previous morning a false alert triggered some of the nation's defenses against a missile attack that turned out to be nonexistent. The alert lasted six minutes; had it lasted just one additional minute, the president and the secretary of defense would have received notice of a possible incoming attack on the United States. An intercontinental missile can reach the United States from the Soviet Union in less than twenty minutes. A president has little time to decide whether to release the codes.

After six minutes, it was discovered that a mechanical error had sent war-game information into the sensing system providing early warning of nuclear attack. If confirmed, this warning would have indicated to military officers that the United States was under attack from missiles, presumably launched by a Soviet submarine, probably located in the northern Pacific. According to the Pentagon, ten jet interceptors from the United States and Canada were scrambled aloft, and missile bases throughout the country went automatically on a low-level alert. Even so, the Pentagon stated that the alert had been viewed skeptically from the outset.

Pentagon officials said there had been a number of false alarms over the years, resulting from computer failures, natural phenomena (perhaps Canadian geese), and test firings. These incidents were more frequent when the system was new, in the late 1950s and the early 1960s.

In 1980, the press noted a Senate committee report disclosing that the North American Air Defense Command (NORAD) experienced 147 false alarms during an eighteen-month period in 1979–80. The alerts were sufficiently serious to require an evaluation of whether they represented a potential attack. Four additional alarms, including two that had not been previously disclosed, were judged to be even more serious and had stimulated orders to B-52 bomber crews and intercontinental ballistic missile units to move to a higher alert status. One alarm was sounded when a Soviet submarine near the Kurile Islands, north of Japan, fired four missiles in a training exercise. Another occurred when a radar station in the United States Northwest detected a rocket body that was disintegrating and falling from space. Outer space is said to abound in such junk.

Perhaps most alarming is the report that a defective silicon chip in a communications device generated false signals of an attack. This false alarm caused considerable controversy at the time. Senator Mark Hatfield, for example, expressed his fear that a false alarm could trigger an accidental nuclear war. The Pentagon's position at the time, as later noted in the Senate report, was that the United States in no way had ever been close to a nuclear war as a result of these false readings and malfunctions.

Nonetheless, the senators urged in their report that the warning system be more tightly organized and controlled. Otherwise, they saw dangers of delays and technical obsolescence. Most shocking of all, perhaps, was the senators' report that no formal study of this problem had been undertaken.

What a study would likely show is that human beings, in search of national security, will increasingly put their fate in the hands of the machines of communication, detection, and computation that technology provides. If nuclear weapons are not to be abolished, their only rational use is for deterrence. What will guarantee deterrence is ultimately uncalculable, but the trend is toward automatic systems. The changes in space, time, and power relationships through changes in technology meant that future decision-makers could become the prisoners of information technology. One faulty silicon chip may cause World War III. The informational assumptions on which many past United States wars have been fought now seem to have been faulty, if not erroneous. Examples are the War of 1812, the war with Spain over Cuba in 1898, and, in a generalized sense, the Vietnam war. It may be that some wars resulted from too little information that was poorly communicated. Perhaps a future war will result from too much (and possibly false) information that is too rapidly communicated and misinterpreted.

One solution is to make massive secret intelligence operations unnecessary by the international sharing of increasing amounts of information. A nation might prefer to keep such information secret. But when it becomes apparent that technology makes this unfeasible, making such information freely available might be more sensible than spending vast resources on counterintelligence. Undeniably, knowledge is power. In a time of distrust that is dominated by a balance-of-power ethic, secret intelligence is likely to remain a major instrument of statesmen pursuing power. Like armaments, perhaps intelligence activity could be scaled down substantially. Yet competition in intelligence technology seems to have an amoebic quality. One cannot be sanguine in predicting that its momentum can be easily slowed. National security, strategic intelligence, arms reduction agreements, and technology are intertwined. Here again, technology often creates part of the problem. But international sharing of the product of technology could also be part of the solution.

Terrorism and Urban Violence

RICHARD CLUTTERBUCK

Internal violence has become the predominant form of conflict in modern society, whether it is domestically or internationally inspired or exploited. It is more important for politicians, policemen, and soldiers to understand the techniques of the propaganda war than those of the shooting war. This development has placed increasing power in the hands of editors, producers, and journalists—supplementing their already enormous economic and commercial power. They have become the new barons of the twentieth century and, like other barons before them—feudal, industrial, or financial—they may find that peoples of liberal societies will demand democratic processes to restrain them if they exercise their power irresponsibly.

The communications revolution has made it possible for news instantly to reach a vast and growing audience all over the world. Violence can dominate the news, and the mass media can magnify a violent incident out of proportion to its scale or true significance. Publicity of street violence, riots, and terrorism also encourages imitation—the "copycat phenomenon." The enormous cumulative psychological and emotional effects of all this may force political leaders to pursue courses of action (whether soft or hard line) that all other considerations would suggest are unwise.

Outside the field of the mass media, the communications revolution has opened up a new range of vulnerable targets for terrorists, especially in the fields of telecommunications and computer systems. On the other hand, technological change has also presented governments and business organizations with new opportunities for countering the purveyors of violence, in the fields of access control, surveillance, and intelligence.

The communications revolution, far from over, is continuing at an ever-increasing pace. Neither terrorists nor antiterrorists have yet caught up with the opportunities offered even by existing technology. These opportunities present dangerous threats to liberal societies, not only of coercion by violence but also of invasion of privacy or curtailment of the healthy influence of a free investigative press. It is incumbent on politicians, officials, and scientists to look ahead shrewdly to the new technological developments, which can usually be foreseen several years before they materialize in practical form, if liberal democracy is to survive the threat from those who are intent on destroying it and from officials abusing their power in misguided attempts to preserve it.

The Media and Political Violence

The biggest single motivation for terrorism and urban violence is to gain publicity by attracting the attention of the mass media. Other motivations include political blackmail to obtain the release of prisoners, the extortion of ransom, and the destabilization of the established government and society. Destabilization may be achieved by provoking overreaction by the government, the police, and the army. Terrorists can thereby alienate a government's popular support by demoralizing it so that it loses both the will and the ability to enforce the law. Consequently, public confidence in the government can be destroyed so that people turn in desperation to some alternative revolutionary, reactionary, or military organization that, however distasteful, offers the hope of restoring order. The resulting regime will be authoritarian or, more probably, totalitarian, like Lenin's in Russia in 1917, or the military regimes that have followed periods of political violence in Latin America.

In recent years, undoubtedly, the immediate aim of political violence has most often been publicity, which usually contributes in any case to the other aims. For their part, the mass media in a free society are motivated by the need to attract an audience, largely because the media stand or fall by selling advertising, though purely professional motivations (as in a noncommercial organization like the BBC) may be just as strong. The journalists who produce successful programs or articles will be given greater and greater professional opportunities. Professional advancement may not always be a healthy motivation but it is part of the price of a free press.

For attracting an audience, nothing can compare with exploiting tension, public anxiety, and violence. So the terrorist (or the rioter) and the media each gives the other what it wants in an unholy and (for the media) a sometimes unwilling alliance. Such an alliance existed for more than a century, since the spread of education and the development of the telegraph first made the popular press a viable institution. Thereafter, rapid technological development of communications—radio, television, the zoom lens, the electronic news-gathering (ENG) camera, which could transmit instant live pictures relayed to the world by satellite—has made the alliance all the more close and, in material terms, rewarding.

To what extent do the media thereby encourage violence and terrorism, unavoidably, irresponsibly, or even deliberately? The journalists face a clash between their duty to report the news and their responsibility as citizens not to exacerbate the violence or to encourage more of it. Their actions become irresponsible if their reports will incite or inflame violence or will put lives at risk.

The deliberate incitement of violence by a journalist in order to create sensational news is criminal, though it is also rare. There was one such case in Northern Ireland in May 1981, when a foreign camera crew, disappointed at the lack of action to film, urged some young Irish Republican Army (IRA) sympathizers to throw missiles at passing vehicles. When they did, a brick hit the windshield of a van that thereupon crashed, killing both the driver and his small child.

Such journalists, if caught, could be convicted of manslaughter, if not murder; but it is not so easy to restrain journalists who are merely reckless or irresponsible. Could the profession enforce its own ethical code, as do doctors and lawyers, by prohibiting those who break the code from practicing their profession? Could editors be compelled to enforce it? If so, how? Should gross irresponsibility itself become a criminal offense, like reckless driving? And how can any of these things be done without inhibiting the vital role of a free investigative press in controlling corruption or the abuse of power?

The mass media have given deliberate violence a vastly increased influence on national and international affairs and have effected a profound change in the balance of forces in democratic society. Is it necessary to adapt traditional institutions, laws, or practices to accommodate the change? And will the need for such adaptions become greater as the communications revolution further magnifies the power of violence or of the threat of violence? If democracy is to survive, these questions must be faced by media people themselves and also by politicians and the voters who elect them.

Political Demonstrations and Riots

Freedom of assembly is as fundamental as freedom of speech and freedom of the press, yet all three can be abused. The right to march, to demonstrate the strength of popular feeling and the extent of popular support for a point of view, has an honorable record. Numbers alone can create news—50,000 people demonstrating against the United States's involvement in Vietnam or 250,000 people demonstrating for nuclear disarmament did have an effect, the more so when they were nonviolent. Demonstrations by smaller groups, however, are less likely to get significant media coverage unless they use or threaten violence. In fact, they are unlikely to attract the cameras at all unless they arouse at least an expectation of violence. Once they see that the cameras are there, the demonstrators are tempted to act in such a way as to attract their attention so that their demonstration will get a place in the main television news bulletins or a picture on the front page of the newspapers. A dangerous cycle of cause and effect may thus be created: a demonstration achieves nothing if it is not reported. If only violence will get it reported, then demonstrators will sooner or later use violence. If the media, in order to discourage it, play down the violence, demonstrators will tend to escalate the scale of the violence until it becomes dramatic enough to force its way into the news.

The same cycle also applies to riots that are a manifestation of deep-rooted dissatisfaction, of conflicts between rival communities, or of hatred by resentful sectors of society for the police. Whether spontaneous or politically organized, the rioters are trying to make a point, and afterwards they will eagerly watch on the television or buy the newspapers to see whether they have made them. If they have not, they may be more violent the next night to make sure that they do.

Radio has provided a dimension to rioting that has recently made it even more important than television. The transistor radio is ubiquitous, on the street as well as in the home. Live commentary on a riot may attract others to the scene of the action within a few minutes. If the riot is a fight against a rival community or against the police, sympathizers may be drawn from their homes to join in. For this reason, many broadcasting organizations have a rule that such commentaries will not be broadcast until after, say, thirty minutes. Other organizations, however, are less responsible, and it must be asked whether legislative action is needed and whether the price of such action in inhibiting reporting would be justified.

The advent of the ENG camera has brought television, potentially at least, into that same syndrome. Instant live reporting of riots and demonstrations is now fully practicable, though an unlikely combination of restrictive action by trade unions (to save the jobs of technicians) and a responsible editorial awarenes of the dangers have restrained its development. Inevitably, however, these restraints will be overcome: first by normal competition among broadcasters, which will become intensified with the multiplication of channels by cable television; then further by the ability of international television organizations to record news live by ENG camera and then to relay it and transmit it by satellite to anyone in the world who has a receiver linked directly or by cable to that transmission. It is thus already technically feasible for foreign broadcasters to aggravate riots by instant live broadcasts, by either radio or television, to the people of the country in which the riots are occurring. This power may present new problems if it is used irresponsibly or with mischievous or malevolent intent.

The more effective such aggravation becomes, whether by domestic or foreign broadcasters, governments will all the more be tempted to increase restrictions on journalists and on the frequencies or channels that domestic sets can receive, and demonstrators and rioters will all the more be tempted to create dramatic situations for the benefit of the cameras. This aggravation will further encourage those who wish to exacerbate either racial or industrial conflict to bring about political change beyond that desired by the people as expressed by democratic processes. Destabilization is largely a psychological process—the collapse of confidence leading to a desire for a restoration of tranquility at any price, that is, to give way to the wishes of a minority or to turn in desperation to an authoritarian alternative. The media can be manipulated for this purpose by any skilled operator who understands the "unholy alliance" between the rioter and the media, and the desire of competing journalists for exciting news.

Racial unrest or conflict between disgruntled communities and the police are particularly easy to arouse, because the seeds of these conflicts between rival communities are always there, and because the police have the task of controlling outbursts of violence, which will inevitably be resented by one or both of the rivals, who will feel, rightly or wrongly, that the police are biased against them.

Racial conflict is particularly likely in times of economic recession, when unemployment is high. There is not only resentment of perceived job discrimination or of the presence of the rival community "taking" the available jobs, but there are also a lot of unemployed young people with time on their hands and not enough money to pay for any reasonable means of enjoying that time. The result is predictable—and exploitable. By creating newsworthy events that will arouse the anger of the rival community, those with evil intent can use the media to exacerbate and exploit the inherent conflicts. Thereafter the media themselves maintain the momentum of discontent by the copycat phenomenon.

The 1981 summer riots in England—the most widespread for two centuries—provide a classic example of the copycat process. The flood of black immigrants into Britain since the late 1950s had created a tense situation in most of the industrial cities in England, especially in the crumbling "poverty rings" around the inner cities where blacks tended to concentrate. High unemployment hit young blacks particularly hard and many turned to violent street crime. This alarmed white residents and led to such heavy policing that the blacks felt that the police were discriminating against them. From 1977 to 1980 this tense situation was exploited by both the far right and the far left, the former organizing provocative marches of whites through high immigrant areas and the latter instigating disgruntled young blacks to attack them. This exploitation intensified the local hostility between blacks and whites, which was what the far right wanted. Moreover, since the marches, no matter how objectionable, were a legal and orderly demonstration of freedom of assembly, the police were obliged to protect them. This protection further enraged the young blacks who felt that, as in the matter of crime, the police were discriminating against them. By 1981 an explosive mixture had been created in many cities that needed only a spark to set it off.

Two such sparks began the conflagration in 1981. The first was in the Brixton district of London, where routine police action against street crime led to an explosion of rioting in which petrol bombs were used in England for the first time and over 400 policemen were injured in two nights of rioting, burning, and looting. The second spark was remarkably similar—in the Toxteth division of Liverpool in July 1981. Petrol bombs were again used, and the police used CS (tear gas), another first for England. Both petrol bombs and CS gas had been in evidence in Northern Ireland since 1969, but they were used with particular intensity during the hunger-strike riots in Belfast and Londonderry early in 1981. One experienced commentator ascribed this use of petrol bombs—and many other aspects of the riots—to the examples seen regularly on television reports from Northern Ireland. He cited a number of American research projects that have documented this copycat response to incidents seen on television. One study found that the ten to thirteen age group was particularly susceptible to television manipulation.[1] This age group was highly active in the 1981 riots.

The most impressive manifestation of the copycat phenomenon, however, occurred immediately after the Toxteth riots. During the subsequent five nights (July 7–12), there were no less than thirty-eight separate riots in English cities, twenty-one of them in a single night (July 10) in twelve different London boroughs and nine provincial cities. No evidence whatever was found of planned or coordinated action. The pattern of the riots, however, was remarkably similar, particularly in the use of petrol bombs and the widespread looting—similar to what had been seen on television screens during the Toxteth riots and every night thereafter in other cities. No English city with a population of more than 300,000 escaped these riots. Though some of the thirty-eight riots were little more than the kind of brawls that often occur in inner cities on Friday and Saturday nights, their scale and extent as a whole, and their similarities, can have no possible explanation other than the copycat phenomenon.

In this respect, much of the television reporting must certainly be described as irresponsible. Some news items seemed like dramatic television commercials, starting with shots of listless young blacks on a dark street corner, then a crash, breaking glass, rising excitement, running feet, the blinding flash of a petrol bomb, a policeman rolling about with his clothes spurting orange flames, then a boot going through a shop window, and cheers as the crowd surged forward, with eager hands reaching in and holding a looted tape recorder triumphantly before the camera—the "pack shot." For an unemployed black teenager, bored, frustrated, and resentful of the police, the temptation to go out with a few friends to join in the excitement—and the looting—was intense.

Terrorism

Both the sophisticated terrorist and the counterterrorist will realize that the war that matters is the propaganda war. The shooting war must support that propaganda war but must never supersede it. The most powerful weapon in the terrorist war is the television camera, which is available to either side. The most crucial of the modern martial arts is learning how to use it.

In the propaganda war, terrorists have one enormous advantage: except in rare cases (such as police raids acting on information), they initiate the violence and choose its time and place. They call violence "the propaganda of the deed" and, like the clever politician timing the propaganda of the word, they time their deeds to dominate the news, early enough for the evening news bulletins but, above all, late enough to ensure that the government press office cannot get in its own account of the incident.

The government is thus at a particular disadvantage. When, for example, the IRA in Northern Ireland ambushes an army patrol and one of its own men is shot, it arranges to have "bystanders" ready with accounts that indicate that the victim was an innocent unarmed civilian "murdered" by the soldiers. If these

[1] Eric Moonman, *Copycat Hooligans* (London: Centre for Contemporary Studies, 1981), p. 3.

stories are later proved false, there is no reflection on the IRA, with which the "bystanders" had no official connection. The army or police press office, however, must check its stories carefully because, if any detail in them has to be corrected, their whole credibility will be questioned. As a result, the official account is seldom released until the IRA story has already had its impact. As Maurice Tugwell has recorded: "Only after many months in Northern Ireland did one experienced reporter [Tony Gerahty of the *Sunday Times*] conclude: 'I speak as someone of Irish extraction on both sides, yet even I am surprised on occasions at the instant and expert mendacity to which journalists, and no doubt other interested parties such as the police and security forces, are treated in episodes of this sort.' "[2]

If the official news agencies' disadvantage is overcome, it is usually only by good luck. The BBC's Martin Bell (now BBC correspondent in Washington) described how, after an IRA vehicle fleeing from an army patrol killed three young children, he found an eight-year-old boy who had seen it happen: "I put him on camera and he gave me a coherent account of what had happened. Believable as it only can be coming from the 'mouths of babes and sucklings'—no one could have told him what to say—he just said it, and this I subsequently learned caused an awful lot of offence to the IRA because it precluded them from making their own version . . . one then had to ask oneself 'is this fellow going to be victimised?' and I figured that even the IRA wouldn't have it in for an eight-year-old kid."[3]

Another problem that disadvantages government sources is that, as soon as someone is arrested or a judicial inquiry is instituted, the case becomes *sub judice*, sometimes immediately after an incident. Thus, while it is possible for the terrorists' propaganda organization to continue to circulate a totally false account of the incident, official sources are banned from circulating their account until the case is disposed of, which may be many months later.

Terrorists will always seek interviews on television if they can avoid being identified. If they or those for whom they claim to speak are wanted for criminal offenses, the interview should be treated as a criminal offense by the media concerned—just as would have been the case if a radio station in Britain or the United States during World War II had provided a platform for Adolph Hitler or Joseph Goebbels. The ability of foreign stations to beam such interviews, both on radio and television, directly to the people of the target country is increasingly exploited and compounds the problem.

Hostage Situations and the Media

Two types of hostage situations must be differentiated—siege situations and kidnap situations. In siege situations, hostages are held in a known location

[2] Richard Clutterbuck, *The Media and Political Violence* (London: Macmillan Publishing Co., 1981), p. 92.

[3] Quoted in Alan Hooper, *The Military and the Media* (London: Gower Press, forthcoming).

(such as an embassy or a hijacked aircraft), which is besieged as quickly as possible by the police, who thereafter hold the initiative. In kidnap situations, the victims are taken to a secret location. The kidnappers retain the initiative and contact the family or the police only when it suits them, usually by telephone.

The media have sometimes been irresponsible, putting lives at risk in siege situations. Captain Frank Bolz of the New York City Police Hostage Squad has described a siege in which he blocked off the street down which his police were about to advance and attempt a rescue. The operators of a local radio station, finding their reporter thus barred, consulted a street directory and telephoned every house in the vicinity until they found a man who could see the operation from his window. They broadcast his telephone commentary live, describing exactly how and where the policemen were approaching the hostage house.

At the siege of the Iranian Embassy in London in May 1980, the police asked all the many camera crews from the world's media to locate themselves across the street in front of the embassy and not to film from behind. They explained that they did not wish to reveal surveillance equipment in the gardens behind; but, understandably, they did not add that, if a rescue was attempted, the army Special Air Service (SAS) rescue team would be sliding down ropes to enter the windows at the back.

All the media respected this request except one British television crew, which smuggled an ENG camera in a suitcase into a window of an apartment looking across the garden from the back. The crew deliberately deceived the police by pretending to be travelers just arrived from the airport, with airline labels on their suitcases. They filmed the soldiers gathering on the roof and sliding down their ropes. These pictures were transmitted directly from the ENG camera to the television van nearby and from there to the studio. Fortunately, no news bulletin was in progress at the time. The independent television news organization later argued that, even if there had been, the editors responsible would not have transmitted the embassy pictures live. As it was, the broadcast did not go out until a news flash four minutes later. But if it had gone out live, there was every likelihood that the terrorists, who had already killed one hostage and had begun to shoot down the others as soon as they heard the soldiers breaking in, would have had time to kill all those they held. This incident illustrates the dangers posed by the ENG camera and by disregarding the requests of the police when lives are at risk.

In countries where kidnaps to secret locations are commonplace, as in Italy, the media have generally been more responsible. There was an exception when the Schild family was kidnapped in Sardinia in 1979. The kidnappers were encouraged to increase their demands and to prolong the kidnap to seven months by inflated and grossly inaccurate newspaper and radio reports of the wealth of the family. This irresponsible conjecture in the British media was repeated in the Italian press and radio and gleefully received by the kidnappers.

An episode that provided an encouraging example of cooperation between the police and the media occurred in London in 1975 when a young girl was kidnapped. The kidnappers, as always, warned the family not to tell the police, but the family discreetly did so. The metropolitan police commissioner, however, confident that the kidnappers did not know this, called all the London press, radio, and television news editors together, gave them the facts, and implored them not to put the girl's life at risk by reporting the case. He thereafter briefed them daily, and they universally respected his request. After eleven days the girl was safely released, the ransom recovered, and all the kidnappers arrested. Only then was the story released—with the media justly earning as much credit as the police.

Even more impressive was the ending of the Schild case, when the kidnappers had released both parents but still held their fifteen-year-old daughter. The entire world press respected the parents' request not to report this fact, and silence was maintained until the girl was released without further ransom two months later.

Sometimes the media themselves are "hijacked," as occurred in the kidnapping of Peter Lorenz in Berlin in March 1975. As one television editor put it: "For 72 hours we just lost control of the medium, it was theirs, not ours. . . . We shifted shows in order to meet their timetable. Our cameras had to be in position to record each of the released prisoners as they boarded their plane to freedom, and our news coverage had to include prepared statements at their dictate. . . . There is plenty of underworld crime on our screens but . . . now it was the real thing and it was the gangsters who wrote the script and programmed the mass media."[4] Brian Jenkins, of the Rand Corporation, has summarized the situation: "Terrorism is aimed at the people watching, not at the actual victim. Terrorism is theater."[5]

The West German government provided an example of the constructive manipulation of the media in a hostage situation during the holding of Hanns-Martin Schleyer by the Red Army Faction (RAF) in 1977. Chancellor Schmidt publicly maintained a "no-deals" policy, but journalists spotted government ministers and officials in such likely terrorist havens as Aden and Algiers. The media took the bait and made the anticipated conjectures. This deception kept alive terrorist hopes of a deal, and they did not kill their victim for six weeks, during which the police twice found hideouts just vacated.

The police might well have been in time on one of the occasions if they had not been flooded with reports from a public wishing to help (3,826 in all), so that the crucial one was not acted on until too late. As a direct result, the West German police introduced a highly effective computerized intelligence system. This system has enabled them to maintain such constant pressure that the RAF has been heavily eroded by arrests, and its surviving members have been so fully preoccupied with escaping the net (by finding new "safe" houses and by committing enough robberies to subsist) that they have been unable to mount any

[4] Quoted in Yonah Alexander et al., eds., *Terrorism: Interdisciplinary Perspectives* (New York: John Jay Press, 1977), p. 145.

[5] Ibid.

major operations since the end of 1977. The RAF has neither kidnapped nor killed anyone since Schleyer. This example is an impressive one of the use of communications technology to counter terrorism.

The Future

As industrial societies develop, they become more vulnerable to terrorism. Wide-bodied jets with over 300 passengers make newsworthy hijack targets. Tankers carrying oil or liquefied natural gas could wreak havoc if a threat to blow them up were carried out, as could an explosion in oil storage and distribution facilities. Electric power and nuclear installations have become increasingly attractive targets. Above all, the growing interdependence of installations and systems makes disruption of any one of them more damaging to the public.

In no field does this danger apply more than in electronic, computer, and communications technology. The opportunity to spread alarm and confusion by seizing a radio or television transmitter will grow along with the cable systems. The seizure or threat of destruction of computer records would be an almost irresistible bargaining counter. So would the disruption of the information systems of an international banking or insurance corporation.

Two major restraints on terrorists, however, will remain: the more complex an operation, the greater the chance of prior detection or failure. And if the effect of carrying out the threat would be so horrific as to be political suicide for the terrorists, they know that it will be easier to call their bluff. These must be the main reasons why terrorists have not so far attempted the use of nuclear devices, though it has been technically feasible for a number of years.

Armament technology has also strengthened the power of terrorists, with lighter, quicker firing, more accurate, and more powerful weapons, laser and other beams, and, above all, electronic remote control and guidance systems. The sophistication of IRA terrorism has vastly increased over the past ten years. Armament development, however, has also increased the power of governments to counter terrorism. So, too, can the development of communications and other electronic technology. Anti-intrusion, surveillance, and access-control capabilities are much more sophisticated than previously. Magnetic or electronic identity documents make forging difficult. Methods of detection not only of metals but also of explosives and other materials continue to develop. If the manufacturing nations can agree on the matter of tagging explosives and detonators during manufacture, they could make it difficult for terrorists to acquire anything but homemade bulk explosives. Bugging and debugging are now highly efficient.

Most effective of all, however, will be the full exploitation of communications technology to improve intelligence capability and to develop hard evidence for conviction. The detention of terrorists without trial is ultimately counter-productive in a liberal society. But conviction, on incontrovertible evidence in a public trial, remains the most effective of all deterrents.

West Germany has proved the effectiveness of a computerized intelligence. Like any other power, computers can be abused, but proved cases of abuse have been very rare in West Germany. Computers more often act to the benefit of the innocent, in the rapid release of those wrongly suspected and, of course, in saving lives. Nevertheless, along with this technological development of intelligence must go the development of better technical, social, and political safeguards against its abuse. Public cooperation and support, without which no intelligence system can achieve its full potential, will thus be ensured.

The media can exacerbate conflict of all kinds. Irresponsible reporting of rioting can cause an explosion of imitations, as it did in England in July 1981. The media can encourage terrorists by giving them what they want and can thus inhibit protection against them and put innocent lives at risk. On the other hand, most journalists, if treated with trust and confidence, will act responsibly and cooperate in preserving lives and apprehending terrorists.

For the few journalists who knowingly abuse their power, effective restraints must be imposed, preferably by the profession itself, as do doctors and lawyers. Perhaps there should be an institute of the mass media equivalent to, say, the Bar Association. Ultimately, those who break their professional code should be barred from practice. If the profession cannot or will not follow lawyers in coming to terms with its power, this restraint must be exercised by legislation, comparable to that against reckless driving.

Legislated regulation, however, is a hazardous path. If the free investigative press is too much inhibited, then corruption and the abuse of power will grow. It is no fluke that the two countries that have survived longest without revolution or unconstitutional change—Britain and the United States—are the two with the strongest traditions of a free press. On no account must either terrorists who wish to destroy democracy or journalists who irresponsibly abuse their freedom be allowed to deprive the democratic countries of that vital safeguard. The new powers of electronic hardware must not be abused by the people using it. Computers can offer choices, but ultimately a human brain must make judgments. Technological development makes these judgments both more difficult and more dangerous. Foreseeing the effects of technological developments in time is the key. Therein lies the challenge for the politicians and the people in the liberal democracies.

Information Control as an International Issue

LEONARD R. SUSSMAN

Information control has become an international issue of great consequence. Three-quarters of the nations of the world regularly censor or in other ways control the flow of information within, into, and out of their countries, for they realize that information is "an asset, a resource, and a commodity with social, economic and political value."[1] In addition, international controls threaten the flow of news that is vital to nations' policymaking, financial and monetary systems, international trade, and national security. Increasingly in international forums limits are imposed on the flow of economic, social, and cultural information (combined under the rubric of development information), cross-border data flows (commercial information), and the transmission of political views from one country to another (public diplomacy). Indeed, in this "Information Age," the control of international information is as compelling as the endeavor in other times to secure information from distant places. This essay will examine technological developments that generate political demands for controls over information, the diversity of information flows affected by these demands, and the varied attitudes toward these demands among the developing countries, the Soviet Union and its bloc, Western Europe, Japan, and the United States.

Information Saturation and Political Response

It is the nature of modern communication that a few people send messages to large audiences that have little chance to respond. In fact, this generally one-way channel has persisted through the development of writing, printing, radio, television, and computerized data flows linked to satellites for broader dissemination. Though several recent applications of communication technology

[1] John Rankine, *International Data Flow* (Washington, D.C.: Government Printing Office, 1980), p. 3.

do provide two-way channels from receiver to sender, these new developments have neither altered the basic information flows within the developed countries nor affected the developing countries or the international flow of communications. Barely twenty years ago, for example, the United Nations Educational, Scientific, and Cultural Organization (UNESCO) predicted that by employing closed-circuit television "satellites could be used" for "person-to-person communication generally."[2] This has not happened. Instead, governments are more wary now than ever of cross-border communication. It will be possible in a few years to manufacture wristwatch telephones linked to satellite relays that could enable a caller in San Diego to speak to a friend in, say, Africa. But even if the technology existed, the political situation is likely to preclude such uncontrolled international communication. Developing countries fear the widening gap between communication-rich nations and themselves, and in the international forums they dominate they vociferously express their dissatisfaction with being in the communications periphery.

The airways are presently a broadcast battleground. The sounds of competing ideologies — some blatant, such as Radio Moscow and Radio Free Kabul; some more subtle, such as the British Broadcasting Corporation and the Voice of America — may be heard twenty-four hours a day. This is public diplomacy. The radios of one nation beam ideas and information over the heads of another nation's leaders to reach the foreign population directly. Is this interference in the national sovereignty of the receiving nation? It is, according to countries accepting the model of centralized government and invoking information rights on behalf of the collectivity, not of the individual. The democratic governments, on the other hand, regard cross-border broadcasting as a means of providing diverse information to individual citizens in other countries and a step in fulfilling the right guaranteed in 1948 by article 19 of the Universal Declaration of Human Rights, which stated that "everyone has the right to freedom of opinion and expression; this right includes freedom to hold opinions without interference and to seek, receive and impart information and ideas through any media and regardless of frontiers."

Despite the statement of purpose in article 19, by 1975, when the Helsinki Accords were signed, the participants were only able to reach an agreement that "freer and wider dissemination of information" should exist within and among countries. That agreement, however, also incorporated the principle of "noninterference in internal affairs" of sovereign states. That by no means nullified the "freer" flow, but it provided a less specific set of communication rights than had the Universal Declaration of Human Rights. Clearly, in the intervening twenty-seven years, the international environment had limited the flow of information.

Similarly, the fear of foreign ideas has permeated recent United Nations

[2] UNESCO, "Space Communications and the Mass Media," in *Reports and Papers on Mass Communication* (Paris: UNESCO, 1963), p. 22.

debates on direct-broadcast satellites. Soon after Sputnik signaled the USSR's early dominance of outer space, a Soviet writer in 1960 predicted: "With the help of a large Sputnik . . . Moscow television programs could easily be relayed not only to any point in the Soviet Union, but also far beyond its borders." But before long, the United States became the world's dominant communicator using satellites. On November 15, 1972, UNESCO's general conference adopted the Declaration of Guiding Principles in the Use of Space Broadcasting for the Free Flow of Information, the Spread of Education, and Greater Cultural Exchange. It is strongly restrictive, stressing sovereignty and permitting each country "to decide on the content" of the program "broadcast by satellite to its people." The declaration was adopted by a 55-to-7 vote (the United States opposing the motion), with 22 abstentions.

Many reasons are given for limiting the free flow of information across national borders: traditional cultures, it is said, must be preserved from commercialized cultural imports; specifically desirable economic-development information must be stressed; confusing or dissident political reports must be stopped at the border. Most often, however, protection of the regime in power is the primary motive for international control over information.

Some countries may soon consider "computer diplomacy" to be as threatening as broadcast or public diplomacy. A few data centers control cross-border information flows. International Business Machines (IBM) produces most of the world's computer hardware. Computers in the United States store much of the business information needed in other countries. The cause of concern in Western Europe is dramatically revealed in the case of the fire fighters of Malmoe, Sweden. Malmoe placed data in a computerized system concerning the structure, use, and inhabitants of most buildings in the city. This information could be retrieved immediately after a fire alarm sounded. The computer, however, was located in Cleveland, Ohio.

American multinational corporations routinely store information in their United States-based computers on the personal histories of their personnel overseas. European legislators, for example, regard the retrieving of data in Chicago about an employee in Brussels as an invasion of the personal privacy of their citizens. Some Third World countries maintain that cross-border data flows are a new form of colonialism that should be regulated. Several have, therefore, begun to regulate cross-border data flows.

UNESCO, a harbinger of broadening communication possibilities, has become in the past decade the principal arena for debating both national and international aspects of information control (though the charges and countercharges leveled there have been repeated in the UN General Assembly, through its Committee on Information and the Special Political Committee). In these debates, the control of information is generally rationalized as a response to patterns of communication that are said to be detrimental to all except the countries that dominate world-news reporting, communication-hardware manufacturing, and the storage and transmission of data—the United States, Great Britain, France, and Japan.

The developing countries regard access to information as essential to their social and economic development. Many also believe that the New International Economic Order (NIEO) will not deliver essential resources unless a new world information and communication order (NWICO) prods the developed countries. In the view of developing countries, information systems are points of vulnerability for developed countries; their information systems can be hampered by controlling the information flow within developing nations and between them and the rest of the world.

That is not to say that all Third World countries issue explicit ultimatums to control information. Indeed, 23 percent of the developing countries have free press and broadcast services and do not restrict foreign correspondents. Even these, however, have joined the demand for a new world information order.

There is an obvious imbalance in the volume of information circulating around the world. A vast quantity of news and data flows daily to and from the developed countries. Although it is sometimes argued that, despite the imbalance in the volume of North-South communication, the content provides a balanced view of events over time, Third World leaders generally do not concede this point. Third World news, they say, is prepared in the normative Western style, based on balance and objectivity as understood in Western terms. Third World spokesmen demand greater parity both in the volume of information carried over the world-news services and in the opportunity freely to express their views over these systems.

The Soviet bloc sees these demands for a NWICO as the opportunity to generate political capital in the Third World. As late as April 1978 at a UNESCO meeting in Stockholm, Leonid Zamyatin, then director of the Soviet news agency TASS (now in charge of information on the Central Committee), derided as "unnecessary" the Third World's demand for a new information order. He argued that the world already has an acceptable order based on the sovereignty of nations. In a statement made at Tashkent in September 1979, however, the Soviet Union reversed its policies and called for an "order" defined by Third World activists at UNESCO meetings. "This new order," said the Tashkent statement, "understood as an integral part of the new international economic order, should be based on the generally recognized principle of international law, in particular as respect for national sovereignty and noninterference in internal affairs of other states." The statement demanded a display of "responsibility" by those providing information. "Responsibility," in turn, would be defined by national and international doctrines. The "free flow of information"—universally accepted since it was incorporated in UNESCO's charter in 1945—was described at Tashkent as a "grossly commercial concept serving the interests of transnational corporations," that should be replaced by a "concept ensuring the interest of all countries."

As early as 1970 the Soviet Union sought international help in banning American public diplomacy—Radio Liberty and Radio Free Europe—from cross-border broadcasting to Eastern Europe and the Soviet Union. Meanwhile, the Nonaligned Movement was also criticizing the world's information systems and discussing alternatives. At UNESCO's 1972 biennial general conference the Soviet Union introduced a draft declaration on the mass news media that provided a press-control model. The title of the draft accurately revealed its objective: to establish intergovernmental criteria by which the "use of the mass media" could by "governed" in order to provide governmentally approved results, such as strengthening peace and combating war propaganda and racism—noble goals but all subject to open-ended interpretations by government censors and ideologues.

In 1976, the Soviets introduced a still harsher draft that declared: "States are responsible for the activities in the international sphere of all mass media under their jurisdiction." This model offered a new universal standard for the flow of information, interposing governments between the transmitters of information and receivers around the world, a dictum that would make the United States government, for example, responsible for news reports published by the *New York Times*. Obviously, the First Amendment of the United States Constitution would preclude that, but the intention of the backers of the draft was to ensure the "sovereignty" of states in the information sphere. This failed attempt by the Soviet bloc and some Third World countries to secure such international controls did not end with a compromise arrangement in 1976. Indeed, the controversies in this field have intensified and become more complex in recent years.

The Present World Information Order

Perhaps the most significant aspect of the present worldwide flow of information is its disorderliness. The developed countries invent and manufacture nearly all the communications systems, as they do most other industrial products. These countries also produce most of the software used in the entertainment fields and in commercial data processing. Three of these countries—the United States, the United Kingdom, and France—also serve as headquarters for the four largest news organizations: the Associated Press (AP), United Press International (UPI), Reuters, and Agence France-Presse.

Western domination of the information flow results not from a conspiracy but from a combination of political, economic, and technological factors that began with the Industrial Revolution; this domination was magnified during the later colonial period. The search for resources distant from the homeland required dependable communications links with the colony. Communications followed the lines of colonial control, from the center to each of the colonies, outward, like the spokes of a wheel. There was no rapid communication between colonies without going through London or Paris, and no open lines between colonies having different European homelands. North-South communications lines persisted even when potential South-South communicators may have been barely a few miles apart.

Immediately after achieving independence, the new nations of the South recognized the importance of information in developing a state and a society. Virtually every new nation acted promptly to exert control over domestic press and broadcast facilities. In some emerging countries the mass media were placed under sharp controls by rulers who only a short time before were able to serve as dissident editors opposing colonial rule. Though the new nations recognized that newsprint, telecommunications tariffs, and broadcast technology were expensive, the volume of information entering the Third World steadily increased after the colonial period ended. More news about the Third World also entered the developed countries. Whether or not citizens in the West now read, hear, or view proportionately more about the Third World than before is uncertain. The volume of information about all topics has increased so greatly that gatekeepers in the news media still assign a small proportion of space or time to Third World matters. But recent studies show that editors in the Third World demonstrate similar judgments in serving their audiences. African readers get little Asian and Latin American news. Asians see and hear little of African affairs. Latin Americans concern themselves chiefly with their own and neighboring regions.

A contrasting and sharply critical interpretation of the current information "disorder" is presented by two Marxist analysts, Kaarle Nordenstreng of the University of Tampere in Finland and Herbert I. Schiller of the University of California, San Diego. "While new flags and frontiers have proliferated in the last thirty years," they say, "less visible but powerful forces have been trespassing over national boundaries on an unprecedented scale." The global "business system" that is centered on the American economy organizes this "border-crossing" through transnational corporations (TNCs). "Most of the TNCs are only indirectly related to the mass media," the authors agree, but state that "they have a decisive role in determining—largely through advertising—the content of media flows and, consequently, the social consciousness prevailing in society, propagating the system's values and reinforcing its authority as the ultimate definer of issues."[3]

From the Marxist viewpoint, national sovereignty is the principal requirement and national interests the primary objectives of an international information system. It was not by accident that the Soviet Union's draft declarations at UNESCO demanded "state responsibility" for mass news media and the listing by governments of the objectives of the media. The USSR rejects political and social systems based on individualism as well as the market system. According to Vladimir Hudec, dean of the Faculty of Journalism of Charles University in Prague, Czechoslovakia, journalism "cannot be 'independent' of society" or "uncommitted to topical social problems." "Faithfulness to facts," he adds, "requires that topical problems should be presented precisely in terms of concrete evidence." Hudec explains that the "facts" should be presented "with a party bias [to provide] the 'ardent evidence of the facts themselves,' and not in a detached

[3] Kaarle Nordenstreng and Herbert I. Schiller, *National Sovereignty and International Communication* (Norwood, N.J.: Ablex, 1979), p. ix.

objectivistic way."[4] The party, then, is to decide the selection and interpretation of the "facts" so that the journalist can prepare an "ardent" report.

It is unarguable that the West, particularly the United States, dominates the flow of information today. What remains sharply at issue, however, is whether communication capability and information can be more widely shared without governmental controls. The desire of Marxist ideologues and their authoritarian allies in the Third World to apply governmental and intergovernmental controls over international information flows should be separated from the understandable desire of moderate Third World spokesmen for greater participation in the world communication system. Even Pope John Paul II unintentionally confused the basic issues by failing to distinguish between reasonable and unreasonable Third World demands. The pope told Nigerian journalists in February 1982 that "the operations of high technology Western media could lead to the ideological domination of the Third World." He said, "I feel it is important that national sovereignty is safeguarded through the correct use of the communications media, precisely because these media can become instruments of ideological pressure."[5]

The pope based his appeal on the defense of national sovereignty—the right of a central government to control information—rather than on the right of individual citizens to secure information. Yet in three-quarters of the world, national governments determine which news and information their citizens may receive. These countries purchase information from world-news services, share it with their elites, and only then pass along selected news to the citizenry. There are 105 national news agencies, mainly operated by governments, clear demonstrations of national sovereignty over information. Little information or entertainment enters Third World countries without the implicit permission of or actual purchase by local elites.

At issue more fundamentally is the conveying of "ideas" through the daily transmission of news. Moderate Third World governments demand, if not the "ardent evidence of the facts" presented "with a party bias," better coverage of economic development and related issues of great concern to young and poor countries. And there has been inadequate reporting in the world-news media of the particular problems facing societies unskilled in modern farm and factory techniques. But that is not to say that many Third World nations will readily permit their own media to express dissenting views, particularly on development issues. They are still less ready to do so on other political matters.

The Structure of Information Control

Kingman Brewster said that "cynical disparagement of objectivity as a 'myth' " is "both naive and irresponsible." He explained: "Any claim of novelty to the

[4] Vladimir Hudec, *Journalism: Substance, Social Functions Development* (Prague: International Organization of Journalists, 1980), p. 32.

[5] Associated Press, world wire, February 16, 1982.

observation that men are fallible at best, corruptible at worst, is naive. Its irresponsibility lies in the conclusion that since the ideal is unattainable it should not be held up as a standard to both [journalistic] practitioners and critics."[6]

This commitment to balance and objectivity as standards is the crux of the world-news controversy. Western journalism strives for them over time, if not in every story. Individual reporters and editors, however, are fallible and may be biased. Offsetting their fallibility is the diversity of the media. Some permit lengthier reports and longer research time than others; some feature serious reportage and analysis rather than just headline news; some provide views in opposition to conventional wisdom.

A Western journalist covering a Third World country is nevertheless hard pressed to avoid treating custom as exotica, or reporting without adequate explanation the limitations of local governance. These problems of covering a story in a foreign country are not new. For the last five years, the major world-news services have been especially attentive to criticism. They have increased the number and quality of reports focusing on the Third World. But they can never correct the false impression made in the Third World assertion that "90 percent of news flowing around the world goes from a developed country to the developing world." Tallied in that "90 percent" are many stories—sometimes one-quarter to one-third of each day's report—that originate in a Third World country. For example, most stories from Latin America are transmitted first to New York (because that is how computers flow most inexpensively) and are then retransmitted—often with little or no editing—to other Latin American countries. On the Latin American desk in New York, moreover, Latin Americans as well as North Americans edit the news. Similarly, reports from Cairo or Singapore passing through London are counted as "news from a developed country."

Further, the four world-news services write about 3.5 million words a day, not the "more than 30 million" words claimed by UNESCO.[7] A group of fifteen regional and Third World national news agencies prepares 1.3 million words a day. About eighty smaller Third World agencies add to this total. The world-news services account for a large proportion of the flow of information because they process each story as many as ten different times for ten different kinds of users (such as radio, business clients, and regional editors). A large part of this volume is consumed within the developed countries themselves. Yet UNESCO statistics repeatedly imply the saturation of the world by Western news, suggesting further that this is an unwarranted imposition of indoctrinational ideas.

Some news reports of the four major services are fashioned for foreign audiences. The services try to transmit news known to be of particular interest to certain regions. Reuters features African news. AP and UPI cover Latin America intensively. Sugar prices and cocoa trading figures are flashed quickly to Africa

[6] *Wall Street Journal*, January 17, 1970.

[7] Dileep Padgaonkar, deputy director, Office of Public Information, UNESCO, to United Nations Association of the USA, September 15, 1981, pp. 3–4.

and the Caribbean. Japan receives daily bulletins on certain stock exchange actions. However, it is unlikely the four major news services will ever again deploy as many correspondents in distant places as in the past, because of the expense. It costs $100,000 to keep one American correspondent abroad for a year. Yet the Third World demands more and broader coverage from Western correspondents even while seeking assistance in creating its own communications infrastructures.

These information controversies have linked the demands for modern infrastructure to both the complaints about the imposition of Western ideas and the threat of information control. This linkage clearly has inhibited the United States and its allies from making available to the Third World significant technological hardware or training in the information field. Congress made its views clear when it amended the State Department authorization bill in October 1981. It passed the Beard amendment that would deprive UNESCO of all United States funding "if that organization implements any policy or procedure the effect of which is to license journalists or their publications, to censor or otherwise restrict the free flow of information within or among countries or to impose mandatory codes of journalistic practice or ethics." The secretary of state was instructed to tell Congress by February 1 whether UNESCO had taken such actions.

A second act, the Shamansky-Fenwick amendment, requires the president to assess for Congress the value of UNESCO's total program in light of United States interests, and the "quality" of United States participation and representation in UNESCO. To underscore his concern, President Reagan wrote the House of Representatives that it was "worrisome" that the right to personal freedom of opinion and expression and the transmission of information "regardless of frontiers" – vouchsafed in the Universal Declaration of Human Rights – should come under attack in UNESCO. The president concluded, "We do not feel we can continue to support a UNESCO that turns its back on the high purposes this organization was originally intended to serve."[8]

Earlier, President Reagan urged all nations to read the declaration by independent news-media leaders of twenty-one nations issued at the Voices of Freedom Conference, held on May 15–17, 1981, at Talloires, France. The conference, organized by the World Press Freedom Committee and the Fletcher School of Law and Diplomacy at Tufts University, was the most representative meeting ever held of print and broadcast leaders. Participants came from Africa, Asia, and Latin America as well as from Europe and North America. The Declaration of Talloires, widely reprinted, was an avowed response to seven years of debate at UNESCO over proposed curbs of press freedom and probably generated the congressional and presidential actions cited above.

The declaration regarded "restraints on the movement of news and information" as inimical to "international understanding" and insisted that "free access,

[8] Ronald Reagan to Thomas P. O'Neill, in *Congressional Record*, September 17, 1981, p. H-349.

by the people and the press, to all sources of information, both official and unofficial, must be assured and reinforced." The authors acknowledged that governments, developed and developing alike, "constrain or otherwise discourage the reporting of information they consider detrimental or embarrassing, and that governments usually invoke the national interest to justify these constraints." The authors believed, however, that "the people's interest, and therefore the interests of the nation, are better served by free and open reporting." The declaration supported "all efforts" by private and public bodies to make communication technology available to "correct the imbalances" in the world. It rejected censorship and other arbitrary controls of information, an international code of journalistic ethics, special protection for journalists or controls in the name of protecting them, restrictions on becoming a journalist, licensing of journalists, and specially mandated responsibilities for the press.

In a paper presented to the Talloires conference, the author reported analyses of government and news-media relationships in ninety-three countries. The report noted that there are increasing demands in UNESCO for the creation of a code of journalistic ethics. Yet voluntary codes already exist in most places where UNESCO would impose a governmental standard—in the West. In thirteen of eighteen centers of independent journalism—72 percent of the countries in Western Europe, the United States, Japan, Australia, and New Zealand—professional news organizations already have their own codes of journalistic ethics. Only one Western European country, Portugal, has a government code. Professional codes are rarely found in countries pressing them on others. In the Third World, professional codes exist in four African countries (11 percent), two Asian countries (10 percent), and one Latin American country (4.8 percent). There are three state-imposed codes, one in Africa and two in Latin America. Government codes are little needed in three-quarters of the countries, however, since the state either owns or controls the print and broadcast media. These nations, however, generally favor imposing codes on independent journalists around the world.

Some press-control measures were set in place after debates began at UNESCO over the need for a new "order." It is difficult, however, to demonstrate a direct causal relationship between these measures and those debates. It is likely, though, that the debates established a broader climate of acceptance for press controls and may have provided descriptive assistance to putative press-controllers.

The 312-page report of UNESCO's International Commission for the Study of Communication Problems is a case in point. Of the commission's sixteen members, headed by Sean MacBride, winner of both the Lenin Prize and the Nobel Peace Prize, only six generally supported a fully independent press. The report, not unexpectedly, is at best ambivalent on fundamental liberatarian issues. It supported both individual and collective rights, speaking of freedom of information as a basic human right but also accepting the primacy of the state and national sovereignty in informational matters. The report discussed all the current threats to independent journalism and the flow of information, and accepted some restrictive measures while ignoring or equivocating about others. It concluded by making eighty-two recommendations, mainly for government action, and listing another twelve "issues requiring further study." Among these are codes of journalistic ethics, the alleged harmful effects of advertising on "cultural identity and moral values," steps to "protect" journalists (totally rejected by Western news groups because such protection is linked to government-regulated "responsibilities" assigned to journalists), and the establishment of an international tax on the "use of electromagnetic spectrum and geostationary orbit space for the benefit of developing countries."

The delivery of the MacBride report at the 1980 UNESCO general conference did not settle the controversy. In 1983, UNESCO is expected to define the new world information and communication order at a general conference that will surely renew debates over information control. Events at a meeting in Acapulco in January 1982 concerning the International Program for the Development of Communication (IPDC) were a harbinger. The IPDC was created to make communication technology and training available to developing countries. Western delegates sought to prevent the IPDC from using its voluntarily contributed funds to extend governmental controls over international information flows, while Amadou Mahtar M'Bow, UNESCO's director-general, accused the Western press of "traumatizing," with false stories, governments that otherwise would have contributed to the program.

An actual case of traumatizing independent journalists by a national government occurred the week following the Acapulco conference. There, a 1,400-page report by the Commission of Inquiry into the Mass Media concluded with proposed legislation to "professionalize the mass media." The four volumes provide a classic rationale for institutionalizing press controls in a country in which journalism has been relatively free for generations. The report stated:

> The purpose . . . is to regulate the whole journalistic mass media operation by the introduction of standards of journalistic performance to be achieved by way of qualifications for entry into that operation by the formulation of norms of conduct and the introduction of machinery to enforce such norms as well as by way of disqualifications for continued participation in the operation.
>
> The necessity for such regulation is the need to ensure socially responsible conduct by all members of the journalistic operation and the protection and advancement of journalistic independence.
>
> The method of achieving such regulation is the compulsory professionalism of the whole journalistic operation. . . .

A second proposal would alter the ownership of South African newspapers, adversely affecting mainly those now published for English-speaking whites. A few weeks after this proposal, the revolutionary government of Nicaragua offered a new restrictive press law that would require all economic news to come from governmental sources. Balanced reporting of economic news would be precluded. All journalists working and living in Nicaragua would have to be Nicaraguans. The international news media would be prevented from assigning resident foreign journalists who are less subject to the legal and social pressures of the country they are covering. Another clause would prohibit the news media from "being a sounding board for the interests of imperialism or reproducing international propaganda campaigns which enemies of the revolution promote against the (revolutionary) process."[9] This vague restriction clearly leads to self-censorship.

The Social Responsibility of the Journalist

Does the journalist have a responsibility to society beyond providing the fairest, most balanced, best researched, clearest report possible and distinguishing straight reportage from analysis or comment? When the Commission on Freedom of the Press, led by Robert Hutchins in the 1940s, raised the question of social responsibility for journalists, it was widely attacked by editors, reporters, publishers, and broadcasters. Yet journalists hailed the publication of the Pentagon Papers as a "vital public service," another phrase for journalists fulfilling a social responsibility. Similarly, the Watergate disclosures and the "new journalism," first developed as a mode of attacking the United States's role in the Vietnam war, were justified by many journalists as employing the tools of their trade to effect desirable changes in the nation and the world—to fulfill social responsibility as they viewed it.

Clearly, journalists who hold these views mean something different by "social responsibility" than those at UNESCO and in other international forums that adopted the "responsibility of journalists" as a slogan for effecting change not only in journalism but in national and international affairs as well. The first social responsibility of a free journalist is to remain free. A democratic society cannot long function without free media, and the determination of the objectives and operating procedures of free information media should be defined only by the practitioners themselves. Their guide should be the priorities of their society and the world at large, as they view them, and their responsibility to truth, fairness, and balance. Equally important is a personal commitment to help those reached by the media to understand the world as it is and to grapple with it more effectively.

This responsibility requires the highest professionalization of those who function in the information media. Enforced government professionalization, whether proposed at UNESCO or in South Africa or Nicaragua, is, by definition, a contradiction. The United Nations General Assembly has proclaimed 1983 World Communications Year, thus recognizing the central role that infor-

[9] Associated Press, March 3, 1982.

mation now plays in all societies. Those who have vast stores of information and the equipment to manufacture and distribute still more should share both the information and the equipment with those who do not possess them. Information is power, yet unlike transferring commodities or weapons systems, sharing information is not necessarily giving up either information or power. In the long run, such sharing may enable both developed and developing countries to engage more freely in two-way exchanges. For the World Communications Year to have such a salutary effect, however, the developed nations should ask for a muting of proposals to expand the national and international controls of information.

New Defense Systems

ROBERT F. COULAM

Heinz Guderian, a former signals officer in the German army, developed one of the great tactical innovations of World War II. The rudiments of Guderian's plan were simple: place a two-way radio in every tank; establish a division communications net, so that the commander could command from any point in the division; place the commander forward in the division's operations, able to respond on the spot to the changing fortunes of battle; make all orders oral rather than written; and delegate authority and latitude for execution of the orders to the lowest possible level.[1] Guderian thus envisioned communications technologies serving an opportunistic doctrine of decentralized command and control for land operations. The blitzkrieg became possible when the German army adopted the essentials of Guderian's plan, with devastating results for the allies through the early years of the war.

The key to the success of the blitzkrieg was the way in which it wedded communications capabilities (simple, even for their time) to a well-conceived set of ideas about who should be where, doing (and expecting to do) what, in the land battle. Therein lies the value of the blitzkrieg for thinking about new defense communications technologies today. There has indeed been a revolution in communications technologies in defense acquisition, centered on the increased use of digital computers and sophisticated sensor technologies. Huge expenditures—and political attention unknown even ten years ago—now are being devoted to the development and procurement of various communications technologies. But there is a lack of well-conceived ideas about how these technologies will actually be used, how they fit probable wartime environments, and how they will affect wartime patterns of command and control. American technology is outrunning the doctrine, organization, and training that govern American military forces.

The first section of this essay describes what is revolutionary about new defense communications systems and how the Defense Department has changed

[1] Franklin C. Spinney, "Defense Facts of Life," staff paper (Washington, D.C.: Department of Defense, 1980), p. 116.

its organization to enhance communications development. The second section discusses communications systems in use or planned for strategic nuclear weapons. The third section discusses tactical applications of these new technologies. The final section considers briefly how the Soviet Union's work in this area compares to that of the United States.

The Communications Revolution in Defense Systems

New communications technologies will have different effects on different communications activities. In some areas where technology will change rapidly, the functions to be performed will hardly change at all. For example, in tactical aircraft operations, the most pressing communications problem is mundane: the need for two-way voice communications resistant to the increasingly sophisticated "jamming" measures an enemy can employ. While dramatic technical changes may be required to solve this problem, these changes are expected to yield sophisticated two-way radios rather than a revolution in communications. An analogous problem affects strategic nuclear forces. In the event of a nuclear war, communications with (and hence command and control of) these forces will be impeded by jamming, sabotage, and various effects of the nuclear weapons themselves. Nothing more exotic in function is required than one-way or two-way radios. The equipment to perform that function will, however, be sophisticated indeed. To the degree that there is a revolution in these areas, it is in the awareness of how an enemy could disrupt communications using electronic and physical means. The United States is pressing technical frontiers so that it can continue doing what it has done (or assumed it could do) before.

There is a second group of defense systems, and for this group technology and the role of communications will change together. These systems all have in common an emphasis on new sensor systems and digital computer technology. Electronic and other sensors are not new to combat environments. But a far wider variety of sensors are planned for deployment in future wars. These range from aircraft-mounted radar, such as the Airborne Warning and Control System (AWACS), to passive battlefield sensors, to satellite sensors. Direct human observation will not be entirely displaced, but unprecedented quantities of data on enemy movements are expected to be generated. Manual collation and synthesis of these data will be impossible in many cases. Thus digital computers will be important for collation, presentation, and analysis. Whereas the standard communication system of past wars was the two-way voice system or its analogues (such as teletypes or telegraphic systems), military communication systems today are being converted into computer systems. The communication system of the future battle will be a network of computer systems connected to one another. The uses of communications are expanding accordingly. It is imperative that wartime uses of these systems be carefully conceived, that the vagaries of combat be adequately anticipated, and that troops be thoroughly trained in the use of the new systems. It is for these computer-based systems, performing what are in fact expanded communication roles, that the problem of matching technology to doctrine—to effective ways of fighting—is most serious.

But the promise of these systems is great. In principle, the movement of everything from troops to tanks to aircraft can be monitored as it happens—automatically—for the first time. An enemy plane can be picked up by AWACS as it takes off. AWACS computers can direct fighter aircraft to intercept it and simultaneously alert surface-to-air missile batteries of the attacking aircraft's presence. An extreme view of the possibilities would virtually remove human decision from these increasingly refined systems of sensors, feedback loops, and automated data processing. A more moderate view preserves the role of human decision but removes grease pencils and map transparencies from command locations, replacing them with computer terminals that provide maps of battle action and more general summaries of intelligence. The precise character of United States objectives in this area is unclear, which helps explain why the utility of these systems in battle remains uncertain.

The United States holds a significant lead over the Soviet Union in most sensor and computer-related technologies and is investing billions of dollars in these programs. The United States began in the mid-1970s to centralize guidance and planning for communications, command, control, and intelligence (C3I) programs in the Defense Department. An assistant secretary of defense for C3I was established in the Office of the Secretary of Defense (OSD). Meanwhile, the Joint Chiefs of Staff (JCS) created a separate directorate of communications, command, and control (C3) systems within the JCS organization. By the early 1980s, C3 systems had become conspicuous. Substantial resources were being devoted to new systems, and organizational focal points for C3 efforts had emerged. The change reflected an expanded Soviet threat to United States C3 capabilities, a greater appreciation of threats that had always been present, and a sense of the dramatic possibilities that new technologies offered.

Strategic Systems

Questions involving communications, command, and control acquire special significance for the most important defense systems, strategic nuclear weapons. That nuclear weapons must be reliably controlled is obvious. Two communication problems present the most serious dangers to this control: reliability and vulnerability.

If C3 systems are not reliable, the probability of "false alarms" increases. False indications of an attack could set in motion tragically mistaken commands to strike. The worries here are not entirely conjectural. In a recent nine-month period, at least five false indications of attack were projected by United States missile-warning radar systems. The projected attacks ranged in seriousness from a mass raid to a single missile launch. The proximate causes of the warning-system failures included: (1) the inadvertent introduction of simulation data into central command computers; (2) faulty components in certain communication-processor computers; and (3) computer misreadings of a Soviet rocket test and of a decayed rocket body reentering the atmosphere. New programs are under way to upgrade and replace the key computer components of the system by the late 1980s. The most important innovation is the development of an overall, integrated computer architecture for missile warning systems. (The computer systems now in place were built through piecemeal adoption of components originally developed for other purposes.) The air force and Congress expect greater reliability and accuracy from the new, specially designed systems. It is too soon to judge their optimism.

Meanwhile, an even more far-reaching set of problems will remain—the potential vulnerability of United States communication systems. According to the General Accounting Office, "today's C3 systems were conceived in the late 1950s and most became operational in the 1960s. They are essentially peacetime systems and depend[e]nt on vu[l]nerable ground communication networks."[2] The main sources of vulnerability can be quickly summarized. First, ground communications facilities that are not well guarded can be easily sabotaged. Second, communications can be disrupted by electronic countermeasures, or "jamming." The effects are uncertain, although the increasing sophistication of the threat is widely recognized. Third, secondary effects of high-altitude nuclear explosions could seriously disrupt the C3 network.

The General Accounting Office described this problem: "The effects of such detonations can disrupt the atmosphere and cause blackout and disruption of radio frequencies. Electromagnetic pulse (EMP), an intense electrical field that radiates rapidly from a nuclear blast, is collected and channeled by radio antennas, powerlines, and other unintended collectors. EMP could damage components of civilian and military communications systems and could scramble digital computers and other electronic equipment. High altitude blasts can spread EMP and other nuclear effects over hundreds of miles with little or no collateral damage. . . .The possibility of high altitude nuclear blasts coupled with communications jamming and possibly even sabotage of key facilities poses a threat to U.S. strategic C3."[3]

Finally, the primary blast effects of nuclear detonations could directly destroy almost every part of the C3 network. John Steinbruner has noted: "Fewer than 100 judiciously targeted nuclear weapons could so severely damage U.S. communications facilities and command centers that form the military chain of command that the actions of individual weapons commanders could no longer be controlled or coordinated. Some bomber crews, submarine officers, and ICBM silo launch officers could undertake very damaging retaliation and hence continue to pose a deterrent threat. Nonetheless, even 50 nuclear weapons are prob-

[2] U.S., Comptroller General, *Report to the Congress: Countervailing Strategy Demands Revision of Strategic Force Acquisition Plans* (Washington, D.C.: General Accounting Office, 1981), p. 20.
[3] Ibid., p. 21.

ably sufficient to eliminate the ability to direct U.S. strategic forces to coherent purposes."[4]

The problems caused by primary nuclear blasts are twofold. It is difficult to predict who will survive a nuclear attack. As a result, the C3 network must be able to accommodate speculative variations in who will be present in the chain of command after an attack. At the same time, facilities will be destroyed. Fixed, ground-based facilities are especially susceptible to damage; indeed, they are so easily targeted that they cannot be expected to survive beyond the earliest phases of a major conflict. Satellite relays, an important part of the system, are also easily targeted and will be vulnerable to nuclear and conventional attacks.

Given all these effects, it is difficult to imagine how communications and control could be maintained in a nuclear war. The implications are serious: if a minimal attack can so disrupt communications and command authority, most traditional ideas about nuclear war are beside the point. Nuclear retaliation will be a militarily incoherent and spasmodic response to an enemy's first strike. Without communication systems and leaders to use them, it is simply unrealistic to expect predictable and purposeful responses, including orders to restrain the forces as well as commands to strike.

Many of the partial solutions to these problems are mundane. Ideas and increased spending, not revolutionary technology, are required to solve them. For example, defense against sabotage will likely require that key facilities be guarded. There is little mystery about how to reduce the vulnerability of fixed, ground-based systems – make them and their support facilities mobile. In fact, back-up command and communication systems in the C3 network do rely on mobility. All of the nuclear commands have airborne command centers. However, only the Strategic Air Command (SAC) in Omaha, Nebraska, has a command center airborne twenty-four hours a day. The other nuclear commands have their aircraft parked on runways, where they will be easy targets unless they receive sufficient warning. There is an airborne command center for the president and other high-level civilian and military officials. However, the center must await the arrival of these officials in a crisis. It is unlikely these officials will be able to get there in time for three reasons: because evacuation procedures are unpredictable (President Carter instigated surprise alerts, which initially took twice as long as planned); because key officials will not be available in the ordinary performance of their duties (for example, the president may be in Chicago and the vice-president in China); and because an adversary can reduce warning times to a very few minutes (by depressed-orbit attacks from submarines, among other means).

The airborne command centers have an airborne communications system available to back up any damaged ground or satellite facilities, the Minimum Essential Emergency Communications Network. This network is designed to communicate emergency action messages (EAMs) to the nuclear forces to order

[4] John D. Steinbruner, "Nuclear Decapitation," *Foreign Policy*, no. 45 (Winter 1981–82), p. 18.

execution of preplanned nuclear retaliatory strikes. The network is basically a one-way system. The heart of the Minimum Essential Emergency Communication Network system is an airborne radio relay network. That network includes: (1) communications facilities of surviving airborne command posts; (2) aircraft specifically intended to relay messages between the command posts and forces; (3) a navy aircraft system called TACAMO, which relays very low frequency EAMs to submerged, missile-launching nuclear submarines (SSBNs); and (4) an Emergency Rocket Communication System (ERCS).

The capability of the postattack command and control system to disseminate EAMs to all forces depends initially on the survival of the aircraft relays. The survival of these relays is as uncertain as the survival of the airborne command centers that the relays support. If the airborne relays are destroyed, the system of last resort is ERCS. ERCS is a SAC communications system mounted on silo-based Minuteman booster rockets. ERCS would broadcast EAMs after being launched on a ballistic trajectory to reach each major nuclear force area. A recorded code can be taped into the payload to provide a broadcast to each of the nuclear forces. The silo-based ERCS, like Minuteman missiles generally, is vulnerable to direct attack by Soviet ICBMs. This threat will increase in the 1980s, as the accuracy of Soviet missiles improves.

Overall, then, the United States strategic network (including all of the emergency back-ups) provides little confidence that the United States will be able to command and communicate with its strategic forces in the event of a nuclear war. The first-line communication system, relying on ground-based facilities and satellites, is extremely vulnerable. Most of the back-up facilities are more mobile, but they could be destroyed on the ground if they did not receive adequate warning of attack. Even with adequate warning, they will require airfields, maintenance facilities, and added fuel to operate more than a few hours. Unfortunately, the fields, facilities, and fuel are themselves ground-based and vulnerable in an attack.

Endless debate has occurred in the United States about the various vulnerabilities of its strategic weapons. This country has demonstrated its willingness to spend more than $100 billion to address, among other things, the vulnerabilities that these often esoteric debates have revealed (the Trident submarine and MX missile programs are the most conspicuous results). Meanwhile, for want of a clear conception of the problem and for want of much less in resources, the command and communications systems that support this country's strategic weapons manifest the most glaring vulnerabilities of all, vulnerabilities that will likely render any retaliation by the United States incoherent and spasmodic. It may be argued that the Soviets would not capitalize on these vulnerabilities. In fact, however, their public literature emphasizes the opportunity and necessity to do so.

The United States is pressing technical improvements in the C3 system, but these improvements address certain details, not the fundamentals, of the vulnerability problem. For example, efforts are being devoted to hardening and shielding various parts of the C3 network against electromagnetic pulse from nuclear explosions. Existing automated data-processing capabilities are being modernized, and new equipment is being introduced into command facilities that now rely on manual means. (For example, the central airborne command center has no computer capability and only a limited, onboard data base. In a crisis, data must be processed manually, a task critically dependent on the speed and memory of the staff onboard.) Various new technologies are being developed or refined to increase the resistance of communications systems to jamming and to facilitate communications with submarines at greater depths in the ocean, where the submarines are more difficult for an enemy to discover or track. For the first problem, such technologies as spread-spectrum modulation are being developed (basically, a method of hiding high-frequency radio signals in background radio "noise"). To improve submarine communication, such technologies as laser beams and extreme and ultra low frequency radio signals are under development. (All of these penetrate the ocean to a greater depth than the high frequency, low frequency, and acoustical signals now used.)

Whatever the success of these new technologies, their goal is to reestablish something the United States heretofore assumed it had—secure one- and two-way voice and data communications linkages. There has been no major technological revolution, although it is true that data-handling capabilities have been considerably expanded. But whatever the success of the different remedies, a key part of the problem remains unsolved—the vulnerability of the people in the chain of command and of key communications equipment they would need to use. These problems cannot be solved by technical means alone. Most important government officials are exposed to attack by the natural imperatives of the American political system. Apart from certain unique crisis scenarios, it will be difficult to protect these officials and thus difficult to preserve the anticipated linkages of authority. In the event of a nuclear conflict, the United States will have an ad hoc chain of command. It is questionable whether existing communications systems will be able to provide the opportunities for review, confirmation, or consultation that those subject to ad hoc authority may demand. This problem is especially acute, given the unpredictable—but likely severe—damage that existing communication systems are likely to sustain in an attack.

The Reagan administration has sensed the urgency of the C3 problem. In late 1981, it placed strategic C3 on the same priority as the strategic weapons the C3 network must support. The priority is understandable, but it has yet to result in new programs and new budget authority. For decades, strategic debate in the United States has focused on strategic weapons and virtually ignored the communications systems needed to command and control these weapons. Until better ideas are developed about the full range of the threat and how it might be met amid the incredible destruction of nuclear war, technological refinements will leave much of the strategic communications problem unsolved.

Tactical Applications

Communications problems and major communications investments are not restricted to the strategic nuclear network. In fact, the vulnerability and jamming problems critical to nuclear conflicts have direct analogues in conventional warfare. For example, major North Atlantic Treaty Organization (NATO) command headquarters in Europe are fixed and ground-based and thus are vulnerable to pretargeted attacks by conventional weapons. At the same time, jamming or electronic countermeasures (ECM) have become especially serious problems in modern warfare. In the Yom Kippur War, for example, jamming by Egyptian forces caused an almost complete loss of voice communications on the frequencies jammed. ECM and ECCM (electronic counter-countermeasures) will be critical to the command of troops in any future battle.

The United States has developed a number of new systems to meet this threat. The main thrust of these systems is to establish digital computer networks as the backbone of American tactical communication systems. Such networks have great promise, but many problems are likely to result, especially if (as is likely) a future war provides little opportunity to refine or replace these systems based on combat experience. The major systems to be discussed here are the World-Wide Military Command and Control System (WWMCCS, pronounced "wimex"), the E-3 (the Airborne Warning and Control System, or AWACS), the Joint Tactical Information Distribution System (JTIDS), the Battlefield Exploitation and Target Acquisition project (BETA), and certain secure voice communications projects.

WWMCCS is a worldwide communications network. More concretely, it is an arrangement of personnel, computers, software, communications channels, facilities, and procedures employed in coordinating and controlling the operational activities of United States military forces. The strategic C3 network, described in the previous section, is a priority component of WWMCCS. But the system reaches far beyond strategic forces, ultimately to all United States military forces around the world. WWMCCS began in the 1960s as a loosely coordinated federation of 158 different computer systems using 30 different software systems at 81 separate locations. Its geographic reach has since expanded and its equipment has been modernized, but fragmented management has prevented the integration of its separate components. Attempts to develop an overall system architecture have been thwarted by the different interests and information needs of its many users. An effective plan to decentralize system development has yet to materialize. Approximately $1 billion has been spent in attempts to upgrade WWWMCCS, with little success to date. The system is said to provide reasonable service for routine information needs, but to be inadequate for any crisis period.

At theater-level operations, the first system to note is the E-3A AWACS. AWACS represents an innovation in tactical operations, especially air operations. Placing a large radar with "look-down" capability on a flying aircraft permits United States forces a much deeper radar view into enemy territory. Matching that radar with computer equipment on board the plane is said to permit active management of the air (and, to an undetermined extent, ground) battle. AWACS could serve as a key link in automated battle decisions—directing missiles to fire and planes to attack, based on what its radars sight and how its computers and operators respond. It could serve as an airborne command center for air and ground operations, but more generally it will report to ground-based command centers. AWACS will be connected to the JTIDS system. AWACS evolved from the American experience in the Vietnam war. By trial and error, the air force discovered that the use of a crude airborne command center dramatically improved its success in air-to-air combat with North Vietnamese airplanes. It also reduced the number of friendly airplanes shot down because of "sky clutter"—the airborne tracking of friendly airplanes was a partial solution to the problem of separating friendly from enemy aircraft amid the chaos of air battles.

The JTIDS system is a computer-based communication system that will allegedly distribute secure, jam-resistant, digital information over a wide frequency band. Several thousand users will be able to share a common communications network. JTIDS exploits so-called Time Division Multiple Access technology, which splits every second of time into fractions, with each communicator pulsing his message into the system as a digital burst when his fraction of time comes up. This system is accessible only to users equipped with special terminals to send and receive these digital bursts. Terminals having three different levels of sophistication are being developed. The most sophisticated terminals are going into AWACS aircraft and ground command centers. Terminals of lesser sophistication are being designed for fighter aircraft, ships, and mobile ground platforms. The simplest terminals will fit guided weapons and, potentially, manpacks. The foxhole of the future will likely have a simple computer terminal, though additional technological development will be necessary to reduce these simplest terminals to a sufficiently small size and weight. This multibillion-dollar, joint-service program has escalated in cost and has experienced serious technical difficulties in meeting planned goals of performance and reliability.

The BETA program is a high-risk, joint-service effort to develop an experimental test bed to perform automated "intelligence fusion"—that is, to analyze and disseminate tactical intelligence data. Systems like AWACS, JTIDS, and various sensors, radars, and other devices will generate and disseminate an unprecedented flood of data, requiring a heavy reliance on automated decision aids. The BETA program is an attempt to develop the requisite technology, but it has been beset by serious problems.

Finally, with respect to other communications systems, there is a wide variety of smaller defense programs designed to increase the security and reliability of telephone and radio systems. The air force is developing systems (HAVE QUICK for the short run and SEEK TALK for the long run) to increase the jam resistance of two-way voice communication with its aircraft. The Defense Department is helping to convert the European Defense Communication System (a system based in part on European domestic telephone networks) from analog to digital systems. This conversion will increase the capacity and reliability of the system for defense communications. The Defense Department is also investing approximately $300 million in its own nontactical voice communication network.

Together, the system developments described above, as well as other sensor development programs, constitute a major investment to strengthen C3 capabilities for tactical operations and other purposes. They present major problems, however. First, in these programs, the Defense Department has construed the C3 problem as primarily a question of the implicated technologies. A reading of the public literature creates the strong impression that hardware and software systems provide the frame of reference as to what "the C3 problem" is. The new technologies promise to make all kinds of information instantly available to almost everyone, from the president to the infantryman in the foxhole. Having instituted development efforts in response to certain manifest problems, the department is now committed to a series of costly, complex, high-performance system developments. These developments and the technical problems they create will channel C3 initiatives for years to come.

Second, little is said about the behavioral implications of these new systems. Systems like JTIDS, whose initial purpose was to provide jam-resistant communications, may have the primary effect of further centralizing command in ways that can only be partially anticipated. Nowhere in public documents does there appear a Guderian-like synthesis of doctrine and communications, in which changes in communication are tailored to changes in conceptions of how wars should be fought. Instead, one reads of more people having more information about nearly everything – because technology makes it possible – with little discrimination as to who needs to know what.

Third, because unprecedented amounts of data are to be communicated through more levels of command, automated data synthesis will play a much larger role than in past wars. Decisions about the meaning of data and the course of combat must be preprogrammed without detailed knowledge of what the combat will be like. This procedure is not something to avoid entirely, but it presents problems. In the relatively stable environment of the corporate world, new management systems often require major redesign before they satisfy the needs of their users. There is little reason for confidence that the complex military information systems of the future – untested in the unstable world of combat – will properly anticipate all critical elements of the combat environment. This problem is especially acute for NATO forces, given the small amount of realistic training those forces receive in C3 matters.

Finally, the institutional settings for these developments give a special reason for caution: many of them, like BETA and JTIDS, are joint service developments. Joint developments have been deemed necessary in order to ensure the "interoperability" of equipment and procedures among multiple user services. Joint developments are always difficult, especially for projects of high risk and complexity. The problem is almost certainly worse at the NATO level, where multiple nations as well as multiple services are involved.

In summary, while the Defense Department is indeed devoting major resources to remedy C3 problems, the department has framed the issues in relatively narrow technological terms. The increased data-handling capabilities of digital equipment and the greater quantities of data available from new sensor systems have given the unfortunate impression that information is costless to obtain and use. So much information can be made available to so many people that there is less pressure to discriminate about what information is needed in combat. There has been no consensus on how the new systems fit conceptions of command and control and almost no consideration of how major changes in information flow will affect command behavior. Central echelons of command will know (or think they know) far more about combat activities at previously remote, lower levels of the services. How will this new information affect their behavior? Will command be more centralized? If so, is that desirable? Or will commands be inundated with information and unable to react? The answers to these questions may not be discovered until the next war, at which point there will be little time to learn how to change the communication systems and command doctrine that regiment and coordinate troops in battle. Finally, in all of the descriptions of new defense communications systems, the combat world seems unreal. While the new systems hold great promise, they are unlikely to eliminate the "friction," as Clauseweitz aptly termed it, the sheer messiness and unpredictability of battle. Little of the information available about the new systems provides reassurance that the frictions of war have penetrated the thinking of communication system designers.

In the blitzkrieg, the Germans joined a simple communications network to an innovative conception of command and control, a conception that was validated by the test of battle. In current approaches to tactical communications, the United States has developed increasingly complex communication systems without the discipline of a clear doctrine of command and control, a clear set of ideas about the command imperatives the communications systems should support. The Soviet Union does not appear to be making the same mistake.

Soviet Approaches to C3

Any discussion of military systems must take account of the likely adversaries against whom those systems may be called to perform. A summary appraisal of the work of the United States's likely adversary, the Soviet Union, provides little reassurance. The Soviet Union may lag behind the United States in many important communications technologies. But its C3 systems tend to be simple and reliable. More to the point, the Soviet Union appears to have devoted far more attention to integrating C3 technology into the operations of its forces.

The Soviet emphasis on C3 (and counter-C3) is no accident. During the early months of World War II, the Germans attacked Soviet telephone switches and open wire lines. Communications were virtually severed at the division, army, and front level. The results were disastrous (for that, among other reasons). The Soviets apparently learned a lesson from that humiliation. By the spring of 1944, the Soviets were demonstrating an "ability to integrate all aspects of radio-electronic warfare into their tactics."[5]

Confirmation of the Soviet attitude toward electronic warfare came during the Yom Kippur War of 1973. Confronting equipment and tactics supplied by the Soviet Union, Israel "found the East to lead in system philosophy and design, with crude, robust, but reliable components. The West, not surprisingly, was found to excel in technology; a virtue of questionable utility in combat."[6]

While the United States's edge in technology is comforting, its failure to integrate that technology into workable operational concepts should discourage complacency. As the blitzkrieg analogy and the experience of the Yom Kippur War suggest, the military effects of communications critically depend on operational ideas about how these technologies are to be used, not simply on the sophistication of the technologies themselves. The Soviet Union's simpler technology, embedded in more careful doctrinal development, should constitute a major source of concern. Comparing United States and Soviet capabilities in this area, Colonel Alan D. Campen has observed: "[We] seem not to have worked to integrate our superior technology . . . . While electronics are clearly essential, it [*sic*] leaves doctrinal, organizational, and procedural issues to chance; a dicey proposition in the short but violent combat scenario now favored for a NATO conflict. . . . We appear to be fielding equipments with only the most superficial understanding of the means for their successful integration into the chosen tactics for combat."[7]

The Soviet Union has its own problems in the C3 area. For example, its highly centralized form of command makes it especially vulnerable to disruption, if communications are severed and combat does not proceed according to its preplanned scenarios. Nonetheless, the Soviet Union has placed its more austere communications technology at the service of what it actually plans to do in combat. It is a lesson the Germans learned well. The Soviet Union has yet to see the United States's revolution in defense communications, but it at least has not made the mistake of confusing technological sophistication with military effectiveness.

[5] Col. Alan D. Campen, "Electronics: Just Another Element of Warfare," *Signal* (April 1981), p. 18.

[6] Ibid.

[7] Ibid.

Index

Proceedings of The Academy of Political Science

ISSN 0065-0684

1981–82
Volume 34

The volume is not indexed. See table of contents of each issue.

The Academy of Political Science
2852 Broadway
New York, New York 10025-0148